THE CONFIRMATION MESS

Also by Stephen L. Carter

*The Culture of Disbelief: How American Law and
Politics Trivialize Religious Devotion* (Basic Books, 1993)

Reflections of an Affirmative Action Baby
(Basic Books, 1991)

!

The Confirmation Mess

CLEANING UP THE FEDERAL APPOINTMENTS PROCESS

STEPHEN L. CARTER

BasicBooks
A Division of HarperCollins *Publishers*

Designed by Ellen Levine

Library of Congress Cataloging-in-Publication Data

Carter, Stephen L., 1954–
    The confirmation mess: cleaning up the federal appointments
process/by Stephen L. Carter.
            p. cm.
    ISBN 0-465-01364-3
    1. United States—Officials and employees—Selection and
appointment. I. Title.
JK736.C37 1994
353.001'32—dc20   93-40377
                                                          CIP

94 95 96 97 ◆/HC 9 8 7 6 5 4 3 2 1

For Thurgood Marshall

CONTENTS

PREFACE

JUST about everybody I told I was writing a book that would criticize the confirmation-time treatment of both Robert Bork and Lani Guinier had one of two reactions: "What are you defending *him* for?" or "What are you defending *her* for?" But those reactions are the reason for the book: we have reached in our confirmation processes a strange pass at which, once we decide to oppose a nominee, any argument will do. Nobody is interested in playing by a fair set of rules that supersede the cause of the moment; still less do many people seem to care how much right and left have come to resemble each other in the gleeful and reckless distortions that characterize the efforts to defeat challenged nominations. All that seems to matter is the end result: if the demonized nominee loses, all that has gone before is justified. Activists working against a nomination can say just about anything, and the news media will report it (as allegation, to be sure, not as fact), only worrying later about whether it was true.

This book is, first of all, about decency. It is about honesty. About why both are important in our choice of public servants and how we can bring them back. It is about the difference between saying "I don't like the way Robert Bork would vote on the Supreme Court" and "Robert Bork is a monster"; the difference between saying "I disagree with what Lani Guinier stands for" and "Lani Guinier is a dangerous radical." It is about the difference between arguing the merits of a proposed appointment and turning the public debate into the intellectual equivalent of a barroom brawl. And it is about the difference between a nation that is willing to accept in the executive branch and the courts complex human beings with the capacity for error and growth and a nation that tries (in its imagination, at least) to limit public service to a tiny handful of genuine saints who can be said to "deserve" their posts. If our choice is for the first, we can only improve both our government and our attitude toward service. If our choice is for the second, we must realize that the true saints are few, which means that we will have instead a government peopled by the great squirming mass of the ambitious, who are not so much unafraid of the reckless but self-righteous assaults that too often characterize our debates as ruthlessly confident that they will not get caught.

The book has a second theme, one with particular application to the Supreme Court. In 1987, when, as a relatively junior law professor, I rushed home to watch the Bork hearings on C-SPAN each night, I was struck by the fact that nobody involved—not the activists who gave daily press conferences for and against, not the senators who asked the questions, not the journalists who covered the hearings, not Judge Bork himself—seemed to consider the possibility that one who disagreed with many of Robert Bork's substantive positions could nevertheless decide that trying to get him to tell the nation how he would vote on controversial cases if confirmed might pose a greater long-run danger to the Republic than confirming him and letting him do what we assumed he would. It seemed odd to me then, and only seems odder now, that everyone is evidently so happy with the idea that the Supreme Court should be limited to people who have adequately demonstrated their closed-mindedness. (The vicious fights we have therefore tend to be over the direction in which the minds of our Justices should be closed.) We seem unwilling to consider the many ways in which we damage judicial independence when presidential candidates promise to pack the Court if elected, and their opponents can offer nothing better than solemn undertakings to pack the Court the other way.

Hence, for both reasons, this book. I should make clear that although the book is entitled *The Confirmation Mess*, the reason is only that *The Nomination and Confirmation Mess* seemed too wordy and *The Appointment Mess* too obscure. But either title would be more accurate, for the presidents who nominate, no less than senators who decide whether to confirm, bear a substantial responsibility for most (not all) of the problems that I will describe.

The book is not intended as a comprehensive history of the confirmation process from the Founders' time to our own. Several quite good historical treatments are already available, and the careful reader of my endnotes will discover them. Nor is it my intention to offer a detailed statistical treatment of what has happened in the confirmation process over the years. That, too, has been done elsewhere, and, once more, the better sources are listed in the relevant notes. The book, rather, is in the nature of an extended essay, remarking on general themes by using familiar examples, and is meant to provoke thought about—and, one hopes, serious reform of—what President Clinton's chief of staff has come to call, with reason, "confirmation hell."

A few paragraphs of chapter 2 previously appeared in a 1993 letter to the editor in the *New York Times*, and some of the ideas in chapter 3 appeared in an op-ed essay in the *Times* later that same year under the title "A Litmus Test for Judges? It Demeans the Court." Some of the themes of the discussion of the Supreme Court in the book's middle chapters are anticipated in my four law review articles on the same subject: "The Confirmation Mess" (*Harvard Law Review*, 1988), "The Confirmation Mess, Revisited" (*Northwestern University Law Review*, 1990), "Bork Redux, or, How the Tempting of America Led the People to Rise and Battle for Justice" (*Texas Law Review*, 1991), and "The Confirmation Mess, Continued" (*University of Cincinnati Law Review*, 1993). The discussion in chapter 5 of the hearings on Clarence Thomas's nomination is anticipated in my review essay entitled "The Candidate," which appeared in *The New Republic* in 1993.

Over the six years that I have been thinking seriously about these problems, I have gained much from the opportunity to discuss some of these ideas at lectures, panels, or workshops at Hamilton College and Williams College and at the law schools of the following institutions: University of Chicago, University of Cincinnati, University of Dayton, Emory University, George Washington University, University of Illinois, Northwestern University, University of Notre Dame, University of Virginia, and Yale University. During the same period, I have had the benefit of useful comments on and criticisms of my ideas from Bruce Ackerman, Derrick Bell, Harold Berman, Joe Biden, Lea Brilmayer, Ethan Bronner, Gordon Crovitz, Harlon Dalton, Bruce Fein, Owen Fiss, Paul Gewirtz, Lani Guinier, Geoffrey Hazard, Randall Kennedy, Christo Lassiter, Jane Ley, Jane Livingston, Ira Lupu, Michael McConnell, Roberta Romano, Alan Schwartz, Charles Shanor, Martin Shapiro, Suzanna Sherry, Rogers Smith, Arlen Specter, Kate Stith, Geoffrey Stone, Mark Tushnet, Ruth Wedgwood, Harry Wellington, and many others whose omission is a signal only of my own faulty memory. I have further had the special benefit of remarkably close and thoughtful readings of the manuscript itself by Akhil Amar, Robert Burt, Lisle Carter, George Jones, Geoffrey Miller, and Laurence Tribe. And, as usual, I owe a special thanks to the dean of the Yale Law School, Guido Calabresi, not only for his always helpful comments, but also for his willingess to support my work in so many ways. Perhaps needless to add, none of these generous readers agreed with all that I have to say, and some of them agreed with very little.

My editors at Basic Books, Martin Kessler, Kermit Hummel, and Jane Judge, have been endlessly patient and endlessly encouraging, and their assistance has been marvelous, as has that of my literary agent, Lynn Nesbit. My students, as always, have been indispensable. In polishing the manuscript, I have had the benefit of excellent research assistance from Heidi Durrow and Lewis Peterson. On some of the earlier articles, I was fortunate to have the equally outstanding assistance of Phyllis Griffin and Denise Morgan. My secretary, Marcia Mayfield, has as usual been tireless, creative, patient, and always good-humored.

Finally, as always, my greatest debt of gratitude is due to my family: to my marvelous, ever-forgiving children, Leah and Andrew, for putting up with month after month of, "In a minute, in a minute, just let me finish one more paragraph," and, most of all, to my wife, Enola, who has shared with me many gifts of unfailing love, patience, and support; of conversation that led me out of many an analytical cul-de-sac; of thorough, incisive commentary on many a draft, often at great sacrifice to her own work; and of her unique sense of balance between the material and the spiritual, between the here and the hereafter. Without these gifts, I am not sure that I could write at all, and to emulate them, and thus to emulate her, is my fondest hope.

Hamden, Connecticut
February 1994

I

BORKING FOR FUN AND PROFIT

1

The Televised Backyard Fence

NATURALLY, the most vicious confirmation fight in our history was waged to keep a black man off the Supreme Court. They hated him, for the content of his politics and the color of his skin, and so they tried everything. They questioned his intellect and his veracity and the choices he made in his personal life. They made up stories about his ethics. They lambasted him for refusing to answer questions about controversial cases and called him a liar when he said his mind was open. They accused him of a disrespect for law and a subversion of the Constitution to fit the political goals of his movement. They warned that he had no respect for long-settled precedents. They challenged the citations in the opinions he wrote as a judge on the federal appeals court and in the briefs he wrote as a practitioner. He lacked the minimum qualifications for the job, they insisted. He was nominated only because he was a crony, they said. Or because the President was packing the Court with ideologues. Or because he was black. They scrutinized every speech he had ever given for evidence of radicalism and took his words out of context to make him seem scary. They talked to everyone who knew him, and lots of people who did not, in an effort to dig up dirt. When they found none, they tried to manufacture it. But he was confirmed despite their efforts, and they hated him that much more for their inability to defeat him.

And when he died a little over a quarter-century later, more than twenty thousand mourners lined up in the bitter cold, waiting outside the Supreme Court through the day and into the blustery winter night to view the casket of Thurgood Marshall, who had passed in those twenty-five years from dangerous radical to national hero. Marshall, said President Bill Clinton, was "a giant in the quest for human rights." Chief Justice William Rehnquist, who has led the recent move to overturn much jurisprudence that Marshall held dear, praised his long-time adversary's "untiring leadership in the legal battle to outlaw racial discrimination."[1] Marshall was perhaps the most admired human being ever to sit on the Supreme Court.

But had Thurgood Marshall been younger, had he been nominated to the Supreme Court in the year that he died, he might never have been confirmed. The chances are that there would never have been a vote, that under today's silly rules, the nomination would have been withdrawn. Too much baggage, too many eccentricities, too many enemies, and too many harmful sound bites. This, after all, was the man who was fond of telling jokes about what black people would do to white people after the revolution. (Shades of Lani Guinier!) He had more than once questioned the fairness of the Constitution itself, and expressed open disdain for settled precedents. (Shades of Robert Bork!) When pressed by members of the Senate Judiciary Committee to outline his judicial philosophy, he pointedly refused. (Who dares!) The only point in his favor (since talent, experience, and wisdom nowadays seem to count for so little) is that he probably was not wealthy enough to afford a nanny.

Thurgood Marshall was subjected to a degree of racist smear that the confirmation process had not seen before and has not seen since. Conservatives who believe that Robert Bork or Clarence Thomas encountered unprecedented animosity should read the transcripts or study the news accounts of the openly racist, but of course not televised, campaign against Marshall. (I discuss this campaign in chapters 3 and 5.) At the time, the news media played it down and there were no television cameras in the hearing room. But the embarrassing truth is that the campaign that failed in 1967 might well have succeeded in 1993.

The Constitution begins with the words "We, the People of the United States," and, in recent years, We the People have taken an unprecedented interest in the process of nominating and confirming the public servants who govern in our name. This is, in the abstract, all to the good. But the sound-bite campaigns against nominees that are now a regular feature of our politics play to the worst in the American character. Our nation's history is full of the names of able and sometimes brilliant public servants who, in today's climate, would have remained private servants. In America today are hundreds, perhaps thousands, of people in private life who might otherwise be brilliant public servants but never will have the chance, because, for some reason, they are not enamored at the thought of having the media and a variety of interest groups crawl all over their lives in an attempt to dig up whatever bits of dirt, or bits of things that could be called dirt, might be discovered.

That, in a nutshell, is what this book is about: what is wrong with our confirmation process, how it got this way, and what we can do to fix it.

ARTICLE II'S EXCITING DECADE

What a wonderful time to be an American, if you care about who serves in government and you watch television! The confirmation battles, which the Founders evidently thought would be private little debates between President and Senate, are now available for all to enjoy. Because you can see it all laid out for you, at least if a breath of controversy attaches: you need not read for yourself the writings of a Lani Guinier or a Robert Bork or a Ruth Bader Ginsburg, because television brings you plenty of partisans who have read the work for themselves (and plenty more who have not) and are happy to describe it to you in terms either lurid and censurious or glowing and righteous, depending on which side of the issue they happen to be on.

Our confirmation debates run from the sublime—the famous national seminar on constitutional law conducted during the hearings on Robert Bork's 1987 nomination to the Supreme Court—to the ridiculous—the journalist who thought it would be a great kick, during those same hearings, to publish a list of the films Bork had rented at his neighborhood video store. The famous "nanny problem," as it became known, that the nation discovered in 1993 reached up and reportedly felled a likely nominee for the Court, federal appellate judge Stephen Breyer, whose public sin was the private failure to pay Social Security taxes on the wages of a housekeeper long retired.

In his fine book on the Bork hearings, the journalist Ethan Bronner reports a poignant moment that captures perfectly the way our modern confirmation madness can devastate the soul. Douglas Ginsburg, a federal judge nominated by President Reagan after Bork's defeat, already under fire because he had smoked marijuana as an adult and because his wife, a physician (his *wife!*), had performed abortions during one of her residencies, telephoned the White House to report what he had neglected to reveal: that his wife was once a contestant in a beauty contest. If this fact came to light, Ginsburg asked a presidential adviser, would it affect his chances for confirmation? The adviser assured him that it would not.[2] But who can tell for sure these days? It was not at all nutty that Ginsburg brought it up; it is nutty that we live in a world in which he thought he had to.

Ginsburg's nomination was shortly withdrawn without a Senate vote. (But not before the Reagan Administration issued a statement assuring the world that Ginsburg's wife—his *wife*—did not currently perform abortions.) In 1993, he suddenly got lots of company. In January, we the people worked ourselves into a fine sense of national moral outrage following the revelation that Zoe Baird, President Clinton's nominee to head the Justice Department, had hired an illegal immigrant as a nanny and failed to pay Social Security taxes on the nanny's earnings. Thus, just two days after his inauguration, Clinton was forced to withdraw Baird's nomination. One form or another of this nanny problem would over the next few months fell another potential attorney general, a possible Supreme Court nominee, and, according to press reports, lots of other people as well, who suddenly found themselves crossed off the lists for the posts they thought were theirs. For example, just after Baird's withdrawal, Clinton's staff floated the name of the federal judge Kimba Wood, which was just as quickly unfloated. Wood, too, was said to have problems surrounding the employment of a nanny, although she had broken no laws.[3] Still, the problems were said to "disqualify" her, as they had Baird. That is very much our modern approach: we presume the nominees to be entitled to confirmation absent smoking guns, and then we look for the smoke in order to disqualify them.

So it should scarcely have been surprising that Clinton's

second nominee for attorney general, Janet Reno, was dogged by scurrilous rumors of drunken driving that spread across Capitol Hill—and the newspapers—like wildfire, repeated without any verification. The rumors turned out to be false, but nobody apologized for printing them: their news value, it seems, and hence the public's fabled right to know, did not turn on whether they were true. (We, the People, have the right to hear whatever rumors our representatives hear!) A lobbyist for a Beltway interest group (the National Rifle Association) admitted spreading them and was dismissed; Reno was quickly and properly confirmed.

Other cabinet nominees (although, as will be seen, not many) have also found themselves "disqualified" over the years. Three of the more recent are John Tower, whose 1989 nomination by George Bush for secretary of defense collapsed under the weight of charges of womanizing and excessive drinking; Robert Gates, whose name was withdrawn in 1987 as a potential Director of Central Intelligence after his name surfaced in the Iran-Contra report (drafted, ironically, by a commission headed by John Tower); and Theodore Sorensen, whose 1977 nomination by Jimmy Carter for the same post was withdrawn in the wake of assertions that he lacked experience, was a pacifist, and had used secret documents in writing about the Kennedy Administration.* That some of these charges may indeed be disqualifying does nothing to alter an alarming trend that turns tiny ethical molehills into vast mountains of outrage, while consigning questions of policy and ability to minor roles.

* After this manuscript was completed, Admiral Bobby Ray Inman, President Clinton's choice to replace Les Aspin as secretary of defense, withdrew his name and accused a syndicated columnist of conspiring with Senate Republicans to sabotage his candidacy. Although Inman had certainly taken some hard shots from the media for his performance while at the Central Intelligence Agency and the National Security Agency, his defensive, accusatory attitude during his press conference convinced many observers that he would in any case not have been a successful defense secretary.

The disqualification trend has spread further down into the ranks. A few months into the Clinton Administration, a number of senators, spurred on by some very powerful interest groups, tried to block the nomination of Roberta Achtenberg as an assistant secretary of Housing and Urban Development on the ground that she is openly and unapologetically a lesbian. What this had to do with her ability to do the job was left unclear, but very little that is discussed in our contemporary confirmation debates has much to do with qualifications, and some members of the Senate were indeed persuaded to vote no. We talk little, nowadays, about a nominee's qualifications. Instead, today's hearings, when anybody pays attention, are mostly about *dis*qualifications. When controversy erupts, we spend little time letting the nominee and her backers make the positive case, and a great deal of time arguing the case against.

During the same remarkable spring, Lani Guinier, Clinton's nominee for assistant attorney general for civil rights, was painted as a dangerous radical by her opponents, who based their assertion on snippets of her writings—in the parlance, she was borked. Her name was then withdrawn in a messy press conference, in the course of which President Clinton admitted having known little about her work before nominating her. A presidential aide hardly made things better by joking, just before the nomination was withdrawn, that Clinton might instead appoint Guinier to the Supreme Court. The columnist Meg Greenfield called it "incredible for a White House official to be playing around with an appointee who was about to be junked and whose friends and supporters believed she was already being treated with unwarranted disrespect."[4]

But that is what the confirmation process does to people on all sides, including putative supporters. As for legal scholars, well, they should simply stay away from public life—at least if their work is provocative and, as we like to say in the academy, takes risks. Otherwise they are all too likely to learn, as Bork did in 1987 and Guinier did in 1993, that the very qualities we reward in the law schools are penalized when one is sitting for confirmation. The trouble is that scholarship, when at all complex, is easily chopped up into smaller bits, just the right size for our sound-bite–mad media to digest and spit out again in a form even more garbled and out of context than when one's opponents first set out to distort the work.

Even religion, which Thomas Jefferson once called "the most inalienable and sacred of all human rights," is not sacrosanct. Once upon a time, religious inquiry was the province of the radical right, which attacked Louis Brandeis for his Judaism and William Brennan for his Catholicism. But no longer. One senator solemnly stated on the Senate floor that he was voting against Robert Bork's nomination to the Supreme Court because he was not sure that Bork believed in God. Some liberal activists announced their opposition to Clarence Thomas on the ground that he was a Roman Catholic—then, when it turned out that he attended an Episcopal church, on the ground that his church was a conservative one. The Senate, they argued, had an obligation to inquire into his religious beliefs.[5]

People on the right are fond of saying that the often vicious assaults on nominees are cloaks for ideology. For example, Robert Bork wrote after his defeat that the loss was a skirmish in a larger culture war. The fight, he argued, "was ultimately about whether intellectual class values, which are far more egalitarian and socially permissive, which is to say left-liberal, than those of the public at large and so cannot carry elections, were to be continued to be enacted into law by the Supreme Court."[6] And now that the Democrats are doing the nominating, people on the left say much the same thing, although they cite a different set of martyrs and villains. Lani Guinier, for example, has insisted that she was opposed so vehemently because of America's inability to overcome its widespread racism.

But although there is something to both complaints, what has happened in the past decade is more subtle. We the people want and need to be involved in the process of selecting those who will govern our ever more complex society; but despite our ability to vote for our representatives, we have precious few opportunities to exercise any real influence. The confirmation process is our chance—often the only one—to make our voices heard. The trouble is, we have no public political vocabulary in which to speak. (Just try to raise public alarm over a nominee's manifest lack of the basic qualifications for a job: it was inside-the-Beltway politics, not national outrage, that doomed the Supreme Court candidacy of the manifestly unqualified G. Harrold Carswell in 1971.) What we have instead is a public notion of the avoidance of sin that has been with us since the Founding. As will be seen, the quintessentially American puritanical streak that has come to govern our confirmation process makes redemption, even of the penitent, all but impossible. Another way to put the matter is this: the reason that opponents try to paint controversial nominees as sinners, as personally venal, is that they know the American people, the world's strongest supporters of capital punishment, like to see the sinful destroyed; we the people of the United States do not like to forgive.

THE ORIGINAL MISUNDERSTANDING

One might say that we have these bitter nomination battles because the Framers of the Constitution, in their glorious wisdom, planned things that way. The document's entire discussion of the nomination and confirmation process occurs in Article II,

Section 2, which sets forth among the powers of the President the following:

> [H]e shall nominate, and by and with the Advice and Consent of the Senate, shall appoint Ambassadors, other public Ministers and Consuls, Judges of the Supreme Court, and all other Officers of the United States, whose Appointments are not herein otherwise provided for, and which shall be established by Law: but the Congress may by Law vest the Appointment of such inferior Officers, as they think proper, in the President alone, to the Courts of Law, or in the Heads of Departments.

The Constitutional Convention, where many members were suspicious of executive power, had to be dragged to this resolution of a long-simmering controversy over appointments. From the records that exist, it appears that when Alexander Hamilton first suggested it, the idea fell flat. But once convinced that the combination of executive nomination and legislative confirmation had worked for over a century in Massachusetts, the delegates, with evident reluctance, went along.[7]

They were reluctant, for the most part, because of their worry that the President might gain the upper hand, particularly with respect to the appointment of judges, thus upsetting the delicate balance of power among the three branches. The solution, they hoped, was a compromise. But the eighty-two carefully chosen words on the subject of nomination, confirmation, and appointment have caused no end of trouble. In particular, since the administration of George Washington, they have occasioned often vituperative disputes, not only over the approval of particular nominees but over what constitutes the "advice" that the Senate is constitutionally required to give. For most of the Republic's first century, this problem was resolved, for most posts other than the Supreme Court, through a system of consultation: the President and the senators would do their horse trading in advance, and the resulting nominees would all be easily confirmed.

That system was not necessarily better than what we have now; it was simply different. The contemporary model, under which the President seeks advice principally from political counselors—all too rarely from the Senate—and then springs names on the nation like birthday gifts, only to grow sullen and snappish when the recipients (we the people) are ungrateful, has certain advantages in efficiency, as well as in news value. But when the President and his advisers misjudge the mood of the nation or the Senate or both—and, in particular, when the President and his advisers misapprehend the significance of any of a variety of facts in the nominee's background—then the current system necessarily collapses into the mudslinging that television covers so well.

President Carter learned this when he was forced to withdraw the nomination of Theodore Sorensen as director of Central Intelligence; administration officials simply had not realized how badly his lifelong pacifism would play in a nation still licking its wounds from Vietnam. President Reagan walked into the same trap in 1987, when officials were evidently unprepared for the public revulsion at many of the positions that Judge Robert Bork had espoused fervently and was quite prepared, in his honest way, to defend on national television. In neither case does it matter whether one thinks the charges were fair; what the cases teach is that the White House should never assume that the difficult points in a nominee's background can be smoothed over or explained away.[8]

Some political scientists who have studied confirmation battles have concluded that a President who presses hard for his nominee will nearly always win, no matter what the controversy, unless the President himself is weak or unpopular.[9] This would explain, for example, the Bush Administration's ability to push Clarence Thomas's 1991 Supreme Court nomination through the Senate, even though some surveys taken at the time showed that nearly half the American people thought he was lying when he denied Anita Hill's charges of sexual harassment—a number of voters that, if expressed in tens of millions, would ordinarily be crushing. By contrast, the Reagan Administration was unable to bring similar pressures to bear for Robert Bork's confirmation because Reagan himself, already weakened by the Iran-Contra revelations, was perceived as a lame duck. Others have suggested that initial spin is what matters, because senators, interested in reelection, take their early cues from public response, and therefore will make a fight of it only if public opposition rises early on.[10] That is why Bork's opponents decided to attack early, cruelly exaggerating the nominee's own positions in order to "freeze" the Senate and allow time for the preparation of a more measured and thoughtful opposition case.

We have built a system in which strategy (especially public relations strategy) is far more important than issues or qualifications. Indeed, we have reached a peculiar uncertainty in picking our top unelected officials. We know that under Article II of the Constitution, the President nominates them and, with the advice and consent of the Senate, appoints them. But we are not quite sure what anybody's role is—the President's, the Senate's, or the public's. From the late nineteenth century through the middle of the twentieth, Supreme Court nominees enjoyed a virtual presumption of qualification, and nearly all of them were confirmed, rarely with a battle, often without a recorded vote—but nobody can say why. From the 1870s through the 1970s, nominees for the cabinet all but waltzed through, as we celebrated a tradition entitling the President to name his "own team"—a tradition without constitutional foundation and based, as we shall see in chapter 2, on historical accident.

Recent events have made clear that both these traditions

are gone—all presidential nominees who will exercise significant power now receive close Senate scrutiny—and that is all
to the good. What makes our confirmation process messy,
however, is our inability to reach any sort of consensus on
what "close scrutiny" involves. That is why we are able to wax
indignant over nannies and Social Security taxes but only
rarely come to grips with the more important questions for
cabinet officials, their qualifications for the job, and the policies they will enforce in office. That is why we oscillate on the
standards for assessing Supreme Court nominees, agreeing not
to ask them how they will vote on the cases nearest to our
hearts but campaigning for or against them in public according
to those likely votes anyway.

Some of this is doubtless the result of our media culture,
which is notoriously weak at transmitting complicated messages but rewards those who possess a genius for reducing the
messages, however inaccurately, to applause lines. More of it
may rest in our well-known national rootlessness, our uncertainty as a polity about how to exercise the power of self-gov-
ernance, which is why we so often behave as commonwealth-
style *subjects,* waiting for government to make things better,
rather than as American *citizens* whose task is to go out and
run things.

But most of it probably stems from our realization that
the federal government with each passing year recedes further
and further from the control of the people of the United States,
in whose name it exercises authority. The confirmation
process, for a Justice, a cabinet officer, an assistant secretary,
is, for most of us, the only opportunity we will ever have to
get some sense of what kinds of people we are allowing to
run the place. Are they honest or venal? Compassionate or
mean-spirited? Saints or sinners? These are obviously important
inquiries; unfortunately, we have developed a modern tradition holding them to be the *only* important inquiries. We have

a forum for national debate on how a potential Justice will vote, but not on whether she is qualified for the job in the first place; we are able to hold a national conversation on a nominee's nanny but not on the policies the nominee would carry out as attorney general. It may be, then, that by inviting the citizenry to aid in governing the country—by asking, often in so many words in surveys, whether so-and-so should be confirmed or not—we have simultaneously surrendered the possibility of keeping our collective eye on the ball. We have reached a point where the confirmation debates are largely about personalities; we must find a way to recover debate about policies and qualifications. The question is how.

THE MEDIA CULTURE

Perhaps it is only our imagination that suggests, in this constantly televised age, that today's confirmation hearings are rougher than those of the past. Probably there has been no era in our history when trashing the candidate—digging up dirt—was anything other than the order of the day. Yet it is difficult to imagine that those who wrote and ratified the Constitution, when they designed the balance of power between executive and legislature in the appointment process, envisioned quite the mess into which we have worked ourselves.

To be sure, vicious confirmation battles have been around since the Founding. George Washington ran into them at least twice, once famously, when John Rutledge, his nominee for Chief Justice, was accused by political enemies of having taken leave of his senses—he later attempted suicide, making their attacks on him look prescient—and on another occasion, when his nominee for chief naval officer for Georgia was brushed aside for no other reason than that the state's two senators had a candidate of their own. Thomas Jefferson regretfully explained to a candidate for an ambassadorship that his was one of many nominations that the Senate was turning down because of a foreign policy dispute with the executive branch. Andrew Jackson's nomination of Roger Taney to serve as secretary of the treasury was rejected by an angry Senate over a policy dispute. And even before our modern era, lots of nominees have been the victims of vicious smears—in this century alone, one thinks of Louis Brandeis and Thurgood Marshall—but all of that was prior to the entry of television into the fray.

Television gave us the Bork hearings. Even without the cameras, there would have been hearings; but the presence of the cameras, the first ever for a full confirmation hearing, transformed an inside-the-Beltway ritual into a full-blown national extravaganza. Fans of the Block Bork Coalition, which combined some startling and uncomfortable truths about Bork's record with some even more startling and uncomfortable lies, have painted the hearings in romantic tones, referring to them as a national seminar on constitutional interpretation. To Bork supporters, however, the hearings were nothing but an effort to extract commitments that the nominee would vote the way that liberals preferred. Either way, it was television that brought the issue to the American people.

We watched television to learn about Zoe Baird's nanny and Roberta Achtenberg's homosexuality. To find out whether Robert Bork wanted to turn back the clock on civil liberties. To learn whether Lani Guinier was a dangerous radical. To discover whether Ruth Bader Ginsburg could possibly be as wonderful as everybody said and whether David Souter could possibly be as stealthy a candidate as everybody said. To see whether Joycelyn Elders could control her barbed wit. And, of course, to decide whether Clarence Thomas had sexually harassed Anita Hill.

A television network executive quoted in *The New Yorker* on the bizarre popularity of made-for-television movies about Amy Fisher echoed the words of any number of cultural critics in recent years: "People used to sit on the back fence and talk to each other. . . . [N]eighbors would talk. Television has replaced the back fence. Americans love to gossip. It's just something that's part of who we are. We get our gossip from television."[11]

Well, of course! That is what television supplies for us in the confirmation hearings, too. You can call it "gossip" or you can call it "the opportunity for the American people to be informed on the character and fitness of those who would serve them in public office." But whatever you call it, you can see how it works, and how, in our neighborless society, it fulfills our need to be involved. Government, over the years, has receded from the citizens it theoretically serves; local governance, which the Founders thought would be more important than national governance, has fallen into desuetude. Not government—governance. A far higher proportion of voters turns out for national elections than for, say, elections for the school board.

The hearings on Anita Hill's charges of sexual harassment against Clarence Thomas made for riveting television as millions of viewers watched and chose up sides; in fact, the spectacle was so riveting that most Americans apparently forgot that there were other issues about the nomination to be debated. Instead, those who believed Thomas's testimony seemed to think he should be confirmed and those who believed Hill's seemed to think he should not. For just this reason, contrary to the conservative image of a left wing cackling with glee when Hill's charges were revealed, many liberal activists say they wish she had never come forward, for they believe to this day that they had a chance to beat Thomas on the issues.

"The issues"—there's the rest of it. At the cabinet level we scarcely care, but for Supreme Court nominees able to pass the media scrutiny evidently aimed at determining their moral fitness for judicial service, another test awaits. It has become part of our routine to press potential Justices to give us—the people—enough information to allow us to predict their likely votes on the cases we care about most. We take surveys on what voters think is the right outcome in cases few of them have read, based on interpretations of constitutional provisions few of them would recognize. All of this, it is said, in the name of a "democratic check" on the otherwise unaccountable judicial power. As for the old law school (and high school civics) image of judges who make up their minds after they hear arguments instead of before, well, it has been dumped into the ashcan of history by joint consent of left-wing and right-wing activists, few of whom seem actually to relish the idea of an independent judiciary.

True, judicial independence from the control of popular majorities is a threat to democracy. It is supposed to be. That is the distinction, as Simeon Baldwin pointed out in 1905 in a fine book entitled *The American Judiciary*, between the role of a plenary legislature and the role of a constitutional legislature. In a plenary legislature, the people, through their representatives, always get their way. In a constitutional legislature, however, the people, through their representatives, get their way only up to the limits that a prior agreement—a constitution— places upon their government. If temporary legislative majorities have the authority to control the directions of the courts, one moves away from the model of the constitutional legislature and toward the model of the plenary legislature. This was Thomas Jefferson's preference; he thought the federal courts so in need of a democratic check that he proposed that the judges face the voters every few years (see chapter 4). Each time another politician or scholar steps into the Jeffersonian tradition and calls for a democratic check on the Supreme Court, we take another step along that road—the last one, I would think, that either liberals (committed to equality and individual autonomy) or conservatives (committed to liberty, property, and tradition) would want to travel.

But a confirmation fight, like a nomination decision, is an opportunity for our elected representatives to signal us, the voters, on their own ideological bona fides. And presumably, since we are the ones who elect them, this is precisely what we want them to do.

CAN THE CONFIRMATION MESS
BE CLEANED UP?

So what do we do? Finding the right answer, as I explain in the chapters to come, begins with understanding what the question is. And the question is why we focus so relentlessly on a nominee's *disqualifications* rather than *qualifications*. Once we know why we behave that way, we will be able to move forward toward a richer confirmation process.

With important exceptions, it is not my purpose in this book to rehash the charges and countercharges that arose in many recent confirmation cases (although I will try to let the reader know where I stand); certainly the book is not a brief on behalf of any particular nominee. Rather, it is my aim to use the controversies over several recent nominations, to both the executive and the judicial branches, to illuminate the notion that an aspect of an individual's past might disqualify her from public service or, at least, public service requiring Senate confirmation. In particular, I shall argue that we must regain the ability to balance the wrongs that a candidate might have done against the strengths that she might bring to public service—an ability that has tended to atrophy in an age that allows the mass media to play the role of guardians of public morality.

The trend toward searching for disqualifying factors means that we have become less interested in how well a nominee for cabinet or Court will do the job than in whether the individual deserves it, as though the vital question is whether the candidate should get the chance to add the post to her resume, which simply reinforces public cynicism about motives for entering public life. We have come to treat public service as a reward rather than a calling, which takes us down a rather dangerous road, for it becomes impossible to bring any sense of proportionality to bear on the evaluation of potential officials.

Further, the search for disqualifying factors potentially leads to a rather freewheeling investigation into the backgrounds of nominees. The possibility of keeping one's private life private becomes virtually nil, as only the tissue-thin wall of news judgment stands between the nominee and the disclosure (and condemnation) of whatever the candidate might least wish to discuss. This might seem just fine, until one takes the time to consider some of the things that might be disclosed in later cases. (Again, one thinks of Bork's videotape rentals.) To be sure, there are some facts about an individual's background that *should* be disqualifying, but I fear that recent history has shown us to be a bit mixed up about what they are; consequently, in the second part of the book, I suggest which purported disqualifications should be curable and how; which should be curable with difficulty; and which should never be curable at all.

In the case of Supreme Court nominees, the disqualification problem is particularly acute: in addition to the personal detritus through which all nominees must wade, the potential Justice also risks defeat if she has written or said things that will anger powerful constituencies who are wary of the way in which she will exercise her commission. In principle, there is nothing wrong with trying to get a full picture of nominees for the Court, especially given the awesome authority that the Justices wield in contemporary society; indeed, neither the President nor the Senate would be acting in accordance with the constitutional design were no weight given to the nominee's outlook. In practice, however, the effort too often deteriorates into a public relations campaign in which the would-be Justice is praised or excoriated for her likely votes in actual cases. At that point, as I will show by example, we are well on the way to electing our Justices, raising a serious question about why we do not just go ahead and do it explicitly. Indeed, as I shall argue in later chapters, if we are not prepared to change the way we think about the Court, we probably should consider electing its members, as is done in most of the states, where the voters know what they want from their judges and how to get it.

I would prefer not to go that far; I would prefer that we make important changes in our national mood rather than tinker around with the Constitution. If, however, we are too set in our ways of envisioning the judicial role to rethink such matters as whether it really is wise to campaign for or against nominees according to their likely votes, then constitutional change might be our only way of avoiding the considerable blood that is too frequently spilled in our confirmation fights.

To understand why our fights are so bloody, for the executive and judicial branches alike, and how we can try to make some changes, a useful time and place to begin is Washington, D.C., in the first six months of 1993, the start of the Clinton Administration and the time when, for a while, every confirmation seemed to go wrong.

2

Of Nannies, Sound Bites, and Confirmation Nonsense

ACROSS the televised backyard fence, we spread the gossip of the difficult confirmation year of 1993. This was the year that the names of two bright and respected lawyers whom President Clinton tapped for posts at the top of the Justice Department turned into household words: Zoe Baird and Lani Guinier. Baird was nominated to serve as attorney general, Guinier to head the Civil Rights Division. Both were subsequently forced to withdraw in the face of a degree of public opposition that helps illustrate much that is wrong with the way we pick our public servants. Baird broke the law in a rather mundane way and was pilloried for it, the punishment in media humiliation far outweighing the "crime." As for Guinier, the matter is a good deal simpler: she was railroaded. In both cases, a moderate, thoughtful dialogue would have served the nation well. In neither case was it allowed to happen, for simple sound bites beat complex explanations every time.

Also in 1993, steeled by the Baird and Guinier battles, we all geared up for the usual blood on the floor when Justice Byron White announced his retirement, giving President Clinton the chance to pick a successor. Conservative activists had proclaimed boldly in the last few years that the next Democratic nominee might face a "payback" for what were deemed the smears of Robert Bork and Clarence Thomas. Because liberal activists had promised their constituencies during the 1992 election that Clinton, if elected, would appoint one of their own to the Court, all the ingredients for a battle royal were in place. Instead, to the nation's open relief, the nomination of Ruth Bader Ginsburg waltzed through the Senate virtually untouched by serious opposition.

In the next chapter, I will use the Ginsburg nomination as a way of introducing both what is right and what is wrong in the way we discuss our Supreme Court vacancies. First, however, it is useful to pause and consider what the debates (if one may use the term) over the appointments of Baird and Guinier can teach us about more general failings in our confirmation process. In particular, because of the mythology holding that the President deserves to name his own team, cabinet nominees usually receive very light scrutiny. In the face of that traditional deference, there is no way to focus public attention on any particular nominee except by blowing her sins far out of proportion—or, if necessary, manufacturing new ones. Thus, our focus becomes *disqualification* rather than *qualification*—for, quite naturally, when one begins with a presumption in favor of confirmation, the only provocative search is for "evidence" with which to overcome it. We are unlikely to change that raw reality until we are able to overcome the tradition that underlies it.

NANNIES, EQUITY, AND DISQUALIFICATION

Anybody old enough to have been politically aware in 1973 doubtless remembers the "Saturday Night Massacre," when, for an ugly moment, the American idea hung in the balance. President Nixon, under investigation for the crimes that ultimately would drive him from office, fired Archibald Cox, the Watergate special prosecutor who was hot on his trail, and sent the Federal Bureau of Investigation to guard his office and sequester his files. But before disposing of Cox, Nixon created two Republican heroes: Eliot Richardson, the attorney general, who resigned rather than follow the President's order, and William Ruckelshaus, the deputy attorney general, who refused to fire Cox and was himself dismissed.

Ruckelshaus came in for deserved high praise. But if 1973 had been 1993, none of the kudos would have been received because Ruckelshaus might not have had his job. He might not have had his job because he might not have been confirmed. He might not have been confirmed because he had what we nowadays call a "nanny problem"—that is, like most Americans who employ household help, he evidently treated the regulations governing that area of family life as ill-conceived, impossibly burdensome, difficult-to-understand nonsense. But nobody seemed to care. His wife, it seems, had set the whole thing up, and Ruckelshaus himself was immune.[1]

That was then, this is now: future generations may not quite believe that in a nation facing as many challenges as this one, we spent the first week of the Clinton presidency debating whether to shoot down a nominee for attorney general because she hired the wrong babysitter. But in the case of Zoe Baird, that is precisely what we did. Baird and her husband hired a nanny and a chauffeur who were illegal immigrants and lacked permits to work. That they did so on the advice of counsel and with the implicit permission of the Immigration and Naturalization Service was a fact that the media generally found insufficiently interesting to report. That they worked to help the nanny and her husband obtain proper documentation was less interesting still. Moreover, they failed to pay Social Security taxes on what they paid the couple. That half or more of Americans fail to do the same thing—in fact, that another member of Clinton's cabinet, already confirmed, had failed to do the same thing—also seemed not to matter. What mattered was that, to reduce the issue to its least complex sound bite, Baird broke the law. And for that she was pummelled.

It was, from the start, an odd pummelling. Some of us old-fashioned law professors still treat the law as important, but most politicians and activists do so only when the law works in their favor. Although nobody knows for sure, one can scarcely resist guessing that many of the same liberals who dumped on a female nominee for obtaining child care in a manner that happened to be illegal would have excoriated conservatives for attacking a female nominee for obtaining an abortion in a manner that happened to be illegal—perhaps on the bizarre supposition that making choices about rearing children is less important than making choices about having them. (See chapter 6.)

Certainly Baird broke the law. But she did not (as some critics seemed to think) commit a crime. Moreover, she worked harder to comply with the law than most Americans do and than most of her opponents gave her credit for. And she had defenders, of course, including some who pointed out that the Immigration and Naturalization Service does not punish parents who hire undocumented workers to care for their children. The tide of indignation, however, rolled right over such arguments.[2] Two days after Clinton's inauguration, it was all over. The Senate read the proverbial writing on the wall and told the President there was too little support. So Baird was out. By that time, no other result was possible: a nominee who has lost the confidence of the nation, whether fairly or not, should be pressed forward only in the rarest case (see chapter 6).

It is easy to understand the public's initial anger. Given the widespread perception that there exists a wealthy elite that cares neither about Americans nor about the laws that most of us must obey, the fury was predictable. But the sound bites that sparked the popular indignation hid a larger and more complex truth, which came to light only after Baird's withdrawal, when a few journalists began to investigate in more detail than is possible when one is rushing to keep up with the public's insatiable appetite for the latest word over the backyard fence. What they reported was rather unsettling. Lengthy articles by Stuart Taylor in the *American Lawyer* and Sidney Blumenthal in *The New Yorker* concluded that there was much less to the sound bites than a superficial review of the public anger might suggest.[3] To take a single example, Baird and her husband* sought legal advice on the employment of the undocumented workers, and were told to report the hiring to the Immigration and Naturalization Service—which they did, right at the start—and to obtain from the INS a letter stating, in effect, that the INS was aware of the situation and did not propose to do anything about it, as long as the couple helped their employees to obtain the necessary documentation. This, too, they did. Indeed, there are many couples in the situation in which Baird and her husband found themselves, and the INS routinely allows them to handle matters in this fashion, and does not seek civil enforcement—again, the violation is not a criminal one—as long as the employees are domestics. As to the failure to pay Social Security taxes, Baird and her husband, unlike many others since confirmed to high federal

---

* Zoe Baird's husband, Paul Gewirtz, is a colleague of mine at Yale Law School.

office,* had a perfectly reasonable explanation. They had always paid properly for their previous nanny, but did not pay this time because they had been informed by a lawyer, sensibly but mistakenly, that until the couple received "green cards" and Social Security numbers, the Internal Revenue Service would not accept payment.

Many more bits and pieces of the Baird "scandal" also turned out to have less substance than the initial media assault made it appear, but I will not belabor them here; those who are interested may consult the sources listed in the notes. What must be pondered instead is not the overblown claims themselves but the cause and nature of our national fury over this issue, when we manage to keep a grim national silence on so many others.

Our sense of reasonable proportion has gone the way of all other accoutrements of public moral dialogue. We are capable in public life of moralizing but not of morality. Our puritanical fervor burns brightly at our oddly chosen moments of national condemnation: in a nation in which public officials have been complicit and sometimes willful in the deterioration of the inner-city schools that are charged with educating millions of poor children, we are incensed because a potential attorney general failed to please all elements of our labyrinthian federal bureaucracy in her employment of household help. That Zoe Baird did wrong is undeniable; where that wrong ranks on the scale of national scandal, however, is something we have been strangely unable to fathom.

---

* The Clinton Administration and the Senate leadership have now developed a working understanding that allows nominees who have not paid Social Security taxes on household employees to proceed to confirmation as long as they pay the taxes and any penalties. As I argue in chapter 6, this resolution is sensible and probably fair, and might even represent a kind of apology to Baird, but does not come to grips with the question of whether the government should in fact conscript parents to enforce the tax laws.

If we are to play the disqualification game, we might at least try to be sensible about it. Right now, the game proceeds in accordance with no rules whatever. The brouhaha over the Baird nomination shows the inconsistency of our moral indignation, which strikes, cancer-like, almost randomly. Among Zoe Baird's recent predecessors as nominees for attorney general was one who was accused of arranging jobs on the federal payroll for individuals to whom he was financially indebted. The story scarcely stirred the interest, to say nothing of the fury, of the American public. Perhaps the story was not even true—Edwin Meese, the nominee in question, certainly denied it, and a lengthy investigation by an independent counsel turned up no evidence of a crime—but it is ' nevertheless remarkable that so little outrage greeted the allegations, if, as now appears, the identity of one's nanny is a matter of national moment.

Evidently, we have been caught up in baby boomdom; in an era when the quest for the perfect resume seems entirely adequate as a definition of a life well lived, we have fallen into the trap of presuming that public service is simply another stop along the route. When we consider who should serve the nation in our governmental apparatus, we treat the inquiry as one involving moral desert: has the individual earned a place? or has the individual exhibited some disqualifying behavior? These nowadays are the questions that we ask and, for cabinet nominees, they seem to be the only ones that matter. For better or worse, we ask Supreme Court nominees for their views on a variety of substantive legal questions (see chapter 3); but cabinet nominations have long been treated with a deference that makes searching policy inquiries seem to be in bad taste. Thus, we may ask the commerce secretary–designate about his position on the best scheme for reducing the trade deficit with Japan and we might quiz the attorney general–designate about her views on protecting abortion clinics from overzealous protesters, but the Senate rarely votes on such issues. The Senate votes the nation's moral fervor instead; we hold referenda on how bad a person the nominee is.

In this sense, our modern approach to the confirmation process is much like the ban on service by homosexuals in the military. The military ban (as of this writing, softened but not repealed) is categorical. It leaves no space for balance. We do not ask what qualities gay or lesbian soldiers, sailors, or pilots might bring to military service or whether they might serve the nation with honor. We ask, rather, whether they have engaged in conduct—sexual love within rather than across gender lines—that offends many people's morality.[4] And that is all we wish to know: once we have found that "disqualification," our inquiry ends.

The presidents who nominate feed the disqualification game with their disingenuous but perfectly understandable insistence that every nominee for every position is the best or among the best qualified. (Frequently they use the very words.) The implication of such rhetoric is that a concrete set of requirements for the job—the paper qualifications—somewhere exists. (I argue in chapter 6 that we would be better off if it did.) Many candidates have been screened, the President is implying, and the nominee best fits. It is as though the nominee's resume is the principal, perhaps the only, justification for the nomination, and, thus, for confirmation and for the appointment itself. If this bit of presidential puffery is disproven, then, one might literally say that the formerly qualified nominee has now been *disqualified*.

But the approach that divides nominees into only two categories, the deserving and the disqualified, is bad for our government. The scrutiny we now require before allowing willing professionals to become public servants is likely to weaken, not strengthen, our institutions. There is much to be said for keeping government free of the taint of scandal, but not for creating scandals in order to keep our government free of people we do not like. Indeed, Zoe Baird's forced withdrawal because of legal violations she admitted and for which she tried to make recompense raises the question of whether we demand of our public servants a degree of sinlessness that would disqualify substantially all of them, were we willing to search with sufficient rigor. Baird, unlike others whom the Senate has treated with less hostility, admitted her offense and took responsibility for it. She made no effort to blame anyone else and said that what she learned from the experience would make her a better attorney general.

We must develop a sense of balance in judging those who would serve our country. Instead of asking if a nominee has done anything wrong, and then trying to decide how great the wrong is, we should strive to weigh the wrongs a nominee might have done against the service he or she could bring. Otherwise, in our rush to treat virtually any bit of wrongdoing as proof of moral unfitness, we will lose the sense of balance that is vital to a vibrant, functioning democracy—a sense perfectly captured in the words of our greatest President, Abraham Lincoln, who said: "On principle, I dislike an oath which requires a man to swear he *has* not done wrong. It rejects the Christian principle of forgiveness on terms of repentance. I think it enough if a man does no wrong *hereafter*."[5]

"HIS OWN TEAM"

The Baird episode was especially remarkable because it did not involve a Supreme Court nomination. We are accustomed to vigorous struggles over potential Justices, and there are no rules about what tactics are allowed. Cabinet nominations, however, have traditionally been handled with kid gloves by the Senate, at least until the last two decades. Until recently, the handling has been so gentle as to make nomination to a cabinet post tantamount to appointment. Even including the rather chaotic first six months of the Clinton Administration, only 7 of over 250 cabinet-level nominees have been defeated or withdrawn since World War II—and, if one excludes the position of director of Central Intelligence, the number of nominations that have gone down the tubes drops to 5. And although the proportion of negative votes on cabinet nominees has risen since the Nixon years, the fact remains that only 1 of every 9 nominations in the second half of the twentieth century has failed to receive the affirmative votes of at least 90 percent of the senators.[6]

There is reason behind these data. The President, we are fond of saying with reference to the cabinet, deserves his own team. Cabinet nominees come to their hearings carrying a strong presumption in favor of confirmation. After all, we point out, the American people elected the President to do a job for them. The Senate should step back and let him hire the people he thinks he needs to do it.

Recent events suggest that cabinet nominees will henceforth face somewhat closer scrutiny. That is as it should be; the tradition of senatorial deference to presidential cabinet choices was never as historically or constitutionally grounded an idea as rhetoric about letting the President select "his own team" has long made it sound. The Founders never intended senatorial confirmation of cabinet officers as anything like the rubber stamp that it has become. On the contrary, the Founders understood what the Congress has only intermittently realized, that the confirmation power was to be a check on the President's freedom to staff the government and, hence, on his policies. Responding in *Federalist No. 77* to critics who warned that the confirmation power might be used to influence the President, Alexander Hamilton wrote: "If by influencing the

President be meant *restraining* him, this is precisely what must have been intended."

Of course, the Founders also hoped that the requirement of Senate confirmation would improve the quality of the individuals who would serve. Wrote Hamilton in *Federalist No. 76:* "It would be an excellent check upon a spirit of favoritism in the President, and would tend greatly to prevent the appointment of unfit characters from State prejudice, from family connection, or from a view to popularity." And it would be nice if we could conclude that the rate of defeat is so low because of the quality of individuals nominated, but we cannot: we have seen in recent decades some truly outstanding public servants, but we have also seen more than a sprinkling of miscreants and wretches, and not a few of them have ended up standing before judges to request leniency.

The interesting truth, if one looks at the seven defeats, is that, at most, one—one!—nominee lost out because of a Senate perception that he lacked the qualifications for the job. That one nominee was Theodore Sorensen, whom President Carter nominated in 1977 to be director of Central Intelligence, and who faced a variety of attacks from his enemies, among them the charge that he lacked relevant background in intelligence work. Opponents also claimed that he had used secret papers in writing his memoirs (just like everybody else) and that he was a self-declared pacifist, which was a code for being, as Richard Nixon used to say, squishy-soft on communism. But the allegation that Sorensen lacked relevant experience for the job was the one that stuck; indeed, Democrats, too, clung to that description, once it became clear that the snowballing controversy would force Sorensen to withdraw, even though there have been other directors—one George Bush comes immediately to mind—about whom much the same could have been said.

Still, as a formal matter—and perhaps as a factual matter

as well—Sorensen lost out on the qualification question. In the case of the first postwar cabinet rejection, President Eisenhower's nomination of Lewis Strauss to be commerce secretary, most commentators seemed to think at the time that the Senate simply got fed up with the nominee's arrogance and self-promotion. Every other postwar cabinet defeat has involved, at some level or other, a scandal. There was moral turpitude of some kind: an illegal nanny, an illegal investment, alleged misstatements in the past. Some of these charges are more serious than others, but we draw few distinctions. Sins that would be venial in a private citizen become mortal in a cabinet nominee. They have to: based on the record, there is simply no other way to defeat a President's cabinet choice except to make the case that the individual has done something terrible in previous life.

This, then, is what the tradition of deference has brought us: a world in which opponents of a nominee have no choice but to bork, because nothing else makes any impact. By figuring out how and when we reached this point, we might be able to pull back. Fortunately, with respect to the cabinet, we are able to put a date and even a name to the beginning of the tradition of deference: the date is 1877 and the name is Rutherford B. Hayes.

When students hear about the Hayes presidency, they usually learn two facts: first, that he stole the 1876 election, which was thrown into the House of Representatives when no candidate received a majority in the electoral college; second, that he put an end to Reconstruction, withdrawing Union troops from the South and, with them, the only substantial protection for the freed slaves. But Hayes deserves study for another reason as well: more than any other President, he established the principle of presidential autonomy in staffing the executive branch, and thereby set the tone for the modern confirmation process. He was the first President to insist on the

right to name his cabinet officers without significant consultation with the leading members of the Congress, which by his
administration was back in the hands of the Democrats. Before
Hayes, there was hardly ever any controversy over executive
branch nominations because, in line with the Founders' conception, the nation spent its first ninety years with cabinet
appointments heavily influenced by the Congress. The leading
members of Congress and the President negotiated the cabinet
before anybody was nominated. One result of this system is
that only four cabinet nominees were apparently withdrawn in
the entire nineteenth century.

Hayes, not satisfied with undoing Reconstruction, also
had no patience with congressional domination of the appointment process. He refused to nominate the candidates pressed
on him by powerful members of Congress, and the Congress
itself, riven with internal turmoil as the Reconstruction era
slipped, like magic, into the Gilded Age, lacked the backbone
to stand up to him. As a result, the legislative branch lost a
good deal of its influence over the appointments process,
becoming more like what it is today: a body that reacts to the
President's nominees rather than one that is consulted in
advance.[7]

The cabinet, too, has lost importance. In the era of cabinet government, before the invention of the unaccountable
monster known as the Executive Office of the President, the
heads of the departments were the President's chief advisers,
as the Constitution clearly contemplates. Moreover, Presidents
typically included political rivals—even enemies—in their cabi-
nets: Washington had Jefferson, Quincy Adams had Clay, Lincoln had Seward and Chase. Given the greatness that history
records for all three chief executives, it is not at all clear that
the new way is better.

Life, of course, is more complicated today, and political
life with it. Government is incomparably larger. (Lincoln had

one full-time secretary and an assistant to do all political and paperwork chores.) Besides, the presidency of the first half of the nineteenth century was far too weak. But the growth of executive power between the Civil War and World War II led to a situation that went too far in the other direction: congressional opposition to any presidential nominees, other than to the judiciary, became rare. Indeed, until after World War II, there were no official background checks to discover whether nominees had financial conflicts of interest, which is why the Senate needed a newspaper story to tell it in 1925 that it was about to confirm as attorney general and chief trust-buster a man who had spent much of his business career as a trust-builder. (Even so, the nominee, Charles Beecher Warren, was defeated by only 2 votes.)[8] Meanwhile, over the past four decades, the scope of federal power has grown immensely—some would say immoderately. So has the number of nonmilitary policy-making positions requiring Senate confirmation, now rushing past one thousand. There is far more for the Congress to oversee, and far less time for the Senate to give all nominees the scrutiny that their positions deserve.

But the cult of personality in which we foolishly wrap the modern presidency means that all of that vast, complex authority must repose in the single individual whom we happen to elect; we can scarcely imagine today a cabinet so independent that the White House does not know until later the details of what the departments are up to. We nowadays expect the cabinet secretaries to be good managers who will carry out the President's policies—"the job he was elected to do"—rather than to be powerful individuals with policies of their own. But with less and less policy made in the cabinet and more and more made within the Executive Office of the President, the identities of the heads of the departments hardly matter (except to political opponents who seize the chance to embarrass the administration). In this sense, too, the Founders' vision of an appointment process that would act as a restraint has been largely lost.

So although limited resources make it difficult, closer Senate scrutiny of as many nominees as possible would plainly be a good thing, for the reassertion of the legislative prerogative moves us closer to the balance of power that the Founders expected. At the same time, a higher rate of rejection paints a positive portrait only if we are rejecting nominees on sensible grounds. In the topsy-turvy first six months of 1993, it is not at all clear that this is what occurred.

LANI GUINIER AND THE SCHOLAR'S DILEMMA

This brings us to the second name passed freely along the televised backyard fence in the first six months of the Clinton Administration. In the middle of 1992, Lani Guinier was a relatively unknown law professor at the University of Pennsylvania. In the spring of 1993, she was tapped by President Clinton, a law school friend whom she had successfully sued when he was governor of Arkansas, to head the Civil Rights Division of the Department of Justice. And in June of that year, with confirmation support crumbling, she became one of many nominees for public office in our nation's history to be forced to withdraw, but (as far as I have been able to discover) only the second to fall victim to a nationwide campaign resting on distorting small snippets of her scholarship.

In the period between her nomination and its withdrawal, she was lambasted as a "quota queen" in an unusually vicious headline on the *Wall Street Journal's* op-ed page.[9] More thoughtful analysts examined her work and found it . . . well, Borkian. She was said to be a dangerous radical.[10] She thought minority voters should have a veto to protect their interests, the public was told.[11] And that a form of proportional representation (guaranteed seats, a quota) was necessary.[12] And that black officials elected by white voters were not authentically black.[13] Some of these characterizations came from journalists, some from political activists, some from conservatives, some from liberals. And none of them were true.

Lani Guinier, not to put too fine a point on it, was railroaded.[14] I do not mean that her opponents were not, for the most part, sincere individuals who thought that by derailing her nomination, they were somehow advancing the cause of racial justice. I mean, rather, that once her objectionable remarks are placed in their context—and once she is granted the freedom to experiment and imagine that scholarship demands—virtually all the critiques of her candidacy fall away, and those that remain do not seem so serious that they should be used to deny confirmation, especially when one considers certain comparisons that will become obvious.

Before proceeding, it is important to explain what the public debate left unclear. Scholarship—the writing that academics do—is part of a conversation. One puts forth ideas, generates a response, rethinks, and presses on again. The best scholarship is well informed and fair, of course, but it is also imaginative and ground-breaking—and it usually takes risks. In the academic world, we insist that risk taking is what we want to reward. But if scholars with ambitions to public service (there are probably too many) learn from the Guinier episode that anything they write, no matter how preliminary, will later be adjudged a statement of visceral moral commitment, the degree of willingness to take risks will naturally be less. I do *not* suggest that it is inappropriate to consider the scholarship of a nominee for public office; scholarship is, after all, the principal product of the scholar. I do think it absolutely vital, however, to consider it with care and, in particular, to remember that a work of scholarship, in the law or any other field, is not an op-ed article.[15]

Lani Guinier's scholarship revolves around a central problem: why is it that the interests of black voters are so often ignored in the political system? Her answer is that black voters lose out because of the implacable force of racism. How does one get around this? Her answer is that one develops political systems in which minority interests are less likely to be defeated. Borrowing from a rich and respected literature on voting, she puts forth a variety of proposals for the working of such systems. For example, in one of her articles she suggests the replacement of at-large elections for, say, a county board of commissioners (in which the majority gets all of its candidates through, every time) with a cumulative voting system, in which each voter gets as many votes as there are slots up for election. It is easily demonstrated that minority voters will have greatly enhanced opportunities to have their interests supported.[16] This enhancement is not a special gift to voters who are people of color: cumulative voting could enhance the strength of anybody who represents a substantial but under-represented constituency, from the Christian Coalition to the Green Party.[17]

Before proceeding to try to understand the criticism, and why it played so well even though it described her work so poorly, I should make plain that I do not agree with all of what Guinier has to say. In particular, I am far less certain than she seems to be that "minority interests" exist in the strong sense that she proposes. If she means this tautologically—a group interest, in the electoral sense, is what most members say it is—then of course she is precisely right. If on the other hand she means that the shared experience of blackness in an often hostile society creates a distinct perspective on the world, then I am less certain.[18] But so what? If one has to accept all of a scholar's premises before deciding that the scholarship makes a useful contribution to debate, then few of us in academia need bother to write at all.

Guinier's critics, in any event, had in mind nothing so

minor as a largely definitional dispute over what it means for a voter to have an interest. Their dissection of her scholarship was intended to show that she was a dangerous radical. Stuart Taylor's several articles about Guinier in *Legal Times* were typical. Taylor, as have other critics, picked two principal bones with her. First, he attacked her for purportedly believing in quotas in the sense of proportional representation: if African Americans are 25 percent of the voters, they should have 25 percent of the seats in the legislature and win legislative votes 25 percent of the time. Second, he warned that she divided black elected officials into two categories—the "authentic," who were elected from majority-black districts, and the "inauthentic," whose constituents were mostly white. Taylor noted, for instance, that Gov. Douglas Wilder of Virginia, whom Guinier mentions as having won by appealing to white voters, would presumably be an inauthentic representative.[19]

Yet Taylor, like many other detractors, read Guinier's work implausibly. The principal evidence for the legislative quota charge is a long article that Guinier authored in the *Michigan Law Review.* But the critics have her argument precisely backward. Guinier's starting point is the theory of pluralism, which political science students learn as freshmen. The theory holds that democracy will not deteriorate into the majority tyranny of which Tocqueville warned as long as there are no permanent majorities and no permanent minorities. In pluralist theory, each voter is simultaneously a member of many different blocs, and therefore is sometimes with the majority and sometimes with the minority. For example, a strong libertarian is likely to be with both the pro–abortion rights liberals and the right-to-bear-arms conservatives. In pluralist theory, no identifiable group should always be on the winning side, unless the perpetual losers are for some reason unusually weak at forming coalitions.

Guinier argues that if a single group—black people, in this case—repeatedly loses in a majoritarian legislature, the theory of pluralism, which says that everybody should win part of the time because coalitions shift, would predict that some concrete factor is preventing those victories. Guinier, as do many other theorists, believes that when the divide is black against white, the factor explaining the disproportionate losses is likely to be antiblack racism. One can naturally dispute this conclusion. For example, one might reject the entire theory of pluralism. Rejecting pluralism, however, means conceding that our democracy has deteriorated into simple majoritarianism. But it is difficult to find anywhere in history a serious political theorist who disagrees with Tocqueville that simple majoritarianism is oppressive and undemocratic. (Our Constitution, for example, is certainly pluralist and antimajoritarian.) Consequently, the only stable and pro-democratic responses to Guinier would be either to rebut the notion that black people lose in the legislature disproportionately to their numbers or to propose another reason for the losses. These difficult tasks, however, her critics could not be bothered to undertake.

Once the problem is conceded, the difficulty becomes how to solve it. Guinier's proposal for cumulative voting I have already described. The device of cumulative voting is of course well known; it has been used in corporate law and has frequently been proposed for elections of a variety of types, because it is more sensitive than simpler balloting methods to intensity of voter preference. Applying cumulative voting as a remedy for racial discrimination in voting is, as far as I am aware, a new idea. It may be a good idea or a bad one, but it is hardly outside the mainstream.* Guinier suggests a number

---

* It is only in this context that Guinier uses the term "veto." According to some of her critics, she argued that African Americans and other minority groups should have a veto over any legislation affecting their interests. In context, however, I find nothing but a suggestion that adopting a cumulative voting plan would *have the effect* of giving black voters, as well as other minorities, a veto in *some* circumstances over *some* legislation because it would enhance their representation.

of other solutions as well, but none of them turned out to be quite as controversial as this one.

Guinier, of course, is a lifelong supporter of affirmative action programs, and some critics tried to turn this, too, into a disqualification, suggesting that her advocacy of any racially conscious remedies places her outside the mainstream. But this objection is sufficiently specious that it should not have needed serious response. We live in a world in which racially conscious remedies are sometimes the only means for bringing about fair treatment, a point consistently recognized in court decisions and congressional enactments. Doubtless there are some who would prefer a chief of the Civil Rights Division whose commitment is to fighting against rather than enforcing the law, but a belief in the laws one is sworn to uphold would seem to be a qualification, not a disqualification, for the job.

The more serious charge against Lani Guinier had nothing to do with the media's silliness about quotas, outcomes, or cumulative voting. The charge was that her writing indicated that she saw some black political figures—evidently, those to whom white votes were essential—as inauthentically, just "descriptively," black. This is a somewhat forced reading of her scholarship. In context, she is setting out to answer a fairly simple question: are there advantages for black constituents who are represented by black legislators? Despite the argumentative turns of some of her critics, who insisted Guinier was dismissing such eminent black elected officials as Douglas Wilder as inauthentic, I can find nothing more in her scholarship than the troubling but understandable assertion that black politicians who have majority-white constituencies have more on their minds than the interests of their black constituents. So although I might sharply dispute Guinier's ready assumption that identifiable black interests often exist, that black voters have a "distinctive voice,"[20] she is plainly correct to argue that if they do, they will be better served by representatives—black or white—who are elected from districts with black majorities.

True, she could have chosen a more elegant phrasing for what she labels authenticity. But even if the critics are correct, and Guinier does harbor some skepticism about black elected officials who are beholden to white majorities, the claim that this is disqualifying is no more than a distraction. Suspicion against black people who succeed in a white world runs deep in the African American community, and although it is painful to acknowledge, it is difficult to hide. So if the case against Guinier reduces to an argument over whether she should have said what she did about some black politicians, the case is not even interesting. The answer is no, if she said what the critics say she did, she should not have said it. So let her have her hearing and let her apologize if anyone was offended, and then let us go on and scrutinize her qualifications.

Actually, we followed precisely that model when conservatives held power, and black people who made equally strident, and equally ill-conceived, attacks on the black civil rights leadership were lionized. Indeed, one of them, Clarence Thomas, was confirmed to the Supreme Court of the United States, even though he had said that the leaders of the civil rights organizations responsible for the battles that allowed a black man to sit where he now sits "do nothing but bitch, bitch, bitch, moan and moan." It is hard to imagine that this is the voice of racial moderation that Lani Guinier's conservative critics have demanded. Yet when Thomas apologized, most members of the Senate considered the matter settled.

Now, of course, had Guinier had her hearing and denied that she meant the words the way some feared—or even just apologized for them—many would not have believed her. As was Robert Bork before her, she would have been accused of a confirmation conversion. But, what of it? At the same time that the Guinier tempest was storming in its teapot, the Senate unanimously confirmed the President's long-time friend Webster Hubbell as associate attorney general, notwithstanding his long-time membership in a Little Rock country club that has no black members. The club was a problem, but, in the Senate's view, only a small one. He was permitted simply to resign from the club and announce his commitment to integration, a commitment there is no reason to doubt. Still, if these much-delayed actions (why wait to resign until facing a confirmation?) and late words were enough to rescue him from a penalty for his lifelong habit of relaxing in the company of those who would rather segregate, then surely a public apology from Guinier should have been more than enough. (I have more to say of discriminatory private clubs in chapter 6.)

Finally, Guinier was accused of viewing white Americans as implacably hostile to black Americans. Such language does appear in her work, albeit in a context where it is unclear whether she is speaking hypothetically. But, again, even if she said it and meant it, turning this particular opinion into a bar is scary. For if the ranks of the federal government are to be closed to all black Americans who perceive white America as implacably hostile and are willing to say so, one might wind up with a government staffed only by black people who are willing to keep their mouths shut.[21] In any event, surely the task of white Americans who object to the black perception that white people are racist is to prove rather than assert it false.

CONSERVATIVE COMPARISONS

Guinier was hardly the first nominee for a subcabinet post to receive such searing scrutiny. Ronald Reagan's subcabinet choices suffered several defeats.[22] Some conservatives (evidently on the turnabout-is-fair-play theory) have compared what happened to Lani Guinier with what happened to one of

those nominees, William Bradford Reynolds, whose nomination by President Reagan to be associate attorney general, the
number-three post in the Justice Department, was rejected by
the Judiciary Committee on a party-line vote after a confronta-
tional hearing. Reynolds, too, was rejected because he was
seen as outside the mainstream—even though he was said to
have stepped out on the right side rather than the left. Perhaps
some of the criticism of Reynolds was overheated. But his situation is still different from Guinier's. Reynolds was rejected
because the committee was unhappy with his stewardship of
the Civil Rights Division; in other words, he was rejected on
the basis of the way he had done his job. In particular, organizations representing people of color—the groups for whose
benefit the division came into existence in the first place—
objected to his performance. Even if one agrees with Reynolds
(I don't) that civil rights groups have pressed the nation too far
down the road of group remedies, the simple point is that
Reynolds lost out because powerful constituent groups did not
like what he had actually done during his time as a public servant—not because a handful of lines from his articles were
taken out of context.

The more frequent, and more apt, comparison is between
Lani Guinier and Robert Bork. Whatever one's views on
whether Bork should have been confirmed (certainly, there
were thoughtful arguments on both sides), it is plain that the
campaign to defeat him lifted snippets of his scholarship and
his judicial decisions very far out of their contexts, distorting or
misleading to raise popular ire. Two anti-Bork partisans,
Michael Pertschuk and Wendy Schaetzel, virtually conceded
this point in their book about the Bork battle, detailing the use
of focus groups to find the most effective way of presenting
Bork's record to get people to worry.[23]

A single episode suffices to illustrate the similarity in the
form of the distortions of Bork's work and Guinier's. A major

piece of evidence against Bork, featured frequently in advertising and commentary, was his opinion in a case entitled *Oil, Chemical & Atomic Workers International Union v. American Cyanamid Co.*[24] The case involved an employer who, unable to reduce toxicity in a portion of its workplace to levels safe for fetuses, adopted a policy requiring women of childbearing age to be sterilized or lose their jobs. It is difficult to imagine a colder or less sensitive solution to the problem, but the question before the federal appeals court did not involve the policy's morality, nor even, in the sex discrimination sense, its legality. The only question before the court was whether the Congress intended the word *hazard* in the Occupational Safety and Health Act to include an employer's decision to put female employees to this choice. Writing for a unanimous panel, then-Judge Bork concluded that it did not.

This plausible if unhappy statutory interpretation became for many of Bork's most committed foes a statement of policy: in the rhetoric of the opposition, Bork seemed almost to be in favor of sterilization. One advertisement described Bork as "giving women workers a choice between sterilization and their jobs," as though it was *his* policy.[25] Nor was the judgment to emphasize *Cyanamid* a casual, unthinking one: in surveys conducted for the Block Bork Coalition, the holding in *Cyanamid* created far more outrage than any of the other "facts" that the pollsters mentioned.[26] Naturally, then, the case bore emphasis, not as a matter of statutory interpretation, where Bork was very likely correct, but as a matter of Bork's own views: he was said to have "approved" an employer's decision to force female employees to the choice between sterilization and unemployment.[27]

Ironically, the fourth paragraph of Bork's opinion in the case decisively answered the principal argument of the anti-Bork activists:

As we understand the law, we are not free to make a legislative judgment. We may not, on the one hand, decide
that the company is innocent because it chose to let the
women decide for themselves which course was less
harmful to them. Nor may we decide that the company is
guilty because it offered an option of sterilization that the
women might ultimately regret choosing. These are moral
issues of no small complexity, but they are not for us.
Congress has enacted a statute and our only task is the
mundane one of interpreting its language and applying its
policy.[28]

Moreover, lest the moral point be missed, Bork's opinion
noted that no one claimed that the company would have violated the Act by refusing to allow women of childbearing age
to be exposed to toxic substances, and counsel for the union
conceded at oral argument that the company would have been
in compliance with the Act had it adopted a policy that "only
sterile women" could suffer exposure. That hypothetical policy, Bork correctly pointed out, "would also have given
women of childbearing age the option of surgical sterilization,"
which means that "[t]he only difference between this case and
the hypothetical is that here the company pointed out the
option and provided information about it." Thus, by the logic
of the opponents who used the *American Cyanamid* opinion
against him, counsel for the union in the same case would also
be disqualified in any future confirmation proceeding.

The use of the *American Cyanamid* decision against
Bork troubled even some of his most committed opponents.
Consider, for example, the views of Laurence Tribe:

To treat the choice that was put to those women as a
workplace hazard was stretching that law to purposes it
was never meant to serve. . . . I think Bork's decision in
that case was defensible and attempts to use it to show

him to be a prosterilization ogre were terrible. It was part
of attempts to stir up fears about him as a person, which I
tried not to do and regret that others did.[29]

Precisely. That was the point: to stir up fears about Robert
Bork as a person. Tribe might have avoided it, but others
embraced it as a strategy. Said Tribe in another interview:
"[Y]ou will simply not find anything in the testimony that questions Robert Bork's personal views on these matters."[30] Not in
the testimony, perhaps, but the hearing room was only one of
the venues in which the battle was waged, and the more
important battle was in the court of public opinion. There the
members of the Block Bork Coalition seemed to have no hesi-
tation about questioning "Bork's personal views." Consider this
blast from the National Women's Law Center: "No amount of
selective citation and interpretation can change Judge Bork's
record on women's legal rights from what it demonstrably is—
one of deep hostility."[31] The nuance is important. The claim
underlying this statement is not simply that Bork's jurisprudence on women's rights is wrong, nor even simply that it is
harmful; no, the claim is that Bork is *hostile* to women's rights,
and that attack is undeniably a personal one.

Bork, to be sure, had much to answer for. In his infamous 1963 article in the *New Republic*, he had referred to
forced integration of public accommodations as "a principle of
unsurpassed ugliness" and had condemned African Americans
involved in lunch counter sit-ins as "a mob."[32] When asked in
his confirmation hearings to name the most-criticized decision
of the Supreme Court, he came up with (to everyone's surprise) *Brown v. Board of Education*.[33] In a speech to the Federalist Society, he contended that precedents not modeled on
his own form of originalism have "no legitimacy."[34] Certainly, a
reasonable senator would want him to explain—and, if
unhappy with the explanation, would worry.

But it is possible to take a perfectly valid criticism of a nominee too far. Lurking beneath the extravagant and occasionally vituperative language of Bork's purportedly radical exterior was a sense shared by many other constitutional scholars that the institution of judicial review was spinning out of control. Bork obviously quarreled with many of the *results* that the Supreme Court had lately been reaching, but even one who generally accepted the trend of the Court's work could shiver at its method—or, more properly, its lack of method. Indeed, scholars across the political spectrum have charged since the 1970s that the Court never identified a set of enduring principles, tied to the Constitution's text or history, to justify what is commonly referred to, albeit with some loss of precision, as its liberal activism. (For that matter, the Court has not identified a similar set of principles to justify its recent conservative activism.) So to the extent that Bork argued that popular liberal precedents in the areas of privacy, the First Amendment, and criminal procedure lacked firm constitutional moorings, resembling instead governance by judicial fiat, he was solidly within the scholarly mainstream.

The reason this matters is that sensible scholars are able to draw a distinction in their criticism of the Court that the lay public, including politicians, journalists, and activists, too often will miss. This is the distinction between a personal moral preference for a particular result and a conclusion that the result is constitutionally mandated. One may perfectly well believe, to take a single example, that the death penalty is an utterly immoral horror and yet reject the proposition that the Constitution forbids its imposition. Or one might be personally pro-choice and yet take the view that the Constitution allows the states to restrict the ability of a pregnant woman to obtain an abortion.

Consider in this connection Edward Kennedy's famous speech on the Senate floor the day the Bork nomination was announced:

Robert Bork's America is a land in which women would be forced into back alley abortions, blacks would sit at segregated lunch counters, rogue police could break down citizens' doors in midnight raids, school children could not be taught about evolution, writers and artists could be censored at the whim of government, and the doors of the federal courts would be shut on the fingers of millions of citizens for whom the judiciary is—and is often the only—protector of the individual rights that are the heart of our democracy.[35]

This speech, which one scholar has described as "a patent fit of gross hyperbole,"[36] was surely beyond the pale. Plainly, once one understands the distinction between a judge's personal opinion and a judge's constitutional vision, the speech is inaccurate: the picture painted is not necessarily a picture of "Robert Bork's America," unless one believes that Kennedy's statements identify Bork's political preferences. At the same time, the rather arresting imagery could hardly be ignored, for it strikes at the heart of much of the American ideal.

The rhetoric about Lani Guinier was equally strident, and equally distorted. Consider this blast from Senate Minority Leader Robert Dole:

If nothing else, Ms. Guinier has been consistent in her writings—consistently hostile to the principle of one person, one vote; consistently hostile to the majority rule; and a consistent supporter, not only of quotas, but of vote-rigging schemes that make quotas look mild.[37]

Once more, the imagery is arresting—and once more the rhetoric is misleading. Dole accused Guinier not of simple error, but of an open hostility to the American ideal. In both cases—Guinier and Bork—activists opposed to confirmation could. not content themselves with stating in reasoned, thoughtful terms the grounds for their disagreements, perhaps because they feared the press would not cover something so dull as a policy dispute.

According to anti-Bork strategists, the purpose of Kennedy's speech was to "freeze the Senate"—that is, to give pause to those senators who might otherwise automatically line up on the other side.[38] And the strategy worked: the senators and their constituents began to take a closer look. Presumably, Clint Bolick's attack on Lani Guinier on the op-ed page of the *Wall Street Journal* the day following her nomination—the article bore the startling headline, "Clinton's Quota Queens"—had the same purpose; certainly it had the same effect. Let the rhetoric be heated enough, it seems, and somebody is bound to sit up and pay attention.

Of course, people on the left look at Bork and Guinier and say, "But what happened to Bork was fair!" And people on the right look at the two of them and say, "But what we said about Guinier was true!" As is so often the case, however, the activists at both ends of the political spectrum are simultaneously sincere and wrong. The trouble is that the opposition is really to a Bork or Guinier gestalt. Activists who campaign against a nomination see a threatening whole that is not easy to describe if one is forced to go piece by piece. Far easier to blow the pieces themselves out of proportion, to get the public to share the indescribable fear by misstating its basis, than to try making a serious, thoughtful case that is sufficiently dry that neither the news media nor the public they target will take any notice.

The short of the matter is that although there were legitimate arguments to be made against Bork, and perhaps against Guinier as well, opponents, in a simple grab for public attention, chose instead the path of shameless exaggeration. The members of the Block Bork Coalition had no patience with trying to convince the public that Bork had merely *misinterpreted*

the Occupational Safety and Health Act—what would be interesting or provocative about that? Better to make some head-
lines by implying personal misogyny. And those who successfully blocked Guinier did not say what was plainly true—that
most of what they opposed in her arguments was already the
law of the land—because how in the world does one get press
coverage by accusing the nominee of wanting to enforce the
law?

    Not long ago, I had a conversation with a respected and
serious journalist, who told me that although it might be true
that the attacks on Bork got out of hand, she was glad nevertheless, in retrospect, that he was not on the Court. Lots of
people of good will feel exactly the same way about Bork.
Doubtless, lots of people of good will feel exactly the same
way about Lani Guinier. Democratic structures exist, however,
precisely to resist assertions that the end justifies the means;
the American idea proposes that we are better than that. True,
the anti-Bork and anti-Guinier campaigns succeeded. The
American people were scared away. Bork lost. Guinier lost.
Nevertheless, the opponents must ask themselves in somber
retrospect whether they are truly proud of the campaigns they
ran. For decent people, perhaps carried away in the heat of
battle, it should hardly suffice to reply that the relentless personal attacks prevailed. "But we won" is not an argument.

But Bork, the reader may object, was nominated for the
Supreme Court, and Guinier for a sub-cabinet post: surely the
standards for the two are different! The answer is yes, of
course they are, although one would hope that in neither case
would we reward the employment of rhetoric that goes
beyond the bounds of decency, to say nothing of accuracy.
Still, selection of a Justice for the Supreme Court of the United
States surely is unlike the choice of any other public official. In
particular, when we choose a new Justice, we turn over to him

or her one-ninth of a seemingly unreviewable power to block popular political initiatives and force unpopular ones—all in the name of a Constitution most Americans revere but few Americans have read.[39] And we grant to those who wield the power, unlike cabinet officers or even presidents, life tenure.

Those last two words bear emphasis, because they give the Court much of its mystique. *Life tenure.* That, along with the immense and frustratingly distant power that it exercises, are what make the Supreme Court so attractive and so frightening. The urge to control it, to reach up to Olympus, as it were, and direct the flow of energy, is natural, and we do it all the time. Indeed, for all the nonsense to which we subject ourselves each time somebody sees political advantage to be gained by opposing a nomination to an executive branch position, there is nothing quite like the firestorm that erupts when powerful interest groups believe that one of "their" votes on the Supreme Court of the United States is at stake. It is to that problem that I next turn.

3

Of Litmus Testers and Stealth Candidates

SHORTLY before joining the Senate Judiciary Committee's unanimous vote in favor of the confirmation of Ruth Bader Ginsburg to the United States Supreme Court, Arlen Specter warned that the time will come when the committee will be forced to "rear up on its hind legs" and reject the nomination of a potential Justice who refuses to answer questions about fundamental issues in constitutional law.[1] Specter had in mind a frustrating colloquy in which Ginsburg declined on grounds of judicial independence to tell the committee what she thought about the death penalty.*

She was pressed closely on the question by Sen. Orrin Hatch, who wanted to know whether she would endorse the position long espoused by Justices Thurgood Marshall and William Brennan that the death penalty was unconstitutional in all instances. And suddenly Ginsburg, who at other points in her very friendly hearing had been quite forthcoming about her views on gender equality, on abortion rights, and on the

---

* This was not Specter's first expression of irritation at the committee's inability to predict a nominee's votes. In 1987, after charging that Robert Bork's testimony was at variance with some of his previously expressed views, Specter said, "The concern I have is where's the predictability in Judge Bork. Where's the assurances for this committee and the Senate of where you'll be?"

intersection between free speech rights and government funding for the arts, said what, in the end, almost all Supreme Court nominees always say: "I don't think it would be consistent with the line I have tried to hold to tell you that I would definitely accept or definitely reject any position."[2]

The reason that nominees always say this is that members of the Judiciary Committee always box them into corners. Somebody, sometime, finally asks how the potential Justice will vote. The reason the question is asked is that without that information, it is difficult for senators—or the public—to obtain a full picture of the sort of Justice the nominee is likely to be. And given the awesome constitutional authority that our Supreme Court wields, the notion of a wild card, a Justice whose philosophy and therefore whose votes cannot easily be predicted, is frightening. We the people grant the judicial commission for life, after all; the least those who seek it can do is tell us how they plan to exercise it.

Indeed, for an institution that sits atop what the late Alexander Bickel (borrowing from Hamilton) usefully labeled the least dangerous branch of the federal government,[3] the Court excites a remarkable degree of cautious and envious affection. We love it, we hate it, we cherish it, we fear it—but, most important, when one of its members steps aside and leaves a vacancy, we all feel as though we own it. It is *our* Court, and, in the rhetoric of the moment of nomination and confirmation, it ought to articulate *our* values. Choosing a new Justice nowadays is a bit like hiring a new servant: one wants to see prior experience, excellent references, verbal discretion, a judicious temperament, and an instinct for knowing the master's will.

Consider: In June 1992, shortly after the Supreme Court decided in *Planned Parenthood of South Eastern Pennsylvania v. Casey*[4] that the states may place certain restrictions on the availability of abortion, an angry commentator fired off an op-ed piece in the *Wall Street Journal* accusing the three Reagan-Bush appointees whose votes decided the case—Justices Anthony Kennedy, Sandra Day O'Connor, and David Souter—of betraying the conservative principles they were put on the Court to uphold.[5] The problem, it seems, is that they voted merely to narrow the scope of *Roe v. Wade*[6] rather than to overrule it.

A few days later, Bill Clinton said publicly that he would, if elected, nominate only Justices who believe in the fundamental right to privacy, which was widely understood to be a code for support for the abortion right.[7] Certainly many Clinton supporters wasted no time in telling their constituents that *Roe* was hanging by a thread and that a Clinton victory was needed to save it—meaning, presumably, that abortion rights supporters, like abortion rights opponents before them, should have the chance to pack the Court with Justices to uphold the principles of their movement.[8]

One might suppose that appointing Justices who make up their minds about how to vote before they hear any arguments rather than after is a threat to judicial independence. Evidently, one would be wrong. The practice of asking nominees about controversial cases is supported by nearly everyone involved in the process, with the notable exception of the nominees themselves. It is justified as a much-needed check on the otherwise uncheckable third branch. Says the constitutional scholar Paul Gewirtz: "The appointment process is one of the few democratic controls on an unelected Court that has broad leeway, whose members have life tenure and whose constitutional interpretations generally cannot be changed without a constitutional amendment."[9] Moreover, we never quite ask nominees to tell us how they are going to vote. We ask instead about something that we are pleased to label "judicial philosophy"—so slippery and elusive a concept that defining it at all is, as Harold Schoenberg wrote of playing chess against former world champion Tigran Petrosian, "like trying to put handcuffs on an eel." Even if we assume that the term is simply an elegant but inaccurate way of referring to constitutional theory, very few Americans are likely to care deeply about the judicial philosophies of individuals who are to sit on the courts. Quite sensibly, most citizens care instead about concrete results. Although we talk until we are blue in the face about the distinction between inquiring into a potential Justice's judicial philosophy and trying to work out how she will vote, it is a distinction that almost nobody takes seriously. Certainly the committed activists on left and right who constantly draw the distinction to justify their own imposition of litmus tests have no faith in it; one can discern this from the words they choose to spark their constituencies into action. They tell supporters precisely what decisions are at stake if the nominee is confirmed or rejected; in so many words, they tell their supporters how the nominee is likely to vote.

Thus, during the 1992 campaign, the abortion rights supporters who called for Justices who would vote their way, like the anti-abortion forces who felt betrayed when "their" Justices voted with the other side, were all taking the view that a vacancy on the Supreme Court is the moment to use political muscle to alter national policy. Given the role of the Court in our national moral and political controversies, one can hardly escape the desire to nudge that power, that independent, mystical force, in one direction or another—or, better still, to give it a hard shove. Yielding to that splendid temptation, we have no choice but to ask the nominees questions that will help us predict their votes.[10]

JUDICIAL "PHILOSOPHY" AND LINCOLN'S DICTUM

So why don't nominees answer?

The cynic would say they decline to answer because they know that every answer is wrong: just look what happened to

Robert Bork, who insists to this day that it was proper to engage in a colloquy about what was termed his judicial philosophy.

The nominees themselves, and their many defenders, offer a different reason. They do not answer, they say, because judicial independence forbids it. They follow Abraham Lincoln's famous dictum on the occasion of his nomination of political rival Salmon P. Chase to be Chief Justice: "We cannot ask a man what he will do, and if we should, and he should answer us, we should despise him for it." They follow the example of the estimable Justice Felix Frankfurter, who declined an invitation to testify before the Judiciary Committee on the ground that anything he would say might compromise his ability to serve as a fair-minded jurist. (Later, warned by more sensible friends that he might otherwise not be confirmed, Frankfurter changed his mind, which started us, some would say, in exactly the wrong direction.) Most important, they follow the example of each other, each nominee being able to cite as precedent the nominee before who in turn could cite the predecessor nominee, who also gave that same frustrating answer in a nearly unbroken chain, all the way back to John Marshall Harlan in 1955, who was, for reasons that will become clear, the first nominee to face a Judiciary Committee determined to ask about his views on the hot constitutional issues of the moment, and who politely declined because "it is something that is a matter of propriety."[11]

And ever since Harlan, with the single notable exception of Robert Bork in 1987, the nominees have all danced around the many substantive questions, sometimes with an engaging skill (one thinks of Anthony Kennedy, whom liberals and conservatives alike described after his hearings as supporting their positions on abortion), sometimes with an inelegant stubbornness (one thinks of Clarence Thomas, and the controversy over whether he in fact denied ever having expressed a view on the correctness of *Roe v. Wade).*[12] But they all say it, in their different ways: "Senator, it is a matter of propriety." And so on, some would say, ad nauseam. One after another, during the forty years that we have been quizzing nominees about controversial precedents and approaches to interpretation, they have lined up and refused to answer. And one after another, over those same four decades, we have confirmed them anyway. True, many Justices have been rejected—more than one of four nominees in the past quarter century—but there is one fact that all the nominees know: Senator Specter's lament on Ruth Bader Ginsburg notwithstanding, the Senate has never rejected a nominee for failing to answer its questions.

And so the nominees dance. Indeed, although commentators across the political spectrum insist on the obligation of nominees to give us the information we need to assess their judicial philosophies, there is a deep tension between our understanding of the Court's power, which makes us wonder how potential Justices might vote, and our respect for judicial independence, which means that we dare not ask what we really want to know. That tension leaves nominees the space to pick and choose their issues, giving a little to both sides. Ginsburg discussed abortion but not the death penalty. In 1991, Clarence Thomas shared his views on affirmative action but not on abortion.[13] In 1987, Anthony Kennedy talked about the right to privacy in general terms but not about abortion in particular.[14]

When nominees find ways to avoid direct answers to questions about what we are pleased to call their philosophy, we usually say they are being evasive. Many commentators and critics take the view that nominees who refuse to engage in discussions about their constitutional vision should not be confirmed. Such liberal legal theorists as Ronald Dworkin and Laurence Tribe have been quite explicit in endorsing this proposition. So has the conservative federal appellate judge Roger Miner: "If I could not get the answers I wanted," writes Miner, "I would vote 'no.'"[15]

Of course, in insisting on answers, we try to be careful about the questions, for none of us wants to violate Lincoln's dictum. So we rarely ask how a nominee will vote—we ask instead what the nominee thinks of particular precedents or how he or she would approach the interpretation of particular language. Says Judge Miner: "While a nominee may not disclose how he or she would decide a particular case, there are a number of questions that he or she should be required to answer." Although the Judiciary Committee has not—yet— found itself sufficiently angry at an evasive nominee that it has, as Specter said, reared up on its hind legs and voted no, we heap a good deal of public scorn on those who refuse us the information we need.

But exactly what does it mean for a nominee to be evasive? Consider the following exchange, from the transcript of the Judiciary Committee's hearings after the nominee declined to express an opinion on whether *Roe v. Wade* was rightly or wrongly decided. (Because I do not want to bias the reader, I omit for the moment the names of the nominee and the questioner.)

SENATOR: Do you subscribe to the philosophy expressed in the majority of the *Roe* opinion?

NOMINEE: I would say again, I respectfully state to you, Senator, that this is certainly a case that is on its way to the Supreme Court right now.

SENATOR: But it is already ruled on. This is the ruling of the Court.

NOMINEE: But there are other cases. The *Roe* case is not the end. . . .

SENATOR: . . . I am not talking about [those cases]. I am asking you now about the Constitution. . . .

NOMINEE: I cannot comment on what is coming up to the
Court.

SENATOR: But this has already been there.

NOMINEE: But there are hundreds of other ones on the way that
are variations of this.

SENATOR: Of course there are, but this is specific and has been
done.

NOMINEE: Well, Senator, I respectfully say that it would be
improper for me to tell you and the committee or anybody else how I intend to vote.

SENATOR: It is not improper, may I say, for me to weigh your
reluctance to answer . . .

[Portion of colloquy omitted.]

NOMINEE: [A]s I say, I can't comment, because it is coming back
up.

SENATOR: I have to wonder, from your refusal to answer, if you
mean the negative.

NOMINEE: Well, that is up to you, sir. But I have never been dishonest in my life.

Although some might protest that these questions come very
close to asking the nominee for an advance commitment on a
case, the senator who posed them would doubtless respond—
in fact, when criticized, he did—that he simply wanted to gain
a fuller understanding of the nominee's judicial philosophy.
The senator's growing anger, as evidenced by his warning that
"[i]t is not improper . . . for me to weigh your reluctance to
answer," is entirely consistent with Arlen Specter's proposal
that evasiveness itself be counted against a nominee.

It is easy to understand the anger that many feel at a
nominee who refuses to answer such questions. Important
constitutional decisions hang in the balance, often by a single
vote; the lives of tens of millions may be affected. If we are
unable to use the moment when a vacancy occurs to get some
sense of where the nominees stand on these vital issues, it is

hard to see how it will ever be possible to impose even a mild democratic check on the work of the Court. The Justices are around long after the era in which they were selected has passed. Says Laurence Tribe: "When we select Supreme Court Justices, we create a judicial time capsule: we freeze an image of the Constitution that one person holds today and send it off to be observed by, and to shape, the future."[16]

The argument that nominees who fence in this manner instead of disclosing their views on controversial cases are being evasive and should not be confirmed is a principled one and has a certain appeal. For those who find that argument attractive when the setting is the present and the case is *Roe v. Wade,* presumably nothing will change when it turns out that the transcript just quoted is from a hearing in 1967 and that the questions the nominee declined to answer were not about *Roe v. Wade* but about *Miranda v. Arizona.*[17] The inquiry about philosophy did not ask about the right to privacy but about the right of a suspect in a criminal case to assistance of counsel. In every other respect, I have quoted the transcript correctly. Consequently, readers who believe that the nominee is being evasive and should not be confirmed, if that judgment is a principled one, should not change their minds when they learn that the senator asking the questions was named McClellan and the nominee refusing to answer them was named Thurgood Marshall.

The correct transcript reads this way:

SENATOR MCCLELLAN: Do you subscribe to the philosophy expressed in the majority of the *Miranda* opinion?

JUDGE MARSHALL: I would say again, I respectfully state to you, Senator, that this is certainly a case that is on its way to the Supreme Court right now.

SENATOR MCCLELLAN: But it is already ruled on. This is the ruling of the Court.

JUDGE MARSHALL: But there are other cases. The *Miranda* case is not the end. . . .

Here Marshall added what I omitted above: "The case itself says in three or four places in the opinion that they do not know what Congress intends to do, they do not know—" At this point, an obviously irritated McClellan once more interrupted.

SENATOR MCCLELLAN: I am not talking about legislation. I am asking you now about the Constitution. . . .

JUDGE MARSHALL: I cannot comment on what is coming up to the Court.

SENATOR MCCLELLAN: But this has already been there.

JUDGE MARSHALL: But there are hundreds of other ones on the way that are variations of this.

SENATOR MCCLELLAN: Of course there are, but this is specific and has been done.

JUDGE MARSHALL: Well, Senator, I respectfully say that it would be improper for me to tell you and the committee or anybody else how I intend to vote.

SENATOR MCCLELLAN: It is not improper, may I say, for me to weigh your reluctance to answer . . .

[Portion of colloquy omitted.]

JUDGE MARSHALL: [A]s I say, I can't comment, because it is coming back up.

SENATOR MCCLELLAN: I have to wonder, from your refusal to answer, if you mean the negative.

JUDGE MARSHALL: Well, that is up to you, sir. But I have never been dishonest in my life.[18]

This line of questioning made Marshall supporters furious. Stormed Jacob Javits, "[T]he opposition, Mr. President, is not on the basis of fitness, but on the basis of disagreement with the kind of decisions which the opponents believe Judge Marshall will make." He added, "Supreme Court cases should not be reargued here."[19] Of course, "rearguing" *Brown* is precisely what McClellan and other segregationists had in mind. Although Marshall, who had won the case, would hardly criticize it, they hoped to box him into a corner—the very corner that supporters of judicial independence believed was none of the Senate's business. Sen. John Tower, grudgingly conceding the point, announced that he would support the nominee on the basis of his qualifications, even though he disagreed with his views on a variety of important legal issues.[20]

The precedent of the Marshall hearings poses an awkward problem for today's advocates of broad inquiry into the substantive views of potential Justices. Although nominees for the Supreme Court have testified regularly since John Marshall Harlan in 1955, a 1990 Congressional Research Service study of questions asked by the senators indicated that although nominees have always been asked about such matters as prior experience or controversies in their backgrounds, no nominee before Marshall was questioned so closely about constitutional interpretation, including his views on major precedents.[21] The questioning, virtually all of it by Southern segregationist senators, was deftly resisted by the nominee, whose refusals to answer were then defended by liberal senators and journalists. In fact, despite all the talk nowadays about not confirming nominees who evade questions about philosophy, the *only* nominee who has ever embraced rather than resisted such questioning was Robert Bork.

In somber retrospect, the Marshall confirmation hearings provide an ironic reminder of the inconsistency of principle. Only two members of the Senate Judiciary Committee in 1967 were still members in 1987 for the Bork hearings: Edward Kennedy and Strom Thurmond. In 1967, defending Marshall, Kennedy had this to say: "[W]e are not charged with the responsibilities of approving a man to be Associate Justice of the Supreme Court only if his views always coincide with our own."[22] Thurmond responded moments later in these terms: "Several Senators have indicated that they do not believe it to be within the purview of . . . the U.S. Senate to question the philosophy of an appointee to the highest court in the land. I do not accept this theory as valid."[23] In 1987, when the contentious Bork nomination forced the Senate to define its role, the two men essentially switched speeches. And one thing the contrast between the Bork hearings and the Marshall hearings made clear is that for left and right alike, outrage about inappropriate questions or tactics turns out to be a matter of whose ox is being gored.

FELIX FRANKFURTER'S SECRET

Although there has never been an era in our history when the President who nominates and the Senate that confirms have not cared about a potential Justice's views and potential votes, the contemporary presupposition that the nominee herself has the responsibility to tell us is actually quite young—and of dubious political pedigree. The notion that the nominee must appear and answer hard questions about difficult precedents was an invention of segregationists in their political effort to undo *Brown v. Board of Education*.[24] In one of those curious American political inversions, it is now liberals who profess to believe what just a quarter-century ago they termed a gross violation of the separation of powers.

For the first century and a half of the nation's existence, no nominee for the Supreme Court testified before the Senate; even though everybody wanted to know how potential Justices might vote, to ask was considered unseemly. The political branches took to heart Lincoln's dictum and never asked. Even so controversial a nominee as Roger Taney, who had made congressional enemies galore while doing President Andrew Jackson's dirty work by scuttling the Bank of the United States, was not asked to appear.

The first nominee to testify was Harlan Fiske Stone, whose 1925 nomination by Calvin Coolidge ran into serious opposition from Sen. Burton K. Wheeler of Montana, whom Stone, while serving as attorney general, had investigated. Stunned by the unexpected ferocity of Wheeler's assaults, the administration hastily arranged for the Judiciary Committee to reconvene, at which point Stone would have the chance to defend himself. He did so with admirable skill, and was easily confirmed, 71 to 6. For the next thirty years, nominees appeared intermittently. Yale's William O. Douglas, feared by many as a dangerous radical, expressed his willingness to testify but was not called. His lifelong judicial rival Felix Frankfurter, on the other hand, declined to testify when asked, citing a concern for judicial independence. Only after friends convinced him that he would not be confirmed if he defied the committee did Frankfurter give in.

The modern tradition of routinely requiring the nominee to appear began after the signal constitutional event of this century, the Supreme Court's courageous 1954 decision in *Brown v. Board of Education*, which began the direct judicial assault on the Southern racial caste system. Furious at what they described as unwarranted judicial interference with state authority, the Southern segregationist senators who dominated the Judiciary Committee demanded that the very next nominee— John Marshall Harlan in 1955—appear before the committee to explain his views on desegregation. A few nervous liberals protested the command performance as a threat to judicial independence, but Harlan acquiesced and a pattern was set.

For the next twelve years, every nominee appeared and every nominee was grilled about the segregation decisions. As the era of the Warren Court continued, the questioning broadened, and potential Justices found themselves asked about their views on everything from communism to defendants' rights to prayer in the public schools. For example, William Brennan, nominated in 1957 by President Eisenhower, faced a series of politically clever if legally naive questions from Sen. James O. Eastland, chair of the Judiciary Committee, about the legitimacy of the Court's methodology in *Brown*. (Typical: "Do you think the Constitution of the United States could have one meaning this week and another meaning next week?") He was also roughed up by Sen. Joseph McCarthy, whose star was by then falling but who still knew how to smear a witness. (Typical: "I have maintained . . . that you have adopted the gobbledygook that communism is merely a political party, is not a conspiracy. . . . Do you consider communism merely as a political party . . . ?") Picking his way through these mine fields, the usually forthright Brennan understandably chose the path of discretion. Like Harlan, he refused to answer directly, and in the end, the committee dropped these lines of questioning. [25]

By the time of Potter Stewart's nomination by Eisenhower in 1959, however, the segregationists saw history as running against them, and the committee, desperate now, was willing to ask its questions more directly, and with less patience for evasion:

SENATOR MCCLELLAN: The question is, do you agree with the premise used, the reasoning and logic applied, or the lack of application or either or both, as the case may be, and the philosophy expressed by the Supreme Court in arriving at its decision in the case of *Brown v. Board of Education* . . . ?

MR. STEWART: . . . [T]he way that question is ph[r]ased I cannot conscientiously give you a simple "yes" or a simple "no" answer.

SENATOR MCCLELLAN: Give me an unsimple one. . . . [26]

But only the diehard conservatives played this game. For the most part, liberal senators sat on the sidelines during this sparring, convinced that they had the votes for confirmation, which they did. Instead, perhaps because they felt secure in their control of the Court, liberals spent the fifteen years after *Brown* protesting that substantive questions to the nominees were not appropriate.

LITMUS TESTS: SOME HISTORY

When we base our appointment of Justices on predictions of their likely votes, we are imposing what have come to be called litmus tests. And just as in the chemistry lab, if you turn the paper the wrong color, we know you're too acid—or not acid enough—for our taste.

Defenders of litmus tests insist that they have existed all through our history. "[T]he Senate," writes Laurence Tribe in his book on the confirmation process, "has long judged candidates on the basis of what they believe."[27] But although this is correct, it is important not to take it too far. Certainly, political considerations have entered into judicial appointments since the start, and sometimes, even in the early years of the Republic, the politics were about the nominee's likely votes. One thinks of Thomas Jefferson's desperate last-ditch effort to persuade James Madison not to nominate Joseph Story to the Court, based entirely on a perception that Story would (as he did) spend his years as a Justice voting against everything that

Jeffersonians held dear. Or the years after the Court handed down the worst decision in its history, *Scott v. Sandford*,[28] which held that the enslaved black residents of the nation had no rights that the white man was bound to respect. For a while, the Senate took the position that no nominee without clearly established antislavery convictions would be confirmed. One thinks of Theodore Roosevelt, who rejected one potential nominee after another because of his fears that too liberal an approach to interpretation of the Constitution would ruin the nation, or of his cousin Franklin, who decided against nominating Senate Majority Leader Joe Robinson on the ground that he could not be trusted to vote the liberal line. And of course, there is the case of Judge John Parker, whose 1930 nomination by Herbert Hoover collapsed under the weight of criticism of his judicial record by labor unions and civil rights groups. (Parker, it should be noted, was the *only* Supreme Court nominee in the twentieth century to lose out in the Senate until Abe Fortas in 1968, whose nomination by a weakened President Lyndon Johnson—an obvious effort to reward a crony while on the way out of office—was bottled up in the Senate until Richard Nixon rose to power and Fortas, publicly humiliated, resigned from the bench.)

At the same time, not every frequently cited example of the practice of prediction actually involved a litmus test. John Rutledge was already a sitting member of the Supreme Court when the Senate rejected his nomination to be Chief Justice in 1795, but the rejection, although political, had nothing to do with his service on the Court and everything to do with his opposition to the Jay Treaty. Roger Taney, nominated by Andrew Jackson, was confirmed as Chief Justice only after a bitter fight. Many of his opponents objected to his role in the Jackson Administration when it waged guerrilla warfare against the Congress's cherished Bank of the United States; indeed, Taney's earlier nomination to be treasury secretary had been rejected because of this dispute, and nomination to the Court was thus a slap in the Senate's face.[29] But, again, it is hard to see how the fact that Taney's political opponents voted against him because of his views means that they objected to his constitutional vision or to the votes that he might cast.

Indeed, until recently, the "politics" involved in selecting Justices has frequently been the politics of achieving regional balance or rewarding party loyalty or punishing executive branch policies or finding a spot for a crony. Besides, there is an important distinction, one that advocates of the prediction-style confirmation contests of recent years tend to miss, between recognizing that the process sometimes does deteriorate into a squabble over the nominee's likely votes and arguing that it should or that the nominee, testifying under oath, should be forced to assist. Prior to the 1980s, there is no example of an administration systematically screening its nominees for their substantive legal positions. Thus, the Truman, Kennedy, and Johnson Administrations, although they appointed perceived liberals to the bench (with the notable exception of Kennedy's elevation of Byron White in 1962), clearly did so to reward personal and party loyalty. Liberal presidents would understandably have liberal supporters. The Eisenhower and Ford administrations followed a twentieth-century Republican tradition of actually screening for highly qualified moderates, with a sprinkling of regional balance thrown in. (Gerald Ford referred to appointments on "ideological grounds" as "a mistake.")[30]

Regional balance, of course, is itself a litmus test of a sort. So is party loyalty.[31] Indeed, it is quite rare for presidents to appoint judges, to say nothing of Justices, from outside their own political parties, although in the twentieth century, only one President (Woodrow Wilson) has exceeded the astonishing 98.4 percent party compatibility achieved (if that is the word) by Ronald Reagan.[32] But party compatibility has almost always been above 90 percent—in this century, only two very weak Presidents, Herbert Hoover and Gerald Ford, failed to attain that level.[33] Usually, serious historians agree, the reason that judges are appointed mainly from the President's party is less to push a particular agenda than to reward loyalty. Judicial appointments have long been a major plum in the political spoils systems and, apart from Jimmy Carter's fascinating experiment with selection committees,[34] most judgeships have traditionally been awarded upon recommendation of the senators from a particular state, provided that they are members of the President's party.

The Reagan and Bush administrations, by most accounts, raised what had been an occasional habit to a science, for they were less interested in party labels as such than in structuring the membership of the courts in ways that would turn back what was seen as a roiling tide of liberal activism. Litmus tests became far more important—and far more consistent—than at any time in the past.[35] It is not only the left that noted this fact with alarm. Federal appellate judge Roger Miner, usually identified as a conservative, and, according to news reports, a frequent finalist for Supreme Court vacancies during the Reagan and Bush years, offered an unexpectedly scathing view of the Bush selection process in after-dinner remarks at American University Law School in 1992. Referring to the office of White House counsel, where the Bush selections were overseen, Miner said, "It is there that the hot flame of ideology burns brightly." That office, he charged, "examines all candidates for federal judgeships for ideological purity." The result, according to Miner? "Merit has been more or less consigned to the back seat."[36] And Miner's comments, though discomforting, may be closer to the mark than one would like to think, for conservative activists, dizzy from the unexpected win of the Senate that accompanied Reagan's 1980 landslide, certainly laid plans to capture the judiciary.[37]

Perhaps the activists had less power than they thought in picking judges, and certainly the defenders of judicial selection under Reagan and Bush have argued with some force that the claims of ideological litmus tests are vastly overblown. At the same time, the sudden stridency in Senate opposition to a variety of judicial appointments during the 1980s—by no means limited to the Supreme Court—is sometimes defended as a response to what has been described, fairly or not, as an unprecedented effort to pack the courts with ideological soulmates, which helps show why litmus testing by Presidents is no less messy than litmus testing by the Senate.

But even if it is true that no administration pursued a vision of the courts quite as results-oriented as the one that often seemed to drive those who picked judges for Presidents Reagan and Bush, it is hardly the right alone that sees the judiciary as a plum to be handled by powerful constituent groups. As already noted, many on the left see the Clinton Administration as their salvation, the chance to do a bit of court packing of their own. On this much left and right seem to agree: when one's ideological soulmates control, for even a brief historical moment, both the White House and the Senate, the moment has arrived to capture the courts.

That very temptation is what led President Franklin Roosevelt to propose his infamous court-packing plan in 1937. Sick of the "nine old men" and their assaults on the New Deal, Roosevelt hit upon what seemed a simple solution: allow the President to appoint one additional Justice for each member of the Court who reached the age of seventy and did not retire. If adopted, the plan would have allowed Roosevelt to add, immediately, six Justices, all of whom would presumably be New Deal supporters. (The plan also applied to the lower courts, and although estimates vary, would probably have allowed Roosevelt to appoint several dozen additional federal judges.)

The plan, of course, blew up in Roosevelt's face, as even many usually reliable congressional allies ran for cover. (One who did not, Sen. Hugo Black of Alabama, was shortly thereafter rewarded with a Supreme Court seat of his own.) But in retrospect, at least if one believes in litmus tests, it is hard to see why it should have. Roosevelt proposed tampering, true, with the magic number of nine, but only statute and a few decades of tradition, not the Constitution, carved that arbitrary figure in stone. He was said to be threatening judicial independence, including by commentators who shared his evaluation of the Court's efforts to block the New Deal. But as William Rehnquist has pointed out, Roosevelt lacked only patience: packing as vacancies arise, rather than all at once, is a task attempted by many a President.[38] Indeed, if appointing people to the Supreme Court in order to have them vote the party line is a threat to judicial independence, then FDR has taken a bad rap, because, nowadays, that kind of threat to judicial independence is seen as a positive good.

THE MODERN ERA

Supreme Court nominees are entitled to no presumption of confirmation. Through much of our history, however, they have received one. Although many commentators have bandied about statistics concerning the rate of rejection of Supreme Court nominees—figures as high as 25 percent have been cited[39]—the figures are misleading. In the twentieth century, prior to Lyndon Johnson's ill-fated attempt to elevate Abe Fortas to the center chair, only *one* Supreme Court nominee (John Parker in 1930) was rejected. (I use the term "rejected" here to refer to both a formal Senate vote to deny confirmation and Senate opposition of sufficient strength that the President is forced to withdraw the nomination.) The Parker case represented the first flexing of muscles by a coalition of civil rights and labor groups that seemed surprised by its own sudden clout. Parker, a Republican who sat on the United States Court of Appeals for the Fourth Circuit, was nominated by a weakened President Hoover, early in the Depression, to fill the vacancy left by the death of Justice Edward T. Sanford. Labor unions argued that he had approved anti-labor tactics in his opinions. Although he had handed down some important pro–civil rights rulings, civil rights groups pointed to a campaign speech ten years earlier in which he insisted that "[t]he Negro . . . does not desire to enter politics" and referred to "participation of the Negro in politics" as "a source of evil and danger to both races."[40] The Senate ultimately turned down the nomination by a two-vote margin. But some historians now consider the rejection of Parker "not only as unfair and regrettable but as a blunder."[41] Indeed, when he resumed his work on the Fourth Circuit—he sat for another twenty-eight years—Parker became known as a progressive voice in civil rights and civil liberties cases: "liberals and conservatives, whites and blacks all agreed that he had been the very model of a federal judge."[42] On the other hand, the racist campaign speech of 1920 could not be denied, and Parker's written apology shortly before the Senate vote was far too technical, evincing little understanding of the passions it had stirred.

Parker was the first nominee to fall victim to his own paper record, and his was the first nomination defeated principally because of the work of organized interest groups rather than warfare between the President and the Senate. The Fortas case was different. Fortas, characterized by many historians as possessing one of the greatest intellects in the history of the high court, was at first largely a victim of circumstance. When Chief Justice Earl Warren announced his retirement in 1968, Johnson tried to move his friend Fortas from an associate justiceship to the center chair. But the President was a lame duck, the Republicans smelled victory in November, and Fortas was seen by conservatives as one of the great villains of the liberal Warren Court.[43] Here was a chance for some revenge. To make matters worse, Johnson nominated yet *another* old friend— Judge Homer Thornberry—to the seat that Fortas would vacate. Fortas, Marshall, and Thornberry: even some Democrats worried that the Court would harbor too many buddies of the President. To make matters worse, it was revealed toward the end of the hearings that Fortas had accepted a lecture fee of $15,000 for teaching for nine weeks at a local university that very summer. Not unreasonable, perhaps, for the services of a Supreme Court Justice, but by then the Senate and the media had had enough. An effort to break a filibuster failed miserably, and Johnson withdrew the Fortas nomination.* When Richard Nixon became President, he nominated as Chief Justice Warren Burger, who was easily confirmed.[44]

Since the withdrawal of the Fortas nomination, the rate of rejection has indeed been high: through Ruth Bader Ginsburg's nomination in 1993, five of seventeen were rejected or withdrawn. These statistics demonstrate the need to draw a line to define the beginning of the modern era—the era in which the rejection of a Supreme Court nominee once more became (as it should be) a serious possibility. The line should not be drawn in 1968 with Fortas, however. One could draw the line in 1967 with Thurgood Marshall, for Marshall was the first nominee to be faced with an orchestrated campaign, largely run through the mass media, to deny him a seat—a campaign

---

* In the spring of 1969, *Life* magazine revealed a more serious ethical breach by Fortas, the acceptance of a $20,000 per year consultancy from a private foundation established by the family of the imprisoned financier Louis E. Wolfson, money raised largely by Fortas's former law partner. Fortas resigned two weeks later.

in which some who still sit in the Senate today gleefully participated. Many of the questions, on the surface, were directed at
showing Marshall to be outside the mainstream, albeit in rather
diabolical ways. Senator Eastland, who chaired the Judiciary
Committee, observed that one of Marshall's judicial opinions
had cited in support of a particular historical proposition a
book by Herbert Aptheker and wanted to know whether Marshall had known at the time that Aptheker "had been for many
years an avowed Communist and was the leading Communist
theoretician in the United States."[45] Marshall said he had not
known. Later, on the Senate floor, Eastland strongly implied
that he did not believe Marshall's denial, adding a challenge to
Marshall's veracity to this slur on his loyalty. [46] Other questions
were more obviously hostile. Senator Thurmond demanded
that Marshall call immediately to mind such minutiae as the
views of Senator Bingham on whether the Congress could
enforce the privileges and immunities clause of Article IV, and
the names of the members of the congressional committee that
reported out the Fourteenth Amendment.[47]

The questions from the senators were the polite versions
of what the right-wing group Liberty Lobby, a major opponent
of Marshall's confirmation, was doing. Eastland's question
about Aptheker matched nicely the efforts of Liberty Lobby to
call into question Marshall's loyalty to the United States. Thurmond's long line of questions about the minutiae of the history
of the Civil War amendments dovetailed perfectly with the Liberty Lobby's effort to convince the Senate panel that Marshall
was not up to the job intellectually—a slur that Marshall, as the
first black nominee, must surely have expected. The only comparable assault was launched against Louis Brandeis, the first
Jewish Justice, who faced particularly strident criticism, including attacks on his qualifications from William Howard Taft, a
former President of the United States who would five years
later be appointed Chief Justice.

However, the attacks on Brandeis and Marshall need not be taken as evidence of problems in the confirmation process; when one compares them with the relatively placid atmosphere surrounding even the Fortas withdrawal, they might usefully be chalked up to the society's (and, particularly, the bar's) difficulties in accepting that those it tried to exclude—Jews in 1916, African Americans in 1967—were rising to positions that were unthinkable earlier. (President Millard Fillmore did try to nominate a Jewish lawyer, Judah P. Benjamin, to the Court in 1852, but Benjamin chose to serve in the Senate instead, and was later a member of Jefferson Davis's cabinet during the Civil War.)[48] The Marshall case in particular included within its complex symbology a last-ditch effort to refight the battles that Marshall himself had already won as a lawyer.

So drawing the line in the right place requires us first to take a step back. Although, until the 1970s, few twentieth-century nominees were actually rejected, approximately half the Supreme Court nominations since *Brown v. Board of Education*[49] was decided in 1954 (ten of twenty-two) have been seriously contested. This makes sense. *Brown,* after all, ushered in the modern era of judicial activity—the use, for the first time in the nation's history, of the courts as a sword on behalf of change rather than a shield on behalf of the status quo. When the Justices stood mainly in opposition to change, or sat on the sidelines and allowed the political branches to fight things out, those who wanted society to be different fought mainly in the legislatures. But once the Court signaled its willingness to be one of the engines of social change, the battleground shifted, both for those who wanted to make society different and for those who wanted to make sure it stayed the same. In other words, it is only since *Brown* that the Court has become a prize worth spending immense political capital to win.

Thus, segregationists worried about the nominations of William Brennan, Potter Stewart, and Byron White, and they bitterly opposed the elevation of their most effective adversary, Thurgood Marshall, to the high bench. By 1969, when the Republicans regained control of the White House, liberal reliance on the Court as an ally—unimaginable just three decades earlier—was firmly established. Consequently, when Richard Nixon began the much-ballyhooed search for "strict constructionists," liberals responded as though the sky was about to fall—and, for the first time, Senate liberals began to give close scrutiny to every nominee. The close media scrutiny that is now accepted as the norm began at about the same time. Thus, as one study of the history concluded, there has always been a degree of public interest in the selection of Justices, but only in the past twenty years has there been a consistently high degree of involvement by interest groups and the public at large.[50]

The line defining the change in the Senate's generally receptive attitude toward Supreme Court nominees should therefore be drawn with the Nixon Administration, which, in 1971, saw two of its nominees, Clement Haynsworth and G. Harrold Carswell, blown away by forceful Democratic opposition. One may call it ideological, one may call it partisan, or one may call it a sensitive review of the qualifications of the nominees. (Richard Nixon himself called it prejudice against Southerners.) However one describes the shift in attitude, it is important to understand its immediate cause: a shift in perception of the role of the Court in the life of the nation.[51]

Yet even when the ascendant Democrats began during the 1970s to patrol the route to confirmation more closely, they did not take the further step of trying to shut off the Court to those who could not be trusted to vote the right way. Thus they confirmed William Rehnquist and Antonin Scalia, the second with ease, even though, according to content analysis of newspaper coverage, both were seen at the time of their nominations as more conservative than Bork in 1987.[52] And although Rehnquist was questioned closely during his 1971 hearings about a memorandum he wrote as a law clerk for Justice Robert Jackson during the pendency of *Brown v. Board of Education*[53]—a memorandum arguing that the rule of "separate-but-equal" should be sustained—he was asked almost nothing on the substantive work of the current Court.

In 1986, matters were somewhat different. Rehnquist, now a sitting Justice, was nominated to be Chief Justice to succeed the retiring Warren Burger, and Scalia was nominated to fill the seat that Rehnquist would vacate. This time, the Judiciary Committee pressed Rehnquist hard on his jurisprudence, and several questioners, led by Sen. Edward Kennedy, argued that Rehnquist's conservatism was well outside the mainstream.[54] Rehnquist replied, in effect, that he was who he was; the decisions he had already rendered, he implied, were the best clue to the decisions he would hand down in the future. In the end he was confirmed by a vote of 65 to 33—the 33 dissenters representing, until Clarence Thomas's nomination in 1991, the greatest number of negative votes ever cast against a candidate who actually won confirmation.

Scalia, by contrast, was asked several quite general questions about constitutional interpretation, but only a little about cases likely to arise.[55] Certainly the questions to Scalia were intended to yield information about his probable votes, which means that we were firmly on the road, and the information gleaned could hardly have been satisfactory to the liberal constituencies that the following year would join together to oppose Bork. Yet the Senate confirmed Scalia by unanimous vote, which means that there was still no modern-day litmus test. For that development, the nation had to wait another year, until the Bork nomination.

MAKING PREDICTIONS

Even defenders of litmus tests have trouble explaining just why it is so important that the nominees themselves be asked the key questions about philosophy. In the first place, nobody ever answers. Nobody would dare. Even though every nominee since 1955 has testified, only one has cooperated in a detailed examination of his views on constitutional law, and after seeing what happened to that one—Robert Bork—future nominees would be crazy to pass up any opportunity to temporize, distract, and evade.

In the second place, the answers do not really matter. If the nominee says roughly what the questioner expects, that is evidence of dangerous radicalism. But the nominee will be accused of a confirmation conversion if she gives the wrong answers. Uh, the right answers. Well, the answers that make it harder to vote "no." In other words, once the questioner has decided what position the nominee holds, the nominee is not allowed to renounce it.

In the third place, if what we really want to do is predict a Justice's votes, we can generally get that information without asking, as the nation did through most of its history. The political scientist Albert P. Melone, after rejecting the idea that senators should ask nominees how they would vote in actual cases, adds, "There is no need to do so. Nominee attitudes and values are discernable and may serve as indicators of likely future behavior."[56] In other words, Don't ask, don't tell—just like homosexuals in the military! And Melone is right. Votes are not that hard to predict.

A popular mythology, fueled by the press, holds that it is difficult to figure out how nominees are likely to vote in controversial cases. But empirical study has cast serious doubt upon this wisdom. Comparing a content analysis of media predictions of judicial philosophy with later votes in civil rights and civil liberties cases, the political scientists Jeffrey Segal and Albert Cover found a remarkable consistency between the two.[57] And although the models used in literature of this kind are weakened by the availability of hindsight in deciding what counts as a predictor, our practical experience bears this out as well. Everybody knew that Thurgood Marshall was the champion of liberalism in 1967, and everybody was right. Everybody knew that Antonin Scalia was the champion of conservatism in 1986, and everybody was right again.

Nor is there much left of the old mythology that new Justices take a while to find their way, unsure which voting bloc to join, what used to be called the "freshman effect." Chief Justice William Rehnquist, in his book on the Court, cites this factor to explain why, in his judgment, court-packing is not easy to do.[58] Melone, writing prior to Clarence Thomas's nomination, was able to cite a number of studies debunking the myth of the freshman effect, at least in the case of Ronald Reagan's appointees, who were selected with voting predictability in mind.[59] As a member of the Court, Thomas has, if anything, made the data stronger: his consistency in voting with Antonin Scalia is the stuff of legend, and is also empirically validated.[60]

But sometimes prediction is harder. David Souter, nominated by President George Bush in 1990 to fill the seat of the retiring Justice William Brennan, was widely described as the "stealth candidate"—the theory being that unlike Bork, he had no paper record through which advocates might comb.* The

* Not everyone agreed that Souter was the stealth candidate: on some ideological radars, he showed up as a dangerous and identified object. For example, the Nation Institute's Supreme Court Watch project issued a detailed leaflet entitled "Judge David H. Souter, Where Does He Stand? A Preliminary Review of his Judicial Record." From its chilling pages, readers could learn, to their presumed horror, that in his six years on the New Hampshire Supreme Court, he had never written an opinion revealing whether he agreed with *Roe v. Wade*. He had, however, written that a criminal suspect did not formally invoke his right to remain silent when he said to the police, "[I]f you think I'm going to confess to you, you're crazy." Souter took the perfectly sensible posi-

theory underlying the criticism seemed to be that the President has an obligation to nominate someone with a paper record, who could then suffer the cruel distortions that Bork's ideological enemies imposed upon him. (This power of cruel distortion is hardly confined to the left or to the courts, as the eminently qualified Lani Guinier learned six years after Bork.) Presidents, however, are wiser than that, and no administration in the near future is going to walk into the Bork trap.

Besides, it is misleading to speak of stealth candidates. Bork cannot be the baseline. Bork was an unusual nominee, because his serious intellectual work was so extensive.[61] (The "Book of Bork" is what the heavy stack of papers was called in the summer of 1987 when it landed on the desks of journalists and law professors across the nation.) When one writes so much, it is a trivial matter to pick one's writings to pieces. But few nominees in our history have fallen into that category. Most have had careers in practice or in public service that rarely yield the opportunities for thoughtful and relatively detached intellectual interchange that present themselves to scholars and produce the written record on which a scholar is judged.

Aside from David Souter, nominees Anthony Kennedy, Ruth Bader Ginsburg, and, to some extent, Clarence Thomas were also labeled stealth candidates, meaning that the public lacked sufficient information on which to base a reliable prediction of future votes. In such a situation, if we want to know, we have no choice but to ask. But practice teaches us that if the nominees want to be confirmed, they have no choice but to refuse to answer.

---

tion that this was a boast, not a request to end interrogation. The Nation Institute, however, saw danger: "This opinion unfairly penalizes a defendant who has heard of *Miranda* warnings before his arrest and, based on the *Miranda* litany, refuses to talk to police."

HAVE YOU EVER . . . ?

But refusing to play the game means being accused of evasiveness. Arlen Specter's frustration with Ruth Bader Ginsburg's testimony tracks the plaint of the many scholars who have argued that no nominee who refuses to give the public the information it needs to assess her approach to interpreting the Constitution should be confirmed. Judge Roger Miner, in his remarks quoted above, singled out for implicit scorn Clarence Thomas, whose answers to queries about *Roe* during his 1991 confirmation hearings are already the stuff of legend, even if controversy remains over precisely what he said.[62] To this day, Thomas's detractors insist, first, that he told the Senate Judiciary Committee under oath in the summer of 1991 that he had never discussed *Roe v. Wade* and, second, that he lied when he said it. His defenders say, first, that he never said anything of the kind, and, second, that if he did say it, it was true.[63] The transcript is susceptible to readings in support of both contentions, for the following three exchanges occurred. Thomas was asked by Sen. Patrick Leahy if he had ever discussed *Roe* during the eighteen years between the date of the decision and the date of his nomination. He answered:

> Only, I guess, Senator, in the fact that, in the most general sense, that other individuals express concerns one way or the other and you listen and you try to be thoughtful. If you were asking me whether or not I've ever debated the contents of it, the answer to that is no, Senator.

Leahy then asked him whether he had ever expressed an opinion on whether the case was properly decided. Thomas replied:

Senator, in trying to recall and reflect on that, I don't rec-
ollect commenting one way or the other. There were,
again, debates about it in various places, but I generally
did not participate. I don't remember or recall participat-
ing, Senator.

An obviously irritated Leahy asked, "So you don't recall stating
whether you thought it was properly decided or not?" Thomas
answered, "I can't recall saying one way or the other, Senator."

Was this a sincere expression of a lack of intellectual
curiosity? A brilliant example of legal footwork, full of denials
leaving lots of wiggle room? Whichever it was, the argument
over what Thomas actually said, for all its bitterness,[64] masked
a tougher question, for what all too few people discussed,
even at the time, is why exactly Thomas's view on the *legal*
correctness of *Roe v. Wade* was anybody's business but his
own. Or why he had to have a view at all. For the devotee of
judicial independence, there is something terribly attractive
about the possibility that a nominee would answer the question about a specific case with this: "Senator, with respect, I
have no settled view on that. When I see the issue fully briefed
and argued in the context of a specific case, I will make up my
mind." The nominee could even add John Marshall Harlan's
line: "it is something that is a matter of propriety." That is not,
of course, what Clarence Thomas said. The next question,
then, is whether it is what he should have said.

4

Of Judicial Philosophy and Democratic Checkery

LET us begin with what is surely common ground: nobody would argue that the nominee's constitutional vision is entirely a non sequitur. On the contrary. The President who nominates a potential Justice and the senators who must decide whether to confirm her should have their own visions, whether shared or not, of the significance of the Court and the Constitution in our national life. They should have a sense of the moral vision that would drive the nominee in performing her constitutional responsibilities. An inquiry into the views of the nominee on these issues is not only legitimate but probably inevitable, unless one wishes the appointment process to deteriorate into a dreary and mechanistic resume review.

The Senate, in short, should not serve as a rubber stamp for court-packing by the executive branch. There are ways to avoid this pitfall, to test the moral and constitutional sensibilities of the nominee without presuming to impose litmus tests. In chapter 5, I will explain how it might be done. First, however, it is necessary to understand how what we do instead—asking about results in particular cases—threatens judicial independence.

THE DEMOCRATIC CHECK

"[T]he appointment of a Supreme Court justice," Dean Harry Wellington has written, "and the confirmation process before the Senate must take account of the following truth: the nature of constitutional interpretation in the process of adjudication inevitably means that constitutional law is shaped, influenced, indeed made by those authorized to interpret."[1] Further, in the words of Laurence Tribe, the interpretation of the Constitution should reflect "*our* values" but will do so "only if we peer closely enough, and probe deeply enough into the outlooks of those whom our Presidents name to sit on the Supreme Court."[2] The trick is to accept this proposition while avoiding a process that rejects the point of judicial review: frustrating the popular will is precisely what the courts are often *for*.

Consider the views of Chief Justice William Rehnquist in his useful 1987 book, *The Supreme Court:* "[A] president who sets out to pack the Court does nothing more than seek to appoint people to the Court who are sympathetic to his political and philosophical principles."[3] Franklin D. Roosevelt, in other words—and, later, Ronald Reagan—were only doing what presidents are supposed to do. Having won the popular election, they were trying to control the courts, much in the manner of, albeit less directly than, the Stuart kings, who in the years before the English Civil War often discussed pending cases with potential judges before deciding on appointments. Rehnquist's evaluation of court-packing is succint: "There is no reason in the world why a president should not do this."[4]

No reason? The legal scholar Mark Tushnet has put his finger on a potential problem:

> [R]elying on the appointment process to check the courts
> simply reintroduces the problem of legislative tyranny. All
> that it can accomplish is the creation of repeated oscilla-

tion between a regime in which judges defer to legislative will and allow the legislature to tyrannize over those who lack sufficient political power and a regime in which judges do not defer and themselves tyrannize on behalf of parties defeated in the legislature.[5]

Once pointed out, the objection seems an obvious one. Why in the world should anyone who believes in the Constitution believe that elected officials should try to check the Court? The institution of judicial review exists precisely to thwart, not to further, the self-interested programs of temporary majorities.

Rehnquist's answer is that the President and the Senate—he mentions both—should possess a degree of influence over the philosophy of appointees because "the manifold provisions of the Consititution with which judges must deal are by no means crystal clear in their import, and reasonable minds may differ as to which interpretation is proper."[6] And after all, as Wellington and Tribe point out, confirmation hearings may be viewed as a part of the interpretive process. The Bork hearings, for example, are frequently described as a useful national seminar on constitutional law. By the time they were over, it was plain that the public did not want a Justice with doubts about the right to privacy.

Because each side of the argument contains a grain of truth, a worrisome paradox emerges. On the one hand, the courts exist at least in part to limit majority sway. On the other, the courts are to be peopled with judges selected at least in part because their constitutional judgments are consistent with those of the very majority whose authority they supposedly limit.

To make matters more complicated, we do not hold our glorious confirmation seminars in secluded classrooms; we hold them in brightly lit committee rooms. The nomination decision and the confirmation hearings take place in a nation deeply divided over fundamental moral questions that we allow the Justices to resolve. Moreover, through the magic of the sound bite, we actively invite the participation of the public in the Senate's deliberations. In a democracy, this is of course inevitable; but it works out so badly in practice that one wonders if we should keep up the pretense that we are engaged in any exercise other than trying to fix the results of decisions in advance.

However, the worrisome paradox may be more apparent than real, because once one moves away from the academy, it seems unlikely that many of the pundits and politicians who talk about a Court reflecting the values of the American people seriously want that. Usually, what they want instead is a Court reflecting *their own* values—that is, they want Justices who can be trusted to vote the right way. Indeed, the views of the American people tend to be the last thing that activists want the Court to heed. Perhaps this explains the phenomenon, which students of the confirmation process have long noted, of senators struggling to find grounds other than ideology on which to place their opposition that everyone understands is really ideological.[7]

This is certainly true on abortion, where pro-life and pro-choice forces alike have insisted on the privilege of packing the Court. Naturally, they have done so not in the name of narrow partisanship but of the American people, who evidently are on their side. Such arguments as these are usually based on shaky interpretations of the polling data, because, in truth, neither side in the polarized abortion debate much likes the polling data. Although the media offer the impression that people are either pro-life or pro-choice, and those twain don't meet, the truth, consistent now for two decades, is that less than a third of Americans think abortion should be an unfettered choice and less than a sixth think it should be banned in all circumstances. The silent majority is solidly where it often is—in the middle, strongly supporting such restrictions as waiting periods and, in the case of minors, parental notification requirements, and just as strongly opposing broad bans that would allow exceptions only in cases of rape, incest, or to save the life of the pregnant woman.[8] Given the result in *Planned Parenthood v. Casey* (discussed in chapter 3), the Supreme Court is already, right now, taking a position consonant with the will of the public. One might not like that result, and one might lobby for the appointment of Justices who will change it, to one more firmly pro-choice or pro-life; but the argument that the reason for the change is to let the will of the people be done is simply false.

Besides, if we really want a Supreme Court that reflects "our" values, there are some cases on which the Justices are more plainly out of step. Hardly anybody likes the Court's jurisprudence on the rights of the accused,[9] and consistent majorities would overturn the decision extending free-speech protection to the burning of the American flag.[10] But probably the single most unpopular series of Supreme Court decisions— by a huge margin—are those that prohibit organized classroom prayer in the public schools.[11] I happen to think those cases were rightly decided,[12] but that puts me in a clear minority. In 1983, Gallup reported that some *81 percent* of those who were aware of the decisions favored a constitutional amendment overturning them. (Lest one challenge the data on the ground that people are unlikely to be aware unless they care, 82 percent were aware of the decisions.) Support has fallen a smidgen but is still of landslide proportions: in 1992, a Gallup survey indicated that 62 percent of registered voters favored the constitutional amendment.[13] Should the Senate and the President therefore have tried in 1983 at the next available vacancy to ensure that these broadly shared values of the American people be reflected in the Court? Should President Clinton, when Justice Byron White retired, have done the same? One would assume so, if the far weaker and shifting pluralities on either side of the abortion controversy deserve not only to be heard but to be recognized by having, in effect, their own seats on the Court, and if, as advocates of democratic checkery seem to suggest, the role of the nomination and confirmation process is to guarantee that the Court will be staffed with jurists who will give voice to the most fundamental aspirations of the American people.

One might object, of course, that the relevant voices are those of the downtrodden, those the society has ignored. A fine idea—except that support for organized classroom prayer is negatively correlated with both education and income. The poor want it. So do the people who are *not* members of what used to be called the power elite. So do people of color. Both the African American and the Hispanic communities tend to support organized classroom prayer in significantly greater proportions than white people do. Women, if they are the relevant downtrodden group, tend to support it more than men; in fact, all of these putatively oppressed groups, including women, are (in most surveys) more supportive of classroom prayer than they are of abortion rights!*

A natural answer to the school prayer argument, once we move beyond the various false consciousness claims available to help one escape, conveniently but often incoherently, from tight analytical squeezes, is that the Court is not supposed to be sensitive to political pressures of this kind; which is another way of saying the Justices should not care what the public, or

* Lest one be deceived into thinking that I have the calculus backward—that the relevant downtrodden when one discusses public school classroom prayer are those who, for whatever reason, oppose it, as I do—two points should be made. First, because support for school prayer is broader outside than inside the legal community, it seems unlikely that the voices of those who oppose it are given inadequate weight in the judicial process. Second, the definition of downtrodden, to make sense of this criticism, would become tautological: the putative downtrodden turn out to be those who support whatever decision the Court has made, the putative downtrodders those who oppose it.

any subset of the public, thinks of their handiwork. But it is at least a *little* peculiar that we are told that scrutiny of "judicial philosophy" is crucial to provide a democratic check on the Justices, but, at the same time, that the Court should not be responsive to political pressure or public protest.

On the other hand, perhaps what seems to be confusion actually reflects something fundamental in the American character. Perhaps most Americans do not draw a distinction between personal moral belief and constitutional interpretation because they do not believe it is real—that is, if you support a woman's right to choose abortion, then, ipso facto, you believe that the Constitution should be read to protect it. After all, the mere fact that a handful of scholars who ruminate on these matters in the old fashion believe that the distinction is real does not mean that anybody else is obliged to think so.

Thus there may be more sense than immediately appears in our strange ritual under which organizations that measure public opinion conduct surveys in which they ask a cross section of the public whether this decision or that one should be overturned, and then solemnly report the results, as though they have some legal significance, as though the Supreme Court should pay attention to this sentiment—notwithstanding that the respondents are not lawyers, that only a tiny fraction of them are likely to have glanced at the Constitution, and that virtually none of them will ever have read the decision in question. After all, the idea that constitutional law is in some important sense *governed* by the constitutional text is not one that has much academic currency, and it may not have much political currency either.

Everyone talks about *updating* the document to reflect *our* values.[14] When pressed by liberals, the argument always seems somewhat disingenuous, unless one means by *our values* "mine and those of my friends"—for if one sincerely believes in a Constitution that incorporates the values of an evolving American public, then one must want a Constitution with organized classroom prayer in the public schools, fewer rights for criminal defendants, and punishment for those who desecrate the American flag. Not too long ago, we had Presidents who ran and won on platforms promising approximately these things. They were accused, with reason, of seeking to politicize the appointment of Justices. Today we are told by many of the same critics that the new administration has an obligation to make appointments that will restore the "balance"—that is, to appoint Justices whose votes will cancel out the votes of the last five appointees. But changing the set of values that one believes the document should reflect provides no defense against this charge; indeed, to the extent that one selects values without basis in either the original understanding or the public will (and I am no fan of the second), one is simply trying, perhaps for reasons of efficiency, to use the judiciary to enforce elite values in the name of constitutional law.

It is easy to see why this approach is appealing: one can envision seats on the Supreme Court as a costless political largess, distributed in accordance with the interests of one's political followers. As for those of us who believe in trying to preserve the autonomy of the law by stressing interpretive rules that make it more difficult for judges to vote the will of the ideological movements that led to their ascension, well, we are regarded by left and right alike as dinosaurs, politically out of step, theoretically naive. Indeed, an important strain of contemporary constitutional theory holds that no distinction is possible, that legal and constitutional arguments are both bootstraps for political results. I do not accept this view, for reasons I have discussed elsewhere and will not labor here.[15] However, because the view is dominant, and because both the lay public and the leadership of the bar seem to think the view correct, it is worth taking time to tease out its implications for the role of the Supreme Court and the way we choose our Justices.

With this in mind, consider for a moment the vote by the American Bar Association's House of Delegates to put the group on record as supporting reproductive choice. One might consider the vote as evidence that the legal community stands behind *Roe v. Wade.* This might be correct (although the ABA's stubborn refusal to poll its members gives one pause), but there is a sense in which it makes no difference whether the House of Delegates was reaching a policy or theoretical conclusion. To understand why this is so, take the case of an individual who, studying the House of Delegates vote, comes to the conclusion that a mainstream lawyer is one who believes the right to abortion to be constitutionally protected. Since we have established that candidates from outside the mainstream are not entitled to sit on the Supreme Court, this newly persuaded individual will naturally want to know what each nominee's position on abortion is.

Now suppose the nomination of a candidate who has written the following sentence in a major article: "It is ridiculous to claim that the constitutional right to privacy has anything to do with abortion, and the Court's reasoning to the contrary in *Roe v. Wade* is simply a travesty." On its face, given the ABA's position, this sounds like a fairly easy case for rejection of the nominee.

But suppose that the next sentence of the same article reads this way: "However, because only women and not men are burdened by restrictions on reproductive freedom, I would hold such limits unconstitutional on the ground that they violate the equal protection clause." And the argument might finally conclude: "I therefore believe *Roe* to be rightly decided, even if very poorly reasoned."

Now, would an individual persuaded by the House of Delegates vote object to this nominee? Would pro-choice organizations? Or pro-choice senators? Of course not—because the nominee plans to vote the right way, to preserve the abortion right. And the goal of the House of Delegates vote, like the goal of screening judicial nominees for their positions on abortion, is to protect the right itself, not to perpetuate a particular line of reasoning as the right way to reach the result.

Consider President Clinton's nomination of Ruth Bader Ginsburg to the Supreme Court. Ginsburg, in a law review article and a speech while serving as a federal appellate judge, made a form of the argument set out in the hypothetical. She criticized *Roe v. Wade* for deciding more than it had to. She questioned the reliance on privacy as the constitutional rationale. And she contended that an equal protection argument would have put the case on a stronger footing.[16]

All of these are common arguments in the literature, although those with judicial aspirations make them at their peril. In the case of Ginsburg, a few pro-choice groups expressed a bit of uneasiness at her criticisms of *Roe*. (One delegate to the annual convention of the National Organization for Women said in a radio interview that she would have preferred Catharine MacKinnon, a feminist law professor who crusades against pornography, but would accept Ginsburg—evidently on a "best-we're-likely-to-get" theory.) But others in the pro-choice camp reminded the skeptics that Ginsburg was on their side—she simply located the abortion right in a different part of the Constitution. And, in the end, no abortion rights group actually opposed her.

Indeed, no pro-choice scholars opposed her either. This in turn suggests that all the thoughtful academic commentary about how screening a judge for her philosophy is different from screening her for the results she will reach is wrong. Otherwise, one would expect some law professors to have attacked her for misreading the same due process clause that Judge Bork was said to have interpreted wrongly when he said that the rights discovered in *Roe* could not be found there. After all, an intellectually honest view that no one in the mainstream could fail to find the rights where the Court found them should hardly be altered simply because the outside-the-mainstream jurist comfortably located the rights somewhere else.

What this hypothetical teaches—if, as I suspect, it reaches a correct conclusion—is that the affection in the legal community for the abortion right has nothing to do with law as such. It is a policy preference, not a legal preference. It is not, in other words, an argument rooted in a consideration of the relevant constitutional language and precedent, because, if the hypothetical is correct, the constitutional language and precedent do not really matter. The result does.

In short, lawyers are likely to prove little better than lay people in distinguishing between policy choices and theories of adjudication. What matters, when the ABA's House of Delegates takes a position like the one it has, is the bottom line—not how the Court reaches its decisions but what decisions the Court reaches. Virtually all the players—and I most emphatically have in mind the opponents as well as the supporters of abortion rights—care only about concrete results. And the point of the game is to get the results you want.

That, at bottom, is the reason that our battles over confirmation of Supreme Court nominees leave so much blood on the floor: so much is seen to be at stake! When a new Justice is selected, what hangs in the balance is nothing so arcane as the correct approach to constitutional interpretation. What hangs in the balance, rather, is the list of rights to be protected or unprotected, depending on one's preference. The public—including, perhaps, much of the bar—does not particularly care *how* the nominee will reach her results. The public cares only about what results the nominee will reach. And as long as that is our national attitude about the Supreme Court—as long as all that matters is the bottom line—our battles over the rare vacancies will all too frequently be bloody.

Still, all of this is in some sense still prologue. The wheel of history has turned. The Democrats have won the White House and, if their comments are accepted at face value, some of them believe they have a mandate to pack the Court, as a way of "balancing" the Republican court packing. This is the reason that President Clinton's nomination of Ruth Bader Ginsburg, who had nothing going for her but the fact that she is a brilliant jurist whom everybody respects, came as so bitter a disappointment to some activist constituencies. If, when a future vacancy occurs, Clinton appoints someone whose votes are more predictable, it will be interesting to see whether the Republicans, as the opposition party for the first time since the Fortas nomination, will claim that the President has no right to nominate to the Court individuals who will vote the party line—and, if they do, it will then be interesting to see whether the Democrats can find a principled ground for objection.

LESSONS FROM THE STATES

Even if everybody is perfectly sincere, pressuring the nominees to answer questions that will enable us to predict their votes raises grave issues regarding impartiality—at least if any potential litigant watches the hearings. True, many nominees will have strong commitments on many divisive questions; but to make the search for those commitments the focus of executive or Senate review is to propose to the public an image of the judicial process in which the prior commitment holds center stage. It is not clear why anyone would want to argue before a judge who not only has made up her mind but was confirmed precisely for that reason.

Here the experience of the state courts provides a useful analogue. In the states, where most judges are elected, the words they are allowed to use in the course of campaigning are narrowly circumscribed by the strictures of the Model Code of Judicial Conduct. Even though the 1990 amendments to the Model Code have granted more freedom than before to judges who must run for their seats, the ambit of permissible speech is understandably still quite narrow. Until the amendments, Canon 7(B)(1)(c) provided that a candidate for judicial office should not "make pledges or promises of conduct in office other than the faithful and impartial performance of the duties of the office" or "announce his views on disputed legal or political issues." Since the amendments, the Canon no longer requires candidates for judicial office to refrain from announcing their views on disputed issues. However, the limits on campaigning are still quite stringent. The revised Canon 5(A)(3)(d) provides that the candidate shall not "make pledges or promises of conduct in office other than the faithful and impartial performance of the duties of the office" and shall not "make statements that commit or appear to commit the candidate with respect to cases or controversies that are likely to come before the court."[17] This revised Canon takes a more liberal approach than the old Canon's prohibition on virtually any controversial comment. Indeed, when joined to the new Canon 5(A)(3)(e), which allows candidates some latitude in responding to personal attacks, the new Model Code plainly aims at opening up campaign debate.

Still, the Model Code continues to prohibit a candidate from even appearing to commit herself to a position on cases that might come before the relevant court—a rule that might come as a surprise to the many politicians and groups who demand to know how potential Supreme Court Justices would vote on controversial cases. The sensible rationale for the rule is that the appearance of impartiality is weakened when judges are known to have made up their minds before they hear arguments rather than after. Thus, we find another magnificent irony. In the state courts, where judges are elected precisely to decrease the scope of their independence (see the next section), we nevertheless clothe them in the raiment of impartiality by refusing to let them reveal any information that might reveal likely votes. But in the federal system, where we appoint the judges instead of electing them because we wish to protect their independence, we demand that they dispense with the illusion of impartiality and give us precisely the information that they are not allowed to divulge when required to face the popular ballot.

Of course, in a sense, we do select the Justices of the Supreme Court by popular ballot. We take surveys on whether each nominee should be confirmed, and, understandably, members of the Senate pay close attention to their constituents' views. The fact that not everybody gets to play—organized interest groups wield greatly disproportionate influence—does not mean that election is not the game. Again, one is put in mind of the Bork hearings, where the tendency in our confirmation rhetoric to say "judicial philosophy" but mean "rights we like" was showcased in the bizarre spectacle of elected representatives of the people of the United States solemnly propounding such questions as whether a Bork appointment would further or hinder the articulated interests (and, implicitly, the political programs) of women, or of people of color, or of a Congress jealous of its foreign policy prerogatives, until in the rush to explain what valued decisions a hypothetical Justice Bork would overturn, the confirmation battle took on the aspect of an election contest in which one party accused the other of seeking to undermine the nation's traditional values.

That charges of this kind were made, and with real venom, hardly makes the Bork battle unique. In fact, the battle was unusual only because the charges were taken seriously and the nominee was rejected. Members of the Senate are practical politicians and hardly want to cause trouble back home. This in turn suggests that the fundamental charge against Bork—that the results a Justice Bork might reach would not match the results that the American people would prefer—was true. Certainly his views as understood by the American people seemed to be out of step with their own. Yet even assuming an identity between the views he was perceived to hold and the views he held in fact, what is the message in his rejection on this ground? It must surely be what I have proposed: that when the people and their President and their senators talk about "judicial philosophy," they have in mind not adherence to a particular theory but reaching the right results. The public demands the information, and the media, the interest groups, the administration, and the candidate all vie to deliver their own versions, because they know what theorists try to deny—that what is taking place is not a confirmation but an election. For that, in the end, is what it means to impose on the selection process our particular version of the "democratic check."

SOME EMBARRASSING HISTORY

Besides, simply to assert that there should be a democratic check on the Court gives no information on what the check should be. We cannot suppose that the confirmation process that now exists is the ideal form simply because it is what the Founders wanted. Allowing public referenda on the Court's decisions would be a check, too—but I doubt that many of those who demand accountability would feel particularly comfortable with it. Certainly I doubt that many activists involved in the more controversial issues that the Court decides would really want to put their positions, in all of their stark simplicity, to a national vote.

The reason to mention this is that the idea of a democratic check on the Court is not new; on the contrary, the United States has lots of historical experience with democratic checks, most of it woeful. For example, the need for judicial accountability was a staple of segregationist legal and political blather throughout the fifties and early sixties, when politicians and commentators who were furious about *Brown v. Board of Education*[18] had their innings at arguing for a democratic check. The journalist James J. Kilpatrick was among those who called for the Southern states to "interpose" their sovereignty against court-ordered integration,[19] the evident idea being that when the Justices went so arrogantly against the popular will, it was up to political forces to resist. In making this argument, Kilpatrick stood in a long tradition, by no means limited to the South, to which I will momentarily turn. Many of the states agreed with Kilpatrick, but, fortunately, the federal courts firmly rejected the interposition argument, noting that their responsibility was to the Constitution, not to public opinion.[20]

All over the South, voters and politicians demanded to know what could be done about those judges, so unresponsive to the public will. Otto Passman, a member of the Congress of the United States, complained with perfectly straight face, "it is not pleasant to contemplate, but it appears to be true that at least some federal judges take their orders directly from the United States Supreme Court."[21] Sen. Russell Long spoke regretfully to his constituents about the difficulties of appointing judges "absolutely committed to segregation."[22] All of this in the name of bringing some accountability to the judiciary.

Naturally, one might wish to set aside the bitter struggle over segregation as a special case, which it obviously was. But the point of democracy within a constitutional structure is that we have a set of rules by which all parties agree to play—not one set for the good guys and one for the bad guys. In other words, if it is okay for the angels to argue that the courts should reflect the popular will, democracy means that the devils should have the same freedom. Otherwise the claim that the opinion of the public matters is a disingenuous effort to avoid having to defend the merits of one's position.

Moreover, even if we put to one side the debate over checking the courts in the era of the assault on segregation, we have lots of other relevant experience with democratic checks, most of it at the state level, where the experience has been so unsettling that the American Bar Association is on record calling for their abolition. Of course, these state-level democratic checks are the real thing—the judges are elected, or face the voters in what is called a retention election a set number of years after initial appointment—rather than the indirect "democratic" means that exist at the federal level. It was in a retention election that the voters of California in 1986 voted out of office three state supreme court justices who were, according to the well-financed campaign against them, soft on criminals in general and murderers in particular.

What is intriguing about the judicial elections in the states is that they are a relatively recent development. When the nation was founded, only one state elected its judges. The switch to elections—a "reform" movement that swept the nation during the nineteenth century—was justified in precisely the terms that are now used by the advocates of elite democratic checks on the work of the Supreme Court. The difference between the democrats of the nineteenth century and the democrats of the twentieth is that the democrats of the nineteenth made no pretense of wanting to protect judicial independence; what they wanted, they made clear, was to ensure that the judges paid attention to the popular will.

In the early years of the nation, the ideal of an independent judiciary held great currency, for the courts were widely seen as all that stood between tyrannical legislatures and the rights (especially, but not exclusively, the property rights) of the people.[23] Although we nowadays tend to think of state judges as elected, at the time of the Founding, only the state of Vermont elected judges above the level of justice of the peace by popular ballot. Elsewhere, judges were either elected by the legislature or appointed by the governor with legislative consent. Judges nearly everywhere held office during good behavior—that is, they were protected by life tenure. The exceptions were the states of Connecticut, Pennsylvania, and New Jersey, all of which provided for short terms of office; indeed, in Connecticut, the term was technically just a year, because the judges held office only as long as funds were appropriated, and funds were appropriated year to year.[24]

Like most public offices, judgeships were reserved for those with qualifications as electors. Nearly everywhere, this meant that the only people eligible to serve on the bench were property owners. (This requirement virtually by definition excluded women and people who were not white.) Almost without exception, the judges tended to be influential members of the community prior to their appointments; in fact, it was more important that they be influential than that they be lawyers, which many were not. The role of the judge was seen as something requiring less legal acumen than a certain wisdom and experience and a sense of justice.

It is important to understand the existence of property qualifications for judicial service to understand the reasons for the move toward selection of judges by the people. The idea of electing judges developed in the early nineteenth century, as a series of democratic movements swept the nation. Judicial elections were promoted by reformers as a means for overcoming elite privilege, government by the few. As the franchise spread to the unpropertied, so the number of public offices to which contenders had to be elected rather than appointed grew in like measure. And as the Jeffersonian and

Jacksonian movements promoted a mistrust of centralized power, the clamor grew to bring the judges within the ambit of the electoral process.

Judges, after all, were about as elite a group of government officials as one could find. In the view of many of those who came before them, whether as plaintiffs or defendants, judges were not simply undemocratic but essentially antidemocratic. Reformers particularly dreaded the judicial power to hold legislative enactments unconstitutional. Not only were the judges not bound by the will of the people but they seemed willfully to go against it. This was the very evil that the Revolution had been fought to undo. In the popular mind, then, the judges represented all the sons of the old order—elitism, corruption, arrogance. And that, in the early nineteenth century, was what many an ideologue set out to change.

There is some reason to think that the movement to elect state judges reflected in part popular discontent with federal court judicial review. In the early years of the nineteenth century, an activist Supreme Court began consolidating its power as it struck down one state initiative after another.[25] As the Supreme Court gathered authority to itself, calls for democratic accountability increased. Thomas Jefferson, for example, proposed that any judge who was empowered to hold statutes unconstitutional should be willing to face the judgment of the people; six years seemed to him a reasonable tenure for the federal bench. From Georgia to Pennsylvania to Maine, governors and legislators protested what they perceived as a judicial usurpation of state authority. The cry for democratization of the judiciary grew and spread alongside the cry for the "nullification" doctrine—the claim made by most of the states in the early years of the Republic that because the Constitution was a compact among free and equal sovereigns, no central authority, least of all a court, could override any individual state's interpretation of the document.

High school history students learn that nullification was a doctrine of the Southern states, embodied, for example, in the Kentucky and Virginia Resolves of 1798. But the North was up to the same mischief. After the Congress adopted the Embargo Act of 1807, the New England states, their trade routes threatened, not only nullified the law but threatened to secede if it was not swiftly repealed. The state of Maine warned that federal courts could not enforce certain debts. The state of Pennsylvania not only defied federal court orders regarding public lands but called out the armed militia to repel federal marshals who tried to enforce them.

"The doctrine of nullification," as one commentator has noted, "although it related directly to the federal courts, must have affected people's ideas about courts generally."[26] Consequently, if nullification of federal court orders was impossible, then at least the states could control their own courts. And they did their best. A number of state legislatures tried to remove appointed judges who held laws unconstitutional. In 1808, an Ohio judge was impeached by the legislature for holding a state statute unconstitutional. (He was ultimately acquitted.) In 1815, after a trial court in Georgia struck down a state statute, the legislature adopted a resolution ordering the judges not to do it again. In Kentucky, the judges were summoned to a legislative hearing to justify a controversial decision. And several states tried to regulate what authorities the judges were allowed to cite for their positions—in particular, banning the citation of the English common law. All of this in the name of a democratic check on unaccountable power.

The most dramatic display of popular dissatisfaction with judicial decisions came in the early nineteenth century, when the Kentucky legislature became so enraged at a series of decisions of the Court of Appeals—at the time, the highest court in the state—that it abolished the court and established a new one. The story of how this happened, and how matters turned out, speaks volumes about the risks that popular democracy poses for an independent judiciary.

THE KENTUCKY COURT DILEMMA

The background of the battle was the United States Supreme Court's 1821 decision in *Green v. Biddle*,[27] in which a Kentucky statute making it more difficult to eject squatters from private land was held unconstitutional. The Commonwealth, denying that the federal courts had jurisdiction to pronounce upon the validity of state statutes, declined to be represented by counsel. Instead, the state sent two commissioners to Washington to try to persuade the Justices not to hear the case. This the Justices declined to do.[28]

Stymied, the legislature adopted a resolution protesting the Court's decision. Then, still angry at the United States Supreme Court, the legislature took out its fury on its own Court of Appeals, which had recently invalidated two other statutes. The legislature adopted a second resolution, this one disapproving of the verdicts of its own court. A motion to remove all the judges was introduced, but it failed because it carried only a majority of the legislature, not the required two-thirds. Next, the legislature ordered the judges to appear at the next session to defend their decisions. This they did. Another resolution of removal was subsequently introduced, and, once again, it failed to receive the necessary two-thirds.

At this point, the enemies of the Kentucky court hit upon a new scheme. Because they could not muster two-thirds of their fellows to unseat the judges, they did what they could with a simple majority: the legislature voted to abolish the state court of appeals and create a new one. (Lest one suppose that such interference with the judicial function was unprecedented, it should be noted that the Kentucky legislature had been one of those that earlier enacted a law prohibiting the courts to cite English common law authorities.)

Plainly, the abolition of a court because of unhappiness with its decisions represents the ultimate triumph of democracy over judicial independence. One might even suppose that in a true democracy, this threat always lurks somewhere in the background, even if legislators are too frightened (or too circumspect) ever to implement it. In the Kentucky case, however, the cure turned out to be worse than the disease, because the old court refused to leave. Indeed, the old court declared unconstitutional the statute that purported to abolish it.

The new court, for its part, also refused to leave. It sustained the constitutionality of the statute establishing it and treated the acts of the old court—which continued to meet and issue decisions—as null and void. The old court returned the favor, refusing to give any weight to the decisions of the new court. The lower courts were not sure which court's mandates to accept. Litigants, faced with contrary rulings and serious questions about authority, either took their chances with one court or the other or played it safe and appealed their cases to both. Here Prof. Simeon Baldwin, whose wonderful 1903 book *The American Judiciary* contains much wisdom, picks up the tale:

> At the next election the question which court ought to be recognized was the dominant one. The result was that the friends of the old court gained control of the House and those of the new court that of the Senate, one of them being also chosen as the Governor. The new court now got possession of most of the papers of the old court. The latter ordered their sergeant to bring them back. The Governor made preparations to use military force to resist the execution of the order. At last, in 1826, an act was passed ... over the Governor's veto, declaring the acts abolishing the old court unconstitutional and void. The Governor

thereupon appointed one of the judges of the new court chief justice of the old one to fill a vacancy which had occurred on that bench, and for the first time for two years the judicial establishment of the State was on a proper footing.[29]

After the 1826 legislation, it need only be added, the old court held the new court unconstitutional, and the new court went out of business.

But the thwarting of Kentucky's fantastic scheme to replace its independent appellate court with one whose decisions would be more predictable was hardly the end of the clamor for a more accountable judiciary. On the contrary, throughout the early decades of the nineteenth century, the forces of Jacksonian democracy were busily demanding that government power be reduced or at least taken from the hands of elites and returned to the people. The campaign for an elected judiciary—a judiciary "of the people"—was a cornerstone of the movement. Court decisions that seemed to the people of many states to consolidate federal power or to threaten popular legislative initiatives were the villains of the campaign.

As a result of these pressures, one state after another moved during the nineteenth century to some form of judicial election or limited terms. For example, Georgia between 1812 and 1818 moved to popular election for virtually all of its judges, who had previously been selected by the legislature. Illinois in 1848 switched from legislative selection and life tenure to popular election for limited terms. Alabama in 1830 changed the term of office for its judges from tenure during good behavior to six years, and it was one of seven states in 1850 alone to switch to popular election for most judicial offices. By the time of the Civil War, only a handful of states, mostly in the Northeast, still provided for a method other than popular election for judicial office. And only four states—

Maine, Massachusetts, New Hampshire, and South Carolina—provided for life tenure. (South Carolina soon abolished life tenure, in its postwar constitution of 1865.) Moreover, every new state that joined the Union from the 1840s on provided for judicial election. In the battle between the forces of democracy and judicial independence, then, it might be said that democracy won by a knockout.

THE SUPREME COURT UNDER PRESSURE

Popular mythology holds that President Andrew Jackson, at continuing odds with Chief Justice John Marshall, responded to a Supreme Court decision he didn't like with the acid comment, "John Marshall has made his decision, now let him enforce it."

The better histories tell us that Jackson did not really make the comment and, indeed, that he never refused to lend federal assistance to the enforcement of the decisions in the *Cherokee Cases*,[30] which restricted the power of the state of Georgia to regulate activities on Indian reservations. To be sure, there was much ferment, in and out of the state, with regular calls for defiance from politicians and the press, and Jackson was plainly unhappy with what he saw as a transgression against state sovereignty. Moreover, he sought to make a political issue of the cases in national elections. But the moment for federal enforcement never actually arrived, so there was no occasion for Jackson to refuse to do anything.[31] Still, the enduring power of the myth makes an important point: the Court, despite all of its formal authority, is in many ways a weak stepchild in the constitutional system, relying on the good common sense of the other branches not to harry it into insignificance. One of the reasons that the rhetoric of democratic checkery is so scary is that it is a cold reminder of the degree of power that the President and the Senate still can wield over the putatively independent third branch, if they but care to do so. There have been eras in our history when the political branches chose to leave the Court alone to do its work. This, however, is not one of them.

Over the Constitution's two centuries, any number of legislative power-grabs have been justified as indispensable democratic checks on the unaccountable judiciary. For example, in 1802, when the Jeffersonian Congress abolished most of the federal courts created by the Federalists—an act we today would presumably think unconstitutional, but which two centuries ago split the nation solely along political lines—supporters of the President cheered: "Judges created for political purposes, and for the worst purposes under a republican government, *for the purpose of opposing the National will, from this day cease to exist.*"[32] Nothing worse, in other words, than courts that refuse to follow the will of the people as expressed through their legislature.

In every era when the Court has been pressured hard by the political branches, it has retreated. During the eighteenth and nineteenth centuries, the Supreme Court exhibited a particular vulnerability to the vicissitudes of partisan politics—and generally was helpless to do anything about it. Several of the examples are quite famous. After the Supreme Court decided in *Chisholm v. Georgia*[33] that residents of South Carolina could sue the state without its consent to collect a debt, a furious Georgia legislature enacted a bill making it a felony, punishable by hanging, for anyone within the state to attempt to enforce the Court's judgment.[34] (Subsequently, the states exercised their ultimate democratic authority and adopted the Eleventh Amendment, which overruled the essence of *Chisholm.*) And after the Court's horrible decision in *Dred Scott v. Sandford,*[35] striking down the Missouri Compromise and refusing to acknowledge that black Americans possessed any rights, the Justices were so cowed by public fury that they did not strike down another federal statute for 62 years. (To be sure, the reaction to *Dred Scott* could not have been the *only* cause for the Court's sudden humility.)

But of course the most stunning example of judicial weakness in the face of legislative opposition was the 1868 decision in *Ex parte McCardle*,[36] in which the Supreme Court dismissed a habeas corpus appeal because the Congress, during the pendency of the appeal, had taken jurisdiction away. *McCardle* involved a challenge by a newspaper publisher to congressional authority to establish military government in the reconquered South. After his arrest for libel, insurrection, and a variety of other charges, McCardle sought a writ of habeas corpus from a federal court. The Congress responded by repealing the statute that granted the high court jurisdiction.

The Supreme Court's opinion was both unanimous and succinct. Did the Constitution grant to the Congress the power to do what it had done? Of course: "the power to make exceptions to the appellate jurisdiction is given by express words." In the face of the repeal, could the Court grant relief? Of course not: "Without jurisdiction the court cannot proceed at all in any cause. Jurisdiction is the power to declare the law, and when it ceases to exist, the only function remaining to the court is that of announcing the fact and dismissing the cause." Although many thoughtful scholars, reading *McCardle* through the glass of the late–twentieth-century celebration of judicial power, have argued that the Justices did not mean what they plainly wrote,[37] the answer, in historical context, is much simpler. The Reconstruction Congress acted under the plain language of Article III of the Constitution to strip the Supreme Court of jurisdiction, for no reason other than to prevent the decision of the case, and the Court acquiesced. Whether the Justices got their constitutional interpretation right is much less important than the realpolitik involved in their recognition that in a power struggle mediated by democratic politics, the unpopular Court would lose.

Lest one suppose that *McCardle* was an aberration, another Reconstruction-era case made the same point explicitly. In *Mississippi v. Johnson* (1867),[38] the plaintiff filed a complaint in the Court's original jurisdiction to enjoin President Andrew Johnson from carrying out certain of the Reconstruction acts. In dismissing the complaint, the Court noted: "[I]t is needless to observe that the court is without power to enforce its process."[39] But it was not "needless to observe"; it was, rather, the whole point of the case.

Even in the 1803 decision in *Marbury v. Madison,*[40] the Court's first important assertion of the power to review the validity of federal legislation, the Justices showed a similar deference to the ability of the legislature to control its output. The decision, it should be recalled, was handed down well over a year after the argument, and the reason was that the Congress had abolished the Court's intervening term precisely to postpone the decision. Although some protested at the time that the abolition violated the Constitution, even the great advocate of judicial power John Marshall dared not issue a decision during a period when the Congress had prohibited the Court from meeting.[41]

The short of the matter is that at least well into the nineteenth century, the federal courts, despite the protection of life tenure, consistently backed away from confrontations with the legislature. Although our modern tendency is to see such deference to the political branches as a threat to judicial independence, it was seen in nineteenth-century terms as a necessary element of judicial accountability. Today's advocates of democratic checkery, if they do not like the nineteenth-century attitude, might do well to ponder whether accountability in the courts is such a great idea after all.

Faced with such arguments as these, advocates of democratic checks usually respond that what they have in mind is much more moderate, a check that does not threaten independence in the manner of nineteenth-century politicians. But this riposte presents fresh problems. The principal distinction between the need for democratic checks in the way Thomas Jefferson meant it when he called for an elected judiciary and the need for democratic checks in the way it is meant today is the identity of the people who get to be involved in the purportedly "democratic" project. For all the talk about the value of a democratic check on the Court, democracy is not what the liberal and conservative activists who call for litmus tests have in mind. They mean a check against *their own* views on the importance or horror of particular precedents. And it is in the service of that goal that they make their predictions about how nominees will vote and then run popular campaigns for or against them.

THE MORAL JUDGE

The reader must not mistake the point of my criticism. All the theorists are of course right to insist that interpretation involves more than simply technique and that judges are not mere mechanics. If they are good judges, they are bound by precedent and by the norms of their profession. At the Supreme Court, they must try earnestly to understand the text and history of the Constitution. (In academia, it is fashionable to proclaim that the text has no meaning and the history is both obscure and irrelevant, but although such scholarly criticism serves a useful cautionary function—judicial hubris is always a risk—no one boldly proclaiming such views is likely to, or should, reach the Court.) Perhaps needless to add, those who struggle at constitutional interpretation are unlikely to hit upon a single best meaning. But the struggle itself helps cabin what would otherwise be an unbridled discretion, for the Justices must never lose sight of the ultimate source of their legal authority: the claim that a current majority is violating a rule that binds contemporary politics precisely because it is part of our constitutional inheritance—*not* because it has recently struck the Justices that it is a good idea.

This does not mean that no constitutional decisions can ever change. It does not mean that the courts are bound to follow the concrete expectations of the Founders. It does mean that each decision must be guided by a broad principle that some super majority, some time in the past, waged a successful struggle to add to the Constitution.[42] In this sense, the judge must value law, in the sense of believing that there are discoverable rules that narrow the scope of judicial discretion, and must also value order, in the sense of believing that following those rules is better than ignoring them. (The fact that most of us hold this instinct about our judges is evidenced by the frequency with which a nominee's opponents insist that he or she brushes aside inconvenient precedents.)

But although an ideal judge must genuinely value order and law, each judge is also a citizen and a thinking human being. Most of us believe in some moral principle that we hold in sufficiently high esteem that we have no patience with democratic forces that may happen to run the other way. Judicial nominees doubtless have such principles too—ethical commitments of such force that they would have great difficulty separating them from their judicial function. We play a silly game if we ask the nominee to assure us that she has none. Consequently, we do better to ask just what those commitments are. Understanding the nominee's commitments is not necessarily the same as imposing our own.

A nominee who insists that she has no commitments that

would ever interfere with her judicial activity is either lying or so devoid of human feeling, so soulless, that she would be a disaster on the bench. On the other hand, a nominee who turns out to have more than a tiny handful of these well-nigh unshakeable commitments—who can hardly wait to become a judge and write all of her moral conclusions into fundamental law, without waiting around for the democratic processes (a conclusion one might draw from scholarship as well as from testimony)—is probably too zealous for honorable service on the bench.

Asking about nominees' strongest moral commitments might give no information at all about the way they would decide concrete cases, for part of the task of judging is to recognize where one's own strongest commitments lie and, often, to struggle against them instead of yielding to them. And sometimes, the judges who seem deeply committed on one issue will pull a surprise on another. Abraham Lincoln insisted that his nominees be openly anti-slavery (after *Dred Scott*, no one else could in any event be confirmed), but that did not mean they would vote the Republican party line. All five of Lincoln's appointees joined the Court's unanimous opinion in *Ex parte Milligan*[43] (one of them, David Davis, wrote it), which struck down the use of military tribunals to try civilians in many parts of the South. Richard Nixon insisted on what he called "strict constructionists" who would slow down the Warren Court's revolutions in civil rights and criminal procedure, only to look on in astonishment as three of his four appointees joined four Warren Court holdovers in voting to strike down state abortion restrictions in *Roe v. Wade*.[44]

More important, allowing public inquiry into the moral vision of the nominee (a possibility that I explore in greater detail in the next chapter) is not the same as allowing public inquiry into the nominee's likely votes. And there the matter is simple: to wrap the armor of countermajoritarian independence around individuals selected on the basis of predictions about how they will vote represents the enshrinement, through life tenure, of the popular political judgments of particular eras about the proper scope of constitutional protections—a peculiar fealty to pay to the notion of a written Constitution. Interpretation of a written Constitution should reflect a dispassionate search for fundamental principles (whatever their source) that transcend the most deeply felt popular passions of a given political moment.[45] Extending life tenure to the judiciary protects the possibility (that's all it is) of that dispassionate search. The states that took away life tenure in the nineteenth century understood the distinction: they *wanted* to abolish dispassion. Similarly, a confirmation process aimed consciously at preserving or overturning particular precedents might be justifiable were the Justices to serve, for example, eight- or twelve-year terms (see chapter 7). But if Justices are selected not because they are wise but because they are right, it is not easy to see why they *should* serve for life. Constitutional amendments— the locking-in of new binding rules—supposedly require something more than the concurrence of the President and a bare majority of the Senate. To concede the propriety of denying appointment to the Supreme Court on the basis of a prediction of concrete results is to encourage efforts to determine constitutional meaning through a different mechanism, one too easily manipulated by temporary political majorities.

The woeful experience of England under the Stuarts was the understandable inspiration for the ideal of life tenure—or, more properly, tenure during good behavior. In *Federalist No. 78*, Hamilton said this of life tenure: "In a monarchy, it is an excellent barrier to despotism of the prince; in a republic it is a no less excellent barrier to the encroachments and oppressions of the representative body." The "despotism" to which he referred was the Stuart habit of removing judges who voted against them—or who they thought might vote against them.

This was famously the fate of Sir Edward Coke, who time and again rallied his fellow judges to oppose the policies of James I. It appears that his successor, Charles I, removed several more.[46]

Removal, however, was not the only vice in the relationship of the Stuarts to the judiciary, and it could hardly have been the only concern of the Founders. During the English Civil War, Charles was accused by the parliamentary forces of having sold judgeships for money. Whether he did that or not, it is clear that he sold them for promises, that is, that he appointed to the bench judges who had sworn in advance to vote the way Charles wanted them to. Of course, the promises were readily enforceable since Charles was able to remove the judges if they voted the wrong way—but the practice would scarcely have been less objectionable had Charles extracted the promises and, in return, appointed the judges for life.

The only interesting distinction between the mischief of Charles I and our contemporary tendency to demand from potential jurists the same information that got him into trouble is that Charles was one man, twisting the bench to his own ends, whereas here we do the same twisting, but in the name of the majority. It may be, as we smugly believe, that a tyrannical majority is less to be feared than an individual tyrant. That hardly means, however, that a tyrannical majority is not to be feared at all. In both cases, the point of the inquiry is to enable the relevant sovereign to elevate to the bench people whose votes can be trusted. In both cases, the effort itself cuts against the grain of the judicial power as a bulwark against the sovereign. So if in the name of a majority, we demand of the judges what Charles did, we may commit a lesser version of the same offense—but it remains the same offense.

Our democratic habit of inviting the public into the process of bargaining with potential Justices makes matters both better and worse: better because the effort to influence is no longer limited to a tiny, faceless elite, worse because of the inevitable blurring of the crucial distinction between majority will and constitutional law. Because we campaign for and against nominees by encouraging voters to demand (or resist) particular constitutional rights, we propose in effect to do as the Stuarts did, only substituting a tyrannical majority that can then run roughshod over opponents for a tyrannical monarch who can then run roughshod over opponents. Thus, the more scientific—and the more populist—our efforts at prediction become, the less sensible it will be in our rhetoric to treat the Court as an independent group of judges deliberating over the protection of individual rights. So if Presidents and senators are encouraged to exercise the prerogative of appointing Justices who will do what the public wants, we can safely predict that the era of the Court as an important bulwark against majority tyranny will end.

Indeed, for all its obvious appeal, the notion of selecting Justices because of the precedents they promise to uphold or overturn ignores the lessons of history. None of the great decisions that have defined the Court as the protector of our fundamental rights were handed down by Justices selected to vote the way they did; had the President or the Senate imposed litmus tests on the crucial issue of racially separate schools, which everyone knew by the 1940s was on its way to the Court, *Brown v. Board of Education*[47] could never have been decided as it was, because nobody who failed to promise to preserve segregation could have been confirmed. The same may be said for the Court's abortion decision, *Roe v. Wade*,[48] and—perhaps most emphatically—for the school prayer cases.[49] Thus, the theory of democratic checkery seems to have matters precisely backward: the Court has done its greatest service to the nation when it has stood against the popular will. In particular, not one of the precedents so enamoured of the democratic checkers (particularly the liberals among them) was decided by a Supreme Court that included Justices selected in the hope that they would vote that way. This does not mean that the votes of the Justices are not pre-dictable—often they are—or that we never try to predict—often we do—but only that the Court has been at its best when the urge to appoint on the basis of prediction has been quiescent.

5

Of *Brown* . . . and Being Morally Off Limits

BUT if litmus tests are bad things for presidents and senators to apply (one might object), then what about the nominee who is supremely qualified on paper but happens to think that *Brown v. Board of Education*[1] is wrongly decided and that it is perfectly within the constitutional power of a state to segregate its citizens on the basis of race?

The *Brown* decision is everybody's counterexample.[2] That fact by itself helps explain why the *Brown*-as-litmus-test argument does not really work. The ubiquity of *Brown* as the exemplar of an unchallengeable precedent illustrates the transformation of racial segregation over the past four decades from a legal issue into a moral one. Nowadays, there is broad national consensus on segregation that simply does not exist on abortion. Prior to Bill Clinton's victory in 1992, the nation seemed unembarrassed about electing, by landslides, three consecutive Republican candidates running on explicitly anti-abortion platforms. Yet although many a code word is available to make clear a candidate's willingness to play racial politics, they are just that—code words. There is an important historical message in the fact that white supremacists are forced to speak in code, whereas pro-lifers are not.

In the case of judicial appointments, a transformation of this sort is precisely what political theory would have predicted. In his classic study *The Theory of Political Coalitions* William Riker argues that systems with more than one powerful actor tend to be stable only when there is a balance of power *and* when one of two other conditions is true: either there is an additional mediating institution that the competing sides agree not to destroy or there is a moral principle by which the sides agree to be bound.[3]

In America, where powerful political movements on the right and the left fight with as many tools as may be at hand, there is much talk of the importance of preserving the independence of the federal courts—our mediating institutions—but the choice to treat court decisions as largess to be distributed to powerful constituent groups is sad evidence that much of that fine talk is simply lip service. Instead, there is broad agreement on a moral vision that the competing sides will not violate through the nomination process: the vision of a reasonable, centrist America. Thus the truest believers on the right and the left simply are not eligible for judicial office, no matter how remarkable their legal acumen, no matter how impressive their resumes. Many saw the Bork battle, for example, as being over exactly that: keeping a dangerous ideologue off the Supreme Court. The term that his opponents hammered home was "outside the mainstream."[4]

Senator Kennedy's floor speech on the day of the nomination (see chapter 2), with its implication that Bork favored segregated lunch counters and back-alley abortions, was designed to raise the moral question directly. And, like other rhetoric of the campaign against Bork (or against Thurgood Marshall or Louis Brandeis or William Rehnquist or anybody else) these words were intended to send two messages: first, that there is a moral consensus that might be defined, in modern terms, as the American idea; and, second, that the nominee is a dissenter from it.

Bork's opponents plainly understood that the charge that Bork was a *moral* extremist would carry an emotional sting that the mere charge that his scholarship was in error would not. Still, some errors in legal scholarship would strike the general public as outside the mainstream. The contours of the legal mainstream are unclear, but a handful of precedents are clearly and firmly untouchable. Foremost among them, in our contemporary political consensus, is *Brown*. We will fight viciously about nearly every other area of constitutional law—privacy, free speech, the balance of power between the federal and state sovereignties. We will entertain argument over the proper role of the courts—whether they are bound by the original understanding, whether they should enforce society's fundamental values, whether they should be social engineers. But we will not attack *Brown*.

Everyone is required to accept it. Devotees of the original understanding, to be taken seriously, must argue that the *Brown* Court rediscovered what the authors of the Fourteenth Amendment expected—even though most historians think it plain that the Reconstruction Congress that adopted the amendment had no intention of authorizing courts to undo segregated schools. Thus even such devoted originalists as Edwin Meese and Robert Bork have insisted that *Brown* was consistent with the original understanding. (In a sense, it was—but the sense in which it was is not the sense in which Meese and Bork seem to mean it.)[5] Implicit in their arguments is a respect for this firm moral consensus, which creates a stability that nobody dares violate: during the Reagan Administration, so it is said, a law professor who has argued that *Brown* is wrong was considered, and quickly dropped, as a potential judicial nominee.

Moral consensus of this kind carries several risks. First, an advocate of public school classroom prayer might say, "Wait! If you can make enthusiasm for *Brown* into a test of moral fitness, then I can make the support of public school classroom prayer, which most Americans want, into a test." However, that objection is beside the point. I am not calling for the imposition of a desegregation test. I am noting that one already exists. That flows from the very definition of consensus: nobody needs to demand that a nominee demonstrate support for *Brown*. Everyone who will be taken seriously for a judicial appointment supports it already.

Second, moral consensus might develop on other, far more troubling propositions. Riker lists a number of quite unsettling examples—for instance, the unspoken agreement that even Southern liberals in the first half of the twentieth century would not challenge the prevailing racial norms held by white citizens. That led to a form of social stability, but only among the competing political factions.[6] By definition, the interests of those without political power (the black people oppressed by segregation) were not considered.

Consider the case of James C. McReynolds, the cantankerous racist appointed to the Supreme Court by President Woodrow Wilson. McReynolds, it is said, often refused even to speak with fellow Justice (and fellow Wilson appointee) Louis Brandeis, and referred to Howard University as "this nigger university."[7] As a member of the Court, McReynolds did indeed sow much constitutional mischief, first by trying to prevent local government regulation of business, later by trying to undo the New Deal. But he was able to do these things only by joining majorities of fellow Justices, which is another way of saying, sadly, that in his era the views he held were very much in the mainstream. In short, there is every reason to think that the political mainstream—the moral consensus—can be evil.

But this objection also is beside the point. If consensus exists on a principle so vicious and ugly as racism, there is a need for political warfare (violent, if necessary) against the society that shares it. Again, my account of the *Brown* consensus (though I obviously favor it) is meant as descriptive. The fact that it is as easy to form consensus around an evil principle as around a good one is at best a reminder of the importance of skepticism of claims that because a moral consensus exists, the consensus is probably good; it does not mean that no moral consensus ever does exist.

The third objection is perhaps the most potent: a moral consensus may be an illusion. Writing of the so-called balance of terror that was said to mediate the existence of vast nuclear arsenals held by powers hostile to one another, Riker warns:

> Not the least of the terrors is that in some place some man of authority may not be terrified. And it is the possibility that the last terror may be justified that renders the system of balance by moral restraint an unsatisfactory protection, even though it may be the only one really available.[8]

Similarly, there may be among the so-called stealth candidates one or more who are indeed dangerously radical—dangerously left or dangerously right. Although we tend in our casual way to refer to "ideology" when we mean "political views," a judicial nominee with a genuine ideology, in Durkheim's sense of a filter through which one must process all of reality before analyzing it, would almost always turn out to be dangerously radical on the bench, for the obsession of the ideologue is making the world fit a preconceived model, not doing justice according to somebody else's rules. One advantage of a hierarchical judiciary is that a single radical judge, sitting alone, can do little damage. For example, Harold Cox, appointed to the federal district court in Mississippi by President John Kennedy, issued half-crazy, generally racist rulings but was regularly slapped down by the appellate court.

But even if a dangerously radical judge can be corrected by a higher court, or a dangerously radical Supreme Court Justice by a majority of the other Justices, it is nevertheless the better part of wisdom for the Senate that must confirm, like the President who must nominate, to be on the lookout. One must simply be careful of defining the mainstream as including all the results one happens to like, and dismissing all dissenters as radicals. At that point, one is no longer looking for a judge who shares the society's moral consensus; one is looking for a judge who will act as a servant.

Of course, once one concedes that the confirmation process is the proper place to undertake an inquiry into morality, one opens the door to all sorts of mischief—as well as to all sorts of useful information to which those who would prefer to keep it hidden will refer as mischief. But it nevertheless will often be useful for the Senate to undertake moral inquiry, both into the world view of the nominee and, if necessary, into the nominee's conduct. The remainder of this chapter is about the necessity, and the problems, of both approaches.

THE DANGEROUS RADICAL

Like the man on the stair who wasn't there, the specter of Robert Bork's defeated nomination to the Supreme Court refuses to go away. Perhaps it is because Bork himself refuses to go quietly into the oblivion to which his most vigorous opponents sought to consign him. At this writing, nearly seven years have passed since the Senate's decisive rejection of Bork by a vote of 58 to 42, both the largest number of votes and the largest plurality ever cast against a nominee. Yet interest in the Bork battle seems never to wane. The Kennedy, Souter, and Ginsburg confirmations were too placid to eclipse it, and the bitter battle over the Thomas nomination became so caught up in the sexual harassment question that judicial philosophy, which was said to be central to the Bork fight, was practically forgotten.

What is it about the Bork battle that continues to hold the American imagination? In his best-selling book, *The Tempting of America,* Bork gives his own account of what happened to his nomination and offers an explanation for the continuing furor. According to Bork, the continuing debate is evidence of a cultural war in which his nomination was advertently snared.[9] Thus, writes Bork, "in the final analysis, the furor and venom were less about me than about the issue of whether the Court would become dominated by the neutral philosophy of original understanding and thus decisively end its enlistment on one side in our culture."[10] In the world as Robert Bork sees it, then, public interest in the battle over his nomination continues because the cultural war, the war for "left-liberal" hegemony, is still being fought.

Anti-Bork activists Michael Pertschuk and Wendy Schaetzel, who rushed out a book of their own not long after Bork's defeat, offer an equally vigorous but sharply different view. Their book, while flawed, is quite valuable, a rare insider's look at how a campaign of this nature is waged. The question presented by the nomination, they argue, was whether Americans "were prepared to refight the terrible struggles of the sixties, which have now largely receded into history."[11] Bork's opponents were inflamed "by his passionate, relentless, assault on virtually everything the Supreme Court had done in the latter half of the twentieth century to strengthen the equality of citizens before the law and the defense of individual rights against the power of the state."[12] This vision of a potential Justice Bork as reactionary monster fueled much of the rhetoric of the opposition; the vision, rightly or wrongly, lingers. In fact, it provides a kind of yardstick: Would a Justice Kennedy or a Justice Thomas (worried activists asked one another) be as bad as a Justice Bork? Evidently, Robert Bork has become the standard against which lesser evils are measured.[13]

But it was the degree of media attention, not the heat of the rhetoric, that carried the contest along a road that would make it different from other equally or more bitter nomination fights in American history. It was not the left-liberal culture war or the right-wing court packing scheme that made the moment auspicious; it was the realization on the part of anti-Bork activists that the power of the media could be harnessed in the same manner as in an election campaign. This was the point of Kennedy's speech (see chapter 2), as well as other immediate comments, such as the National Organization for Women President Molly Yard's statement that Bork was "a neanderthal": to "freeze the Senate," to slow the momentum for the nomination by making the media and the public stop and take notice.[14] And the media and the public *did* stop and take notice. In this sense, the effectiveness of the campaign was a historical accident; had the President been a Democrat and the nominee a liberal, the right would doubtless have reached the same epiphany. But whatever the first cause, matters would never be the same.

Having said this, I should make clear that I do not share all of Bork's constitutional vision and I worry about his tendency to launch ideological assaults on those who disagree with him. At the same time, I do believe, quite strongly, in accuracy, fairness, and simple decency. The campaign against Bork included many thoughtful, fair-minded individuals with no desire to distort, such stalwarts as the prominent Republican attorney and veteran civil rights litigator William Coleman, the devastatingly effective lead-off witness for the opposition. But it also included many others whom that description would not fit. Not satisfied with arguing against Bork on the basis of his predicted votes, they insisted on trying to paint him as a radical monster—far outside the mainstream of both morality and law.

Indeed, our processes for selecting Justices are dominated by the notion of a mainstream—a place where those who aspire to the office should swim—and a variety of tributaries, which they should avoid. The Kennedy "freeze the Senate" speech set the tone for the effort to demonstrate not simply that Bork was wrong but that he was dangerous. This is not the place to catalog all the distortions that were part of that effort; that work has been ably done by others.[15] It is worth noting, however, that even some of those who opposed Bork actively recognized how badly some others went off the track. The *Washington Post,* which would subsequently come out against the Bork nomination, nevertheless attacked the campaign for engaging in "intellectual vulgarization and personal savagery."[16] Pertschuk and Schaetzel, in their book about the hearings, note that some members of the Block Bork Coalition "believed that, while it was critical to sound the alarm, it was a mistake to engage in extreme rhetoric." They add, "The use of words like 'neanderthal' to characterize Bork tended to mark the speaker, not Bork, as the extremist."[17] The Harvard law professor Laurence Tribe, discussing the effort to use Bork's *American Cyanamid* opinion against him (see chapter 2), said later, "It was part of attempts to stir up fears about him as a person, which I tried not to do and regret that others did."[18]

But the "others" were legion, and their efforts to stir up fears about Bork as a person are legend. It is hard to say whether the effort succeeded, because it is not altogether clear just why Bork lost.[19] Perhaps the American people feared his philosophy, perhaps they feared his likely votes, perhaps they feared him as a person, perhaps he came across as arrogant on television.* Perhaps he lost because of the campaign against him, perhaps he lost in spite of it. Whatever the reason, two things are clear: first, the campaign got out of hand; and second, the same thing could easily happen again.

THE DANGEROUS RADICAL, REDUX

The Bork confirmation fight eerily echoed the battle over Thurgood Marshall's nomination two decades earlier, except that the players took different sides. Indeed, Marshall himself, in the last years of his life, remarked to an interviewer that Bork had been badly treated.[20] To say that there were echoes in the arguments of the opponents is not to say that the nominees themselves were of comparable merit. That is not Robert Bork's fault. Bork was undeniably a fine lawyer and scholar; Marshall, however, was one of the most influential lawyers of this century, and, certainly, one of the greatest individuals ever to sit on the Court. To note the parallels, then, is not to write a brief on behalf of Bork; it is, rather, to recognize the consistency of political style and the inconsistency of political outrage.

Marshall, like Bork, came to his hearing with a magnificent resume: phenomenally successful litigator (twenty-nine

---

* Although the White House strategists evidently believed that Bork would charm the Judiciary Committee and the nation, they were wrong. Notes one observer: "Bork's personal appearance and demeanor seemed as suspect as his ideology. His devilish beard and sometimes turgid academic discourse did not endear him to wavering Senators or the public. Nor did his detailed, scholarly, lecturelike answers to every conceivable question posed to him by the Senate Judiciary Committee." Henry J. Abraham, *Justices and Presidents: A Political History of Appointments to the Supreme Court,* 3d ed. (New York: Oxford University Press, 1992), p. 358.

victories in thirty-two Supreme Court arguments), judge on the Court of Appeals for the Second Circuit (in those days unquestionably the nation's second-most important federal court), and solicitor general of the United States. Beyond all that, he was the grandson of a slave who rose to become the leading legal figure in the most important social movement of the century. In short, at the time of his nomination, Marshall was already one of the great figures of twentieth-century American law, one of only a handful of Justices who would have been in the legal hall of fame, if there were one, even without service on the Court. (In this century, that could be said with confidence only of Oliver Wendell Holmes and Benjamin Cardozo.) An appointment to the Supreme Court was the fitting capstone to Marshall's remarkable career. His hearings should have been a bit like a coronation. Instead, there was an air of lèse-majesté about the thing, as senators nitpicked through his record, searching for evidence that he was the dangerous radical they desperately needed him to be.

Thurgood Marshall, as we have already seen (chapter 3), faced determined racist assaults that no other nominee has been forced to confront and that Bork certainly was spared. But once we place to one side the many ways in which the Marshall hearings were unique, the parallels between Marshall's hearings and Bork's turn out to be many and depressing. Opponents of Bork said that he was a narrow ideologue rather than a principled conservative. Change "conservative" to "liberal" and the same proposition can be found in criticism of Marshall. Marshall's nomination, like Bork's, was opposed on the ground that it would upset the delicate left-right balance on the Court. Critics of Bork complained that the moderate swing vote of Lewis Powell would be replaced by the vote of a right-wing ideologue. Critics of Marshall complained that the moderate swing vote of Tom Clark would be replaced by the vote of a left-wing ideologue.[21]

Like Bork's critics, who focused the "swing-vote" argument on *Roe v. Wade*,[22] Marshall's critics had a particular case in mind when they spoke of the Court's alignment. They worried publicly that Marshall might have turned around the 5 to 4 vote in *Walker v. City of Birmingham*,[23] the decision earlier that year that sustained the contempt citation and jail sentence of Martin Luther King, Jr., and his associates for parading in Birmingham without a permit and in defiance of an injunction. Had Marshall been on the Court when *Walker* was decided, so the worried opponents insisted, Dr. King might have gotten away with his defiance.[24]

Marshall's critics, like Bork's, took him to task for blaspheming any number of icons—only they were icons that faced to the right rather than to the left. Bork was attacked for his disrespect of Supreme Court precedent, and, sometimes, for disrespecting constitutional theories—for example, the theory that the Ninth Amendment provides judicially enforceable rights—that the Supreme Court has never quite embraced.[25] Marshall was criticized for urging the Supreme Court to overturn venerable precedents and for disrespecting other constitutional theories—for example, the view that the Fourteenth Amendment permits separate-but-equal school facilities—that the Supreme Court had recently rejected. Segregationist Sen. Sam Ervin, who just six years later would suddenly become a liberal hero for presiding over the Watergate hearings, accused Marshall of embracing theories "which repudiated or ignored the history of the 14th and 15th amendments [and] overruled or misconstrued or ignored former decisions interpreting the amendments in accord with the purpose of those who framed or ratified them."[26] Compare Ervin's overheated rhetoric with this blast from the anti-Bork testimony of the prominent attorney John Frank: "Judge Bork, quite truly, makes law as though precedent were meaningless and the Congress in permanent recess."[27] Senator Ervin further warned that Marshall would "join other activist Justices in rendering decisions which will substantially impair, if not destroy, the right[s] of Americans for years to come."[28] Once more, the rhetoric mirrors that of Bork opponents: "Bork's current constitutional jurisprudence is essentially directed to a diminution of minority and individual rights."[29]

There is no need to labor the comparisons, not least because I am drawing only an analogy, not an identity.[30] There was much more substance behind the extravagant criticisms of Bork than behind the overheated assaults on Marshall, and the different results in the two cases do much to bear that out: after all, Bork's nomination was defeated. And for all the respect obviously due Robert Bork for his record as lawyer and judge, he was no Thurgood Marshall; but then, nobody is. Still, the rhetorical strategies of the two campaigns were quite similar in their farfetched efforts to show that the nominees were outside the mainstream. In neither case were the opponents willing to tell the American people what was plainly true: he may be inside the mainstream, he may not be, but we don't like the way he's going to vote!

Bork, as I have noted, was not forced to confront the racism of the segregationists. But the fact that the attacks on Marshall were worse does not mean that the attacks on Bork were justified or fair. The trouble, in both cases, was the perception by opponents that the cause—defeating the nominee—was so important that the question of fairness was a distraction. Efficacy, not accuracy, mattered most, which, as Judith Shklar once pointed out in a discussion of hypocrisy, is precisely the trouble with causes—"they can be used to purify any sort of conduct."[31] In too many campaigns against nominees for high office, this tendency becomes a principle.

Of course, although our confirmations are getting much messier, campaigns of this kind remain the exception, not the rule. After all, one can hardly dismiss every nominee as a monster—a prudential concern, to be sure, but one with a point. At least as explained to the public, the Block Bork campaign rested on a faulty premise. A single monster is not very dangerous, not when there are lots of brave soldiers to keep him in check; that is why the Supreme Court has nine Justices. It takes a minimum of five to "turn back the clock" or "deny us our basic liberties" or any of the other colorful slogans that are available to characterize nominees whose predicted votes are inconsistent with a particular critic's desires.* If Bork was really outside the mainstream—if no one so ideologically narrow had lately been nominated to the Supreme Court—then surely he would have made little difference if confirmed. The other eight Justices, well within the mainstream, would have ignored him.

But nobody believed this would happen. The Block Bork Coalition assumed that a Justice Bork would *join majorities* bringing on the parade of horribles. The trouble, then, was not that he would be an outlaw Justice; the trouble was that he would be one of *five* outlaw Justices. Thus the Coalition's quarrel was not really with Bork at all; it was with the other Justices already on the Court. But because those other Justices had already been confirmed, in all cases but one by unanimous or near-unanimous votes, it was difficult to argue that they were monsters too. So nobody was prepared to say what everybody understood, that the battle was not really about Bork but about the votes already accumulated. A Bork who was like half the members sitting on the Court could hardly be painted as a Justice to fear. So he had to be worse.

In this sense, Bork has a point: he was indeed a victim of circumstance, and much of the vituperation directed at him

---

* The "turn back the clock" language has lately enjoyed a peculiar rhetorical rebirth, with conservatives warning that Clinton appointees might turn back the clock on civil rights—meaning that they might endorse rather than frustrate affirmative action programs.

was really directed at sitting members of the institution he was so eager to join. I do not suggest that the Senate necessarily reached the wrong result on Bork, only that the opposition to him, like the opposition to Marshall, was characterized by a belief that no argument that might be effective could possibly be illegitimate. What the two campaigns had in common was a very simple, very cynical political vision: the only way to get the American people to join an ideological crusade is to scare them. And the way to do that, in the case of a Supreme Court nominee, is to demonstrate that he or she is not only wrong but actually dangerous. To show that Marshall and Bork were dangerous, opponents tried to demonstrate the immorality of their world views. My judgment is that in both cases the attacks were unfair, although much more clearly so in the case of Marshall. Others may disagree. I do think it clear that for a senator sincerely persuaded by the charges of dangerous radicalism, a negative vote would have been appropriate.

Of course, the morality of one's ideological vision is only one of many possible moral inquiries. Moral inquiry may take another form as well: an investigation of the morality of the nominee's conduct. And that leads us, finally, to *the* confirmation fight of the modern era, the one that will be debated, with real anger, for decades to come.

THE HIGH-TECH LYNCHING THAT WASN'T

The generation of intellectuals that came of political age in the fifties and early sixties had—and still has—as its litmus test the "Pumpkin Papers" case that pitted Alger Hiss against Whittaker Chambers. Even today, nearly half a century after Chambers testified that Hiss was a spy, intellectuals who came of age during the controversy continue to spar over who was telling the truth—and who smeared whom. For many baby boomers, the emotions that continue to rage around that defining political event seem inexplicable. But the emotions are no less vehement for being hard for those who weren't there to understand: if you were a genuine member of the left, you believed that Alger Hiss was unfairly smeared and Whittaker Chambers was a cowardly liar. If you were a genuine member of the right, you believed that Whittaker Chambers spoke Holy Writ and Alger Hiss was a traitor. There was no middle ground then and, for true believers of that era, there is no middle ground today.

Among members of the generation that came of political age over the last decade, Clarence Thomas and Anita Hill are, and probably will always be, figures of similar defining magnitude. Are you a bona-fide liberal? Obviously, Anita Hill told the truth and Clarence Thomas perjured himself in denying her allegations. Are you a bona fide conservative? Obviously, Clarence Thomas was unjustly smeared by a liberal conspiracy in which Anita Hill was eager participant or unwilling dupe. Future generations will doubtless look at the vicious arguments over Hill's testimony of sexual harassment with much the same mystification with which today's baby boomers regard the bitter debates over the relative veracity of Chambers and Hiss. For there is no middle ground today and, for true believers of our era, there will be no middle ground thirty or forty years from now.

Thomas was nominated by President George Bush to fill the seat of the retiring Justice Thurgood Marshall. Although movement conservatives were delighted, and many African Americans cheered the continuation of the "black seat" (as there was once a "Jewish seat"), many others saw a deliberate slight in the decision to follow the greatest legal figure of the civil rights movement with a less prominent figure from the conservative movement—especially when Thomas had been so harsh in his criticism of the very movement Marshall had led. At the same time, many pro-choice organizations saw a threat to *Roe v. Wade*,[32] possibly even a fifth vote to overturn it. In short, all the ingredients for fireworks existed long before the national media had heard of Professor Anita Hill.

Thomas's defenders are quick to point to the existence of a nationwide campaign to gather "dirt" on the nominee, whose movement conservatism made him many enemies. According to some reports, advertisements were taken out in newspapers asking for harmful material. If this happened, it was despicable—but certainly not out of the ordinary. A friend of mine reports receiving a rather sobering telephone call from opponents of a more recent judicial nominee, asking, in so many words, if he was aware of any dirt. Given the perceived stakes in these battles—*results hanging by a thread!*—it is scarcely surprising that there turn out to be no rules.

Opinion surveys throughout the summer showed moderate to strong support for Thomas in the black community. Many African Americans who might have disagreed with him on the issues nevertheless thought it important that a black presence be maintained on the Court. As for his conservatism on many civil rights measures, supporters argued that the experience of racism would nevertheless inform his decisions; as one syndicated columnist put it, when forced to choose between a conservative who had been called "nigger" and one who had not, African Americans should prefer the first.[33] Because of that same conservatism, however, Thomas was subjected to a cruel barrage of criticism suggesting that he had somehow sacrificed his blackness by taking positions with which many black activists disagreed.[34] At the same time, the principal liberal interest groups were reluctant to get involved in the struggle against Thomas without the leadership of a black civil rights organization—preferably, the National Association for the Advancement of Colored People. When at last the NAACP came out against Thomas, the other groups breathed a sigh of relief and fired up the coalition again, in the hope of scoring another Bork-style knockout.

But Thomas was, in many ways, a more elusive target. In the first place, his skin color and impoverished background apparently immunized him from some charges that he might otherwise have faced from white critics—charges of insensitivity to the plight of people of color, for instance, or of not understanding the perspective of the downtrodden. Moreover, he lacked the dramatic paper trail that the scholarly Bork had left behind. Although everybody understood that Thomas stood squarely in the mainstream of the conservative movement, it was not so easy for his opponents to pin him down. As a result, we all settled in for a long summer of charges and countercharges and efforts by members of the Judiciary Committee to extract enough information to enable them to make a case either way.

In that respect, we were not disappointed. We learned from Thomas's opponents that he was a dangerous radical because he thought it possible for a judge to rely on natural-law reasoning (as many of the Founders did) to resolve knotty problems of constitutional interpretation.[35] His compliment to a prominent pro-life businessman who had endowed the auditorium where Thomas gave a speech was transformed by his opponents into a statement of his life principle. He was, not surprisingly, accused of a variety of "confirmation conversions." And some on the black left vied with one another to see who could come up with the nastiest reference to his race: and so we learned from his critics that Thomas was an Uncle Tom, a turncoat, and full of self-hatred.

Putting aside for a moment the sexual harassment charges, the question remains: Was the campaign against Thomas justified? Was it fair? The answer is that in many respects it was not justified, for a black nominee of Thomas's views provoked a special degree of fury that is unlikely to have confronted a white nominee. But that simple truth is balanced by another, that a white judge of Thomas's limited experience would not have been nominated for the Supreme Court—nor would Thomas himself likely have been nominated for a seat other than the one vacated by the retirement of Thurgood Marshall. Doubtless Thomas's supporters will attribute the record 48 negative votes to racism and ideology; but the closeness of the vote, a razor-thin margin that was expected even before Anita Hill's name became a household word, might also be evidence that many members of the Senate recognized what the former solicitor general Erwin Griswold pointed out in his testimony: that although Thomas might, in time, have acquired experience needed for service on the high court, he did not have it at the time of his nomination. (The American Bar Association's Standing Committee gave Thomas the weakest endorsement of any nominee since its inception.)

Besides, even if some of Thomas's black opponents went beyond the bounds of decency in their attacks, he could hardly have expected the hand of friendship from civil rights leaders whom he had spent much of the previous decade excoriating in vicious terms—most famously, in his 1984 comment that civil rights leaders would rather not work for constructive change as long as they could "bitch bitch bitch, moan and moan, whine and whine."[36] Fairly or not, but certainly understandably, they gave it back in kind.

When the hearings ended in September, it appeared that Thomas had enough votes for confirmation, although even then, the head counts suggested he would receive more negative votes than any successful nominee in the history of the Court. It was at this point, when confirmation seemed certain, that someone with access to the committee's confidential file leaked to two journalists the startling news that Anita Hill, a former aide to Thomas at both the Education Department and the Equal Employment Opportunity Commission, had charged him with sexual harassment in interviews with the Federal Bureau of Investigation.

Before proceeding, I must comment on the leak itself. The leak has been described in several places as an act of courage, but it wasn't that at all. It was, rather, a splendid example of what John le Carré has referred to as "the selfless and devoted way in which we sacrifice other people." As evidence, consider the fact that despite the passing months, the gallant soul who decided to use Hill for his or her own ends by leaking her charges to the press, setting her up for the nasty abuse that she received, remains somehow too modest to step forward and accept the adulation of the public.

What happened next is already the stuff of legend. To many Thomas supporters, by airing the charges at all, the committee was lending itself to a smear—or, in Thomas's words, a high-tech lynching. It is difficult, however, to see how the committee could have avoided a further hearing on the matter, given the force of public indignation and the credibility of the witness. The relevance of the charges was obvious. If the Senate has a responsibility to inquire into the character and fitness of judicial nominees at all, a charge that the would-be judge has mistreated subordinates can hardly be ignored. In fact, if one accepted the characterization of the allegations by some Thomas supporters (Senator Orrin Hatch said that only a "psychopath" would have used the language alleged), a full investigation became indispensable. Moreover, the credibility of the accuser made the charges that much harder to ignore. Among those attesting to her character and veracity was the Yale Law School professor Geoffrey Hazard, head of the American Law Institute, a supporter of Robert Bork's nomination, and therefore unlikely to be part of a left-wing conspiracy against Thomas.* When all of this is taken together, it is hard to see how the committee—which had initially decided not to pursue the charges—could possibly have avoided reopening the hearings. (Friends and supporters of both Hill and Thomas thought the hearing should have been held in closed session, but it is doubtful that an aroused populace or an eager media would have allowed it.)

At the same time, the glee with which too many Thomas opponents (particularly white ones) greeted the revelation of Hill's charges was not merely dismaying—it was actually quite frightening. For some, the relief at finding a smoking gun was evident, as though it was a good thing for the nation that Hill had been sexually harassed, since her suffering would provide the ammunition to defeat monster Thomas. Their glee was balanced, if that is the word, by the anger of many black people, by no means all Thomas supporters, who believed that Hill should not have come forward with her charges after almost a decade of silence, least of all in a context that would (were she believed) deny a Supreme Court seat to a black man.

More than that, the conflict between Anita Hill and Clarence Thomas illuminated the new battle lines of the women's movement, as the conditions of work rather than the opportunities for work move to the fore. Sexual harassment, like what has come to be called comparable worth, represents an effort not simply to gain the right to avoid discrimination but a demand to remake the conditions of the workplace itself. To many traditionalists (here, the term *conservative* would only mislead), this notion is a profoundly threatening one.[37] In short, Anita Hill's charges touched so many searing cultural and political controversies, crossed so many theretofore impregnable boundaries, that it was probably inevitable that the

---

* I also provided the Judiciary Committee with a sworn declaration attesting to Anita Hill's veracity.

choice to believe her or not would be heavily influenced by prior commitments on those same issues.

This is not the place to detail the committee's dreary dance around the charges, the effort to avoid a hearing, or the committee's shameful treatment of Anita Hill in the hearing itself. I should, however, state my bias: I believe the charges. Anita Hill is a personal friend of long standing, and, to me, the notion that she would invent such a story is ludicrous. I recognize that tens of millions of perfectly reasonable people believe otherwise—and yet, for all the contempt lavished upon Hill, it remains difficult to figure out *why* she would have participated in the anti-Thomas conspiracy that his supporters insist was afoot. Indeed, despite the rather desperate stretch by Thomas supporters to find a motive for a Hill fabrication (vengeful spurned lover? pitiful erotomaniac? ruthless publicity hound?), nobody has quite come up with a reason why the fabrication should be so meager: if you are going to tell a lie, runs the widsom, tell a big one. So, if Anita Hill (and co-conspirators) really wanted to "get" Clarence Thomas, why stop at inventing a tale of abusive language, which so distinguished a scholar and social critic as Harvard's Orlando Patterson could plausibly (although, I think, incorrectly) defend as simply a norm in the African American subculture?[38] Why not concoct a true morality play that everyone would recognize and condemn—for example, an explicit threat of professional retaliation for refusing sex? Why manufacture a story of continued abuse over time, which led some to wonder why Hill would remain in Thomas's employ, when one could instead claim that the harassment came suddenly and late?

In short, Hill's testimony was simply too unadorned to be either a vengeful falsification or the result of a bizarre erotomaniacal fantasy.[39] Besides, she passed a polygraph test. True, the Judiciary Committee chair, Sen. Joseph Biden, ruled the test result inadmissible on what seemed to be civil libertarian

grounds (courts do not admit them, after all), but this ruling
was, in its context, quite peculiar. In the first place, the committee allowed into its record all sorts of innuendo and
hearsay that are not admissible in courts either—that is, it was
allowed into the record when it cast doubts upon the character
of Hill. But when it cast doubts upon the character of Thomas,
the committee suddenly balked. Moreover, the reason lie
detector tests are not admissible in court is principally their
tendency to give false positives—that is, to register false
responses when people are actually telling the truth. It is
somewhat more unusual, experts say, for the tests to register
false negatives, to incorrectly show that people who are lying
are actually telling the truth.[40] Furthermore, whatever the limits
of the tests in court, security agencies, from the local police to
the federal government, use them, with high degrees of confidence, all the time.

The lie detector test was no last-minute strategy. When
the FBI agents asked Hill after she first told her story whether
she would be willing to take a polygraph examination, she
said yes.[41] At the time of the hearing, she once more offered to
take an FBI-administered test, if Thomas would do the same.
Thomas supporters argued that nominees should not be
coerced into such testing, and they are correct. Nevertheless,
the offer was there on the table—but those who insisted that
Thomas was telling the truth were reluctant to pick it up.

David Brock, in his mean-spirited book about the
Thomas hearings, insists that the man who administered Hill's
lie detector test, the former FBI agent Paul K. Minor, had made
mistakes before and could easily have been fooled. But
Minor's full resume belongs on the table. Paul Minor is widely
regarded as one of the leading specialists in the field. He spent
ten years as supervisor of polygraph testing for the FBI, and
personally conducted more than 2,500 examinations for the
federal government. It was presumably for this reason—

Minor's reputation among law enforcement professionals—that Hill's lawyers selected him to administer the test. Nobody, they supposed, would think that Minor was part of a left-liberal conspiracy to deny Thomas the seat that was rightly his.[42]

The polygraph story concluded in spring of 1992 with an ironic twist. Former Defense Secretary Caspar Weinberger voluntarily took a lie detector test in an effort to avoid indictment in the Iran-Contra mess—a test, as it happened, also administered by Paul Minor, who the previous year had been all but declared incompetent by conservatives who refused to credit the results of his examination of Anita Hill. Weinberger, like Hill, passed the test; only this time, conservatives declared the fact to be evidence of his credibility, not his delusional character.[43]

THE UNCRITICAL WILL

Thomas partisans, of course, will be unconvinced by anything that I have said. Indeed, the fascination of future generations will not be the searing questions that divide us today—who was telling the truth, who was lying—but the quite different question of why we attach to a simple question of veracity such epochal political importance that choosing the right side becomes a litmus test for one's commitment to a political philosophy. In the same sense, the rising generation no longer cares about Hiss and Chambers, even though the emotions the dispute generated continue to mystify. Perhaps Bork is right: Thomas, Hill, all of us are caught up in a war over the future direction of the Court. But if he is correct, the right behaves no better than the left, and much of the time it behaves a good deal worse. In the interest of gaining or holding control of the Court, right and left alike are ready to sacrifice anybody's reputation, because *our side cannot possibly be allowed to lose!* It is not, however, a war fought in the spirit of Tom Wolfe's fine definition of the right stuff—the uncritical willingness to face danger. It is, rather, a war that demands the uncritical willingness to place others in danger.

The obvious problem with this approach is that one can easily become so caught up in contemplating how best to achieve the goals of the movement that one ignores the importance of the integrity of the institutions in question. Conservatives in particular have in the past evidenced a reverence for the integrity of the traditional institutions of government. In the Thomas battle, however, that integrity was ignored, as personal vindication—a much more liberal and individualistic value—became the goal. The way it worked out was this: An innocent Thomas should be confirmed. To vote against him was like finding him guilty. But that argument is a peculiar one. Even if Thomas was telling the truth, one could conclude that he was so wounded by the hearings that he could not be an effective Justice—not that he would lack the intellectual aptitude or the emotional fortitude, but that he would join the bench mired in scandal and widespread public disbelief. Even if, as some surveys at the time of the hearings suggested, more than half of American adults believed his denials (those data have since shifted),[44] that still left tens of millions who did not. Consequently, one could sensibly, and conservatively, conclude that the Court and the nation would be better served were a different individual appointed, which is why even some of his supporters whispered that Thomas, like other nominees caught up in scandal, should have stepped aside.

Thomas, of course, chose not to do so. His partisans have argued that if a nominee must withdraw whenever charges of misconduct are made, the invitations for smear might as well be mailed out along with the announcement of the nomination. But it is not clear that this is correct. The Thomas case was unusual not because charges were made but because they were so widely believed. For just this reason, I wonder whether conservative supporters of Thomas might have missed their issue in their rush to insist that since he was one of them, he could not possibly be lying. Had Thomas's supporters (and Thomas himself) been willing to concede the substance of Hill's charges, and had the concession been handled in a conciliatory and apologetic way, they might have had the opportunity to conduct a national seminar on repentance, contrition, and forgiveness. To be sure, many people, Thomas supporters and opponents alike, believe that the charges themselves were disqualifying on their face. Perhaps they were. The continuing abuse that Hill described would be chilling even among peers—but to be so addressed by one's supervisor must have been horrifying.

Still, we would have seen a quite different hearing had the committee and the nation confronted not the defiant Thomas but a Thomas able to say, "Yes, it happened, much as described, and I am dreadfully sorry. But it was a very long time ago, it was a difficult time in my life, and I was a very different person. I ask your forgiveness, and Professor Hill's, and ask you to confirm the person I am now, not the person I was then." Would the result have been different? Perhaps not—but we will never know, because that is not the Clarence Thomas that we got.

Joining the Court under a cloud need not ruin Thomas's career. Hugo Black took the judicial oath under a far more ominous cloud, the revelation that he had once been a member of the Ku Klux Klan, and had even received an award from that organization. Yet Black persevered to become a great champion of civil rights and civil liberties and, in the estimation of some authorities, one of the great Justices in the Court's history. As Sen. Paul Simon put it in his book about the Bork and Thomas hearings, "Supreme Court Justices are not saints any more than Senators."[45] So although the early returns are not encouraging, Thomas, too, might emerge from the cloud

through the sparkle of his jurisprudence. Certainly one hopes
that is what his supporters expect.*

THE SOUL OF DEMOCRACY

And yet, looking back on Thomas, on Bork, on Marshall, and
perhaps further, one might reasonably ask whether, if we are
to investigate the moral fitness of nominees, the Senate is the
right place to do it. The answer is simple: not only is the Senate a sensible place for inquiries of this kind; in our system of
government, it may be the only place. The Senate is less
directly responsive to political pressures than is the House of
Representatives because members of the Senate stand for election every six years rather than every two. In any given year,
the entire House is never more than two years away from facing the voters, but two-thirds of the Senate is always a *minimum* of two years—usually more—from the next election. In
theory, then, the House, designed to respond to the popular
will, is and should be swayed by passions when the American
people are swayed by passions, generous when the people are

* Fallout from the Thomas-Hill explosion continues to pollute the confirmation process. As this manuscript was being completed, some conservatives
were resisting the nomination of Janet Napolitano (a former member of Anita
Hill's legal team) to be United States Attorney for Arizona. The peculiar
ground of the opposition was that the Senate had the right to know at least
the lawyer's side of a conversation Napolitano had with a witness (Judge
Susan Hoerchner, a friend of Hill) during a break in testimony before the
Judiciary Committee. A small group of Clarence Thomas's supporters (the
author David Brock prominent among them) suggested that Napolitano might
have used the break to persuade Hoerchner to alter her testimony. But there
was not a shred of evidence to support this smear. Besides, even apart from
the breach of lawyer-client privilege that would occur were a lawyer forced
to divulge conversations with a client, legal ethics experts were quick to point
out that attorneys frequently consult with their clients during testimony: it's
part of the job. See "Thomas-Hill Days Dog U.S. Attorney Nominee," *National
Law Journal*, Nov. 15, 1993, p. 5. When the assistance of counsel sharpens
the witness's recollection, we don't usually cry foul—we usually say the
lawyer has done exactly what she is supposed to.

in the mood to keep what is theirs. The Senate is more capable than the House of reflective and deliberative consideration of the issues confronting the legislative branch. The House of Representatives might be considered the heart of the democracy. The Senate, then, must surely be the soul.

The Senate, responsive to public will but also sharing some of the distance of the courts, has the ability, if it chooses, to give voice not simply to the passions of the moment but to the enduring and fundamental values that shape the specialness of the American people.[46] The institutional design of bicameralism makes this balance possible: what the House votes in its haste, the Senate may reconsider at its leisure. The Senate has no special institutional perspective and no relevant special characteristic but this one. If the senators cannot successfully bring to bear on the confirmation process the characteristics that make their institution unique, then there is scarcely an argument available for resting the confirmation power in the Senate rather than in the House, or in the Congress as a whole.

Giving voice to the deepest common values of the American order does not mean masquerading as either a professional standards review board or a law school appointments committee.[47] It means doing what responsible members of the Senate do best: representing their constituents by reaching conclusions based on a relatively disinterested dialogue, which may be a principally internal one, about the policy most congruent with the fundamental aspirations and long-term interests of the American people. This dialogue would have little to do with predicting results in specific cases. A reflective Senate would refuse to speculate about a potential nominee's likely votes, and would eschew any inquiry into judicial philosophy, not merely because the body might be institutionally incapable of evaluating a nominee's philosophy but also because the long-term interest of the American people requires what, at a deep level, most Americans probably want or believe that they have: an independent judiciary. If indeed it exists, this shared understanding on the desirability of a particular institutional design—courts that are beyond political manipulation—does not, of course, rise to the level of a sophisticated theory of law or politics. Deeply shared values of this kind form a more reliable basis for judgments likely to affect the course of the nation for years to come than do vague and elusive theories about constitutional interpretation. A reflective Senate would understand the threat to judicial independence that is posed when the appointment process is used, by Senate and President alike, as a means for pursuing the short-term partisan end of validating or overturning particular lines of cases.

The tough question is what the Senate should do if its members feel bound (under the argument presented here) to give only slight weight to the results the potential Justice is likely to reach, when they know full well that for the President who has offered the nomination, that factor has been dominant. One result, which would require the summoning of considerable institutional will, would be to reject the nominee out of hand, citing the President's illegitimate conduct, rather than to damage the judiciary further by adding another layer of substantive review. That would be the proper occasion for the Judiciary Committee, in Senator Specter's phrase, to rear up on its hind legs and say no.

JUDICIAL INDEPENDENCE

The ideal judge in the federal system deliberates largely in the absence of distinct political pressures, and the ideal Supreme Court Justice must be the most independent of all. Although there plainly is substance in Alexander Bickel's metaphor of the judicial process as "endlessly renewed educational conversation,"[48] the picture of a Supreme Court that reins itself in because the specter of popular disobedience lurks somewhere beyond the horizon seems less apt in the contemporary climate than it might have been in an earlier age. Circumvention of unpopular opinions has become a sophisticated science, but a secret one. Public proclamation of defiance is over; it ended when liberal suspicion of judicial power evaporated during the civil rights era, the brief historical moment when the courts were reliably on the side of the angels.

Thus there is no longer what Bickel envisioned as the ultimate security against abuse of judicial power: a judicial struggle to preserve legitimacy in the sense of effective authority, authority that will be obeyed. So, for example, even such broadly unpopular decisions as those banning organized classroom prayer from the public schools or protecting flag burning as free speech (I think all these decisions were right) are not met by organized and officially sanctioned disobedience. The same is true for outcomes that the left does not like. When the Supreme Court in *Rust v. Sullivan*[49] upheld regulations restricting the ability of personnel at federally funded family planning clinics to tell patients about abortion services, the liberal response was not to counsel the doctors and other providers to do it anyway, but to lobby the Congress for a new statute. In short, we no longer live in America as it was from the Founding through the mid-twentieth century, when governors and legislatures and sometimes even Presidents conspired to thwart judicial edicts. The late twentieth century is an era in which we the people obey even decisions we dislike—and that fact greatly enhances judicial power.

Yet the dialogic metaphor still has much to recommend it.[50] A sensible and morally reflective Supreme Court, as it works over time to sharpen and refine its doctrine, will consider principally the fundamental tools of its trade: the Constitution's language, structure, and history, and the wealth of precedents that give the document its meaning. But the Justices are not mere mechanics, and the Constitution does not interpret itself. As they breathe life into a compact some two hundred years old—the most successful governing document in human history—they simultaneously give voice to a set of values deeper and more abiding than the political passions of the moment. It is this commitment to what John Rawls calls "public reason"—"what the political conception of justice requires of society's basic structure of institutions, and of the purposes and ends they are to serve"—that sets the Court apart from other institutions of government. The role of the Court in a liberal democracy, says Rawls, is "to give due and continuing effect to public reason by serving as its institutional exemplar."[51]

Although it is axiomatic that such an institution cannot give decisive effect to public opinion—as the political branches so often must—a broadly held public view, consistent over time, might nevertheless carry important truths for a Court that acts ultimately in the people's name. And although popular disobedience is no longer fashionable, the public, if persistent, manages over time to work its will, whether by praying in those public school classrooms where nobody objects, by creating a network of abortion clinics to serve the poor women whom the government, with court approval, turns away, or by moving to the suburbs to avoid court-ordered integration. Thus, the force of Bickel's metaphor is his realization that a judicial opinion is nothing more than an argument for the proposition that an initiative is right or wrong, and an argument can only slow someone down. It is at best a plea for rational reconsideration: a brake, not a wall.[52]

Judicial review is effective law, because when courts hand down controversial decisions, even the political actors who criticize the decisions most vigorously obey them on pain of being painted as disrespectful not simply to the Court but to the law on which their own authority is founded. This obedience is another example of a deeply shared commitment to a public value (here, the rule of law) that binds political action despite, or perhaps because of, its lack of theoretical sophistication. No doubt there are lines that bound permissible legal discourse, bounds beyond which no rational Justice would go, but the specification of those lines is a question of politics. The nature of the system for the selection of nominees—indeed, the nature of the people doing the selecting—ensures that no one with views truly beyond the bounds of politically acceptable discourse could ever be considered seriously as a nominee.[53] (Robert Bork was described this way, but, as I have argued, although he might have been wrong about certain things, he was anything but outside the mainstream.)

Thus, while the Senate certainly should set itself the task of keeping off the Court nominees whose views stray too far beyond the discourse of the mainstream, this duty will but rarely involve a call to arms, for the senators are policing for criminals unlikely to appear. If a nominee's ideas fall within the very broad range of judicial views that are not radical in any nontrivial sense—and Bork had as much right to that middle ground as just about any other nominee in recent decades—we enact a terrible threat to the independence of the judiciary if we pretend the views are extremist when we really mean simply that we disagree with them. Back in the era when the Court was leading the fight against racial segregation and only conservatives insisted on answers to substantive questions, liberals seemed to understand the point. We would only strengthen our constitutional democracy by once more making it our rule.

THE NOMINEE'S MORAL VISION

The dilemma, then, is this: how can the Senate carry out its responsibility to give voice to the deepest values and aspirations of the American people while at the same time not compromising the necessary independence of the Justices? The answer lies in a fuller understanding of the judicial role, which in turn would point the Senate toward attempting what its members often seem mysteriously reluctant to undertake— trying to get a sense of the whole person, an impression partaking not only of the nominee's public legal arguments but of her entire moral universe.

The rhetoric of judging insists that judges should put aside their personal beliefs when called upon to decide what the law requires. In constitutional adjudication especially, however, no matter how much judges strive to interpret without regard to their background morality, they cannot hope for a complete separation of judgment from judge. In this sense, constitutional interpretation is like the interpretation of any other text. The words of the Constitution do not, by themselves, determine everything, and all who must strive to interpret and apply the text, no matter how great their intellectual force or legal sophistication, must at some point make leaps of faith not wholly explicable by reference to standard tools for interpretation.[54] Is flag burning "speech" within the meaning of the First Amendment?[55] Do segregated schools deny "equal protection of the laws" within the meaning of the Fourteenth?[56] Can the President bomb Iraq without the consent of the Congress?[57] Can the Congress subpoena executive branch documents without the consent of the President?[58] All these questions require judgment in the finding of answers, and in every exercise of interpretive judgment, there comes a crucial moment when the interpreter's own experience and values become the most important data. That moment cannot be spotted in advance, any more than the pressing issues of ten years hence can be predicted today. But it is certain that the moment will come, and the Senate can help the nation to be ready when it does.

The issue, finally, is not what sort of theory the nominee happens to indulge but what sort of person the nominee happens to be. There are two senses in which this judgment ought to matter. First, the nominee ought to be a person for whom moral choices occasion deep and sustained reflection. Second, the nominee ought to be, in the judgment of the Senate, an individual whose personal moral decisions seem generally sound. In moments of crisis, we call upon the Supreme Court for a statement of law; more often than we sometimes care to admit, we receive instruction in practical morality instead. At such times, what matters most is not what sort of legal philosophers sit on the Court but what sort of moral philosophers sit there. Even when times are less difficult and the issues less divisive, the judge's background moral vision and degree of moral reflectiveness nevertheless play significant parts in shaping her interpretive conclusions. This background moral vision and the capacity for moral reflection are among the most important aspects of the judicial personality, and it is for these that the Senate, which enjoys the political space to reflect on the fundamental values of the nation, ought to be searching.

Thus the political task in the real world of real interpretive problems is to people the bench not with Justices holding the right constitutional theories but with Justices possessing the right moral instincts. In this sense, it is far less useful to know that a nominee has ruled that private clubs violate no constitutional provisions when they discriminate against nonwhites than to know whether the nominee has belonged to a club with such policies, and for how long. A legal theory leading to the conclusion that private clubs are not regulated by the Constitution is a matter of debate, a matter of reasonable differences, a matter on which one may take instruction, a matter for a later change of mind. But a lifelong habit of spending one's leisure time with those who prefer not to associate with people of the wrong color tells something vitally important about the character and instincts of a would-be constitutional interpreter, something not easily disavowed by so simple an expedient as, for example, resigning from the club (see also chapter 6).

Legal theories, like legal institutions, are ultimately no better than those who take them in charge. Within the universe of mainstream legal discourse (a universe for which the system will usually screen quite effectively) a morally upright proponent of an unpopular or eccentric theory will likely turn out to be a better Justice than one who propounds an acceptable theory but whose personal morality is cynical or mendacious.[59] But "better" is used here in a special sense: the morally superior Justice will be better than the one with the right philosophy in the sense that her instincts will be morally sound, and those instincts, when brought to bear on concrete cases, should be of salutary rather than destructive effect on the Court and the country that it serves.

The Senate would not, of course, be able to predict the particular results that the morally upright Justice would reach in concrete cases, and the reflective Senate would not try. There would be no litmus tests and no campaign promises. And yet, over the very long run, as new and unexpected issues arise, there should evolve a healthy convergence between the moral direction of the Justice and the fundamental moral vision of the nation the Justice serves. The popular sense should come to be one of a good, trusted, upstanding individual sitting on the bench, so that even when the people dislike her work, they will obey her—not simply because of her legal authority but because she is someone held in respect. This prospect might in turn reduce today's tension between the ideal of judicial independence and the demand that the courts support particular political programs. And in the worst of times, when fresh and unexpected issues present grim moral choices, the times when the courts might be most desperately needed, the morally superior individual will almost certainly be the morally superior jurist.

There is a risk, moreover, to an approach that seeks to evaluate the personal moral judgment of the nominee: the wall between the public and the private domains, a wall that is dear to liberal and libertarian theory, might be breached. "Has this nominee violated marital vows?" the senators might demand. "Has that one voted Republican? Used marijuana? Had an abortion?" None of these queries can be dismissed as entirely irrelevant, unless one wants to suppose a theory of human motivation that rigorously separates the moral premises for actions on the two sides of the wall. Relevance, however, is not the same as propriety, and the question is who will decide what lines of relevant inquiry are nevertheless inappropriate. Perhaps the Senate is too risky a place to lodge the power of decision. And yet, if members of the Senate who must reach a moral judgment on the nominee are not to be trusted to draw a line between what may legitimately be considered and what may not, then it is not easy to see why they ought to be trusted with any other aspect of the confirmation decision. For if there is a line between the two, its very location—like the location of the line that bounds rational discourse—is a question not of abstract theory but of politics. Senators inclined to vote "no" because the nominee has had an abortion, or because she refuses to say whether she has or not, must make their decisions in light of the practical political consequences. The political consequences of rejecting a nominee because she has had an abortion would probably be severe, which is why not even the most avowedly pro-life senator would dare ask, which in turn says something important about the kind of moral judgment that the American people are prepared to respect.

This perhaps is too idealized a notion of the relationship between the American people and the Supreme Court.[60] Perhaps results really are all that matter. Presidents often act as though they value only results, the interest groups that campaign for and against each nomination seem bent entirely on prediction, and the Court itself is hardly immune to the criticism that the result in many cases is all that drives its analysis.

But even if there is in the end less truth than aspiration in the vision of an independent and reflective Supreme Court, the Senate of the United States, designed to combine a degree of political sensitivity with the distance necessary for reflection and deliberation, should be the last institution of government to surrender the myth.

II

GOVERNING INSTEAD OF GOSSIPING

6

The Disqualification
Problem, Revisited

I have argued from the outset that the greatest problem with our approach to the confirmation process is the tendency to search for disqualifying factors. This, I have suggested, is a product of our indulging the fantastic notion that nominees— even for the Supreme Court—should enjoy a presumption in favor of confirmation, that members of the Senate must have a solid reason to vote no, and otherwise should vote yes. If we reverse that presumption, if we force the supporters of a nominee to carry the burden of coming forward—of making the case—we will create a climate in which it is possible to reject a nominee on no other ground than that the affirmative case has not been made. This, in turn, would go a long way toward easing the pressure to search for that single tantalizing disqualifier with which one hopes to spark a firestorm of criticism.

This is not to say that no single factor should ever be taken to disqualify anybody from any post. But we should not presume that because we have found wrongdoing, we already have the answer to the disqualification question. Instead, to make our confirmation process work in a way that is both sensible and fair, we must learn to balance the wrong that an individual might have done against the good service that he or she might bring to the nation. The well-known weakness of balancing tests is that they rarely indicate the relative weights to be assigned to the different factors that are balanced. In the interest of trying to alleviate that difficulty here, I will set forth a spectrum of potentially disqualifying behaviors, ranging from those that should require the most additional evidence before they can be cured to those that should require the least.

First, I should say a word about what I am not discussing—disqualifying factors beyond the scope of this analysis and, indeed, beyond the reach of practical solutions. I exclude cabinet nominees who are defeated or withdrawn because of explicitly stated policy disagreements between the President and the Congress, even if caught in a crossfire between President and Congress over other, possibly unrelated issues. Consideration of disputes of this kind is entirely appropriate in casting a vote, and I only wish the Senate would do it more often.[1] Although one naturally feels sorry for nominees who are shot down for reasons unrelated to their own qualifications—sometimes unrelated to the departments they would serve—such losses as these are a consequence of politics and therefore both unavoidable and, in a sense, healthy. Further, although I believe firmly in seeking diversity in appointments, I exclude from this discussion the possibility of rejecting candidates because they are of the "wrong" race, sex, or religion.[2] Disqualifications on that ground are never justified.

But the plausible grounds for rejection that remain cover a vast area. For the sake of convenient understanding, I propose to divide potentially disqualifying factors into five categories and to explain, in each case, why the concern is serious and what it should take to cure the problem. The list that follows, which is in order of hardest-to-cure to easiest-to-cure, is not meant to be exhaustive but should serve as a useful aid to analysis.

CATEGORY 1—QUALIFICATIONS FOR THE JOB

My reference here is entirely to the candidate's resume. Does the candidate have the mental ability and relevant experience? How does the candidate compare with others who have held the same position?

This is the single point that ought never be curable, that is, a nominee who is patently unqualified for the job should never be confirmed. Oddly, however, in the absence of ideological warfare or simple racism, we seem unable to argue in these terms. Thus, for example, Senate opponents of Thurgood Marshall, unembarrassed about defending racial segregation, were not reluctant to claim that he lacked the minimum qualifications for the job, even though, in light of his resume (see chapter 5), the claim was utterly ridiculous. It was simply a smoke screen for politics—and for simple racism.

In recent years, the question of what should constitute the set of minimum qualifications for service on the Supreme Court has received much attention. In particular, a number of observers (I am among them) have argued that seats on the Court should be reserved for those who have spent many years as appellate judges in the federal system or on the highest court of a state with a heavy and diversified work load. On the other hand, the Supreme Court that unanimously decided *Brown v. Board of Education*[3] some forty years ago included no Justices with extensive judicial experience. Indeed, if one examines the roll of great Justices, one might be tempted to agree with Felix Frankfurter's famous observation that "the correlation between prior judicial experience and fitness for the Supreme Court is zero."[4] Some have argued that the Court needs people from a balance of backgrounds—political service, the mainstream bar, public interest work, the academy, and so on. Others contend that it is high time we professionalized our judiciary, adopting the European model, selecting the Justices, as in the civil service, from those who have served long and well in other judicial posts.

Plainly, this is a matter on which the nation is a very long way from closure—but we ought to try. Instead, the question of minimum qualifications, even for the Supreme Court, is usually treated as something too insulting to mention. No one is ever not smart enough, not experienced enough, not educated enough, not even-tempered enough, not open-minded enough.[5] So when the venerable Erwin Griswold, a former solicitor general and senior member of the establishment bar, testified against Clarence Thomas's confirmation on the ground that Thomas, who had been an appellate judge for a bit over a year, lacked adequate experience, some commentators were outraged, reacting as though Griswold had testified in some foreign language—which, in effect, he had. One Senator, perhaps hoping Griswold would back off, asked him to compare Thomas's experience and qualifications with those of Justice David Souter, whom the Senate had confirmed by a vote of 90–9, despite his thin record of federal judicial experience, just one year earlier. Griswold was unabashed: "Senator, this is embarrassing. He [Souter] was a former student of mine, and if there were deficiencies, perhaps I have some of the responsibility, but I would not have regarded him as a distinguished nominee."[6] Griswold was not alone in this concern. The conservative political commentator Bruce Fein has argued vociferously that a clear majority of the Justices sitting at the time of the Thomas nomination—perhaps all but Antonin Scalia—lacked the basic intellectual qualifications for the job.[7]

Were these criticisms fair? Were they beyond the pale? The trouble is, we have no public language in which to answer such questions as these. We as a nation, like the Senate as a body, share no consensus on what qualifications a nominee ought to have, for the Supreme Court or for anything else.

And that, of course, is why we have to spend so much time arguing over whether candidates are *disqualified* instead of whether they are *qualified*.

The American Bar Association's Standing Committee on Federal Judiciary should, in theory, be of assistance on this point. Its role is to assess the qualifications of judicial nominees, in many cases prior to their nominations. It almost lost this role during the Reagan and Bush administrations, however. The first problem was a concern that ideological considerations were entering into its judgments (clearly they were), which raised the question of whether the committee deserved a special role, different from that of other interest groups.[8] Second, a lawsuit that joined liberal and conservative interest groups in a common cause challenged the committee's secrecy, arguing that under the Advisory Committee Act, it was required to hold public meetings. The Supreme Court, in an impenetrable but probably inevitable decision, upheld the committee's closed-meeting policy.[9]

The work of the committee is deceptively simple. For most federal court appointments, it ranks a nominee as "Exceptionally Well Qualified," "Well Qualified," "Qualified," or "Not Qualified." At the Supreme Court level, it uses the ratings "Well Qualified," "Not Opposed" (or "Qualified"), and "Not Qualified." Those who are rated "Not Opposed" or "Qualified" are defined by the committee as "minimally qualified"; those rated as "Not Qualified" are said to lack the "professional qualifications for appointment to the Supreme Court."

The committee's record is uneven. Several members voted that Robert Bork was "Not Qualified," the explicit reason being that they feared the votes they thought he would cast. Bork was the first nominee ever to receive substantial negative votes from the Standing Committee. Even G. Harrold Carswell, a Nixon nominee to the Supreme Court who was widely viewed as unqualified and whom the Senate swatted aside with almost casual ease in 1971, was passed unanimously by the committee.* In a neat twist, many scholars nowadays argue that the Carswell rejection was on ideological grounds, that the arguments over his qualifications were simply smoke screens for differences over the direction the Court should take. But if we have no language with which to argue the proposition that Carswell was less qualified than Bork, then we are unlikely to take seriously what Griswold in his testimony insisted that we must: the possibility that a nominee might lack "the distinction, the depth of experience, the broad legal ability which the American people have the right to expect from persons chosen to our highest court."[10]

Although there have been efforts to set forth the basic qualifications that federal judges should have, they have foundered on the rocks of consensus building. When the Reagan Administration was accused of packing the courts with young conservatives, many of them law professors with little or no experience in the practice of law, several Democratic members of the Judiciary Committee drew what looked like a line in the sand: it was time, they said, to stop the easy confirmations of nominees who had never tried or argued a case in the courts. But they never defended the line, which is hardly surprising, given that there is considerable dispute over even this single, minimal qualification rule.

Many of the states have adopted a variety of the "Missouri Plan," under which judges must be picked from a list provided by a (theoretically) nonpartisan commission. President Carter, determined to reform the federal judicial selection process in the late 1970s, tried a version of the same idea, selecting his nominees for the courts of appeals based on recommendations from special committees. Some critics have

---

* At the time of Carswell's nomination, the Standing Committee used only two categories for Supreme Court nominees, "Qualified" and "Unqualified."

charged that Carter's merit-selection criteria were manipulated in the quest for racial and gender representation; others have insisted, to the contrary, that the resulting nominees were insufficiently diverse. In addition, some detractors claimed that Carter's merit-selection panels, like those in many states, began evaluating a judge's likely votes as an indicator of merit.[11] Whatever the accuracy of the allegations—for the most part, they sound like ideological carping—the controversy over the Carter Administration merit-selection panels serves as further evidence of our inability to find a public language in which to discuss the qualifications of potential judges for public office.

As to the cabinet, we have so thoroughly bought the myth that the President is entitled to his team that we do not give qualifications much thought. In the rare case in which an alleged lack of qualifications *is* mentioned—for example, President Carter's failed nomination of Theodore Sorensen as director of Central Intelligence—it is almost always a code for something else. In Sorensen's case, the real fear, difficult to articulate but easy to understand, was that because he was a self-described pacifist, he must be soft on the Cold War and could not possibly head the CIA.[12]

Our inability to hold public conversations in which we accuse nominees of lacking the basic qualifications for the job may even lead to reverse smoke screens. One Washington insider told me of an episode in the 1980s when a Senate committee was quite convinced that a sub-cabinet nominee lacked the most elementary qualifications for the job in question and therefore frantically called around looking for evidence of wrongdoing, evidently convinced that it would look better to reject the man for some trumped-up scandal than to say what all of them believed, that he was unqualified. (No wrongdoing was found; he was confirmed.)

We might spare our nation much agony—and much official incompetence—if the Senate were to develop the simple courage to say to the President from time to time, "No, you may not have this person in your cabinet. It is not that your nominee is immoral. It is not that we do not like your nominee's politics. It is not that we are throwing our weight around. It is simply that your nominee lacks what we consider the minimum qualifications to do the job." To make this approach work, the Congress that creates all the positions that require confirmation should specify in the relevant legislation just what the necessary experience is. In some cases, we already do so. For example, until 1981, the surgeon general was required by statute to come from the ranks of the Public Health Service corps, but the requirement was waived that year—wisely—for C. Everett Koop, who turned out to be one of the best at the job. (Waivers are fine, as long as they are rare and based on thoughtful consideration of the merits of individual cases.) The solicitor general of the United States, in quaint language that is borrowed from the 1789 Judiciary Act, must be "learned in the law."[13] But these are the exceptions rather than the rules. For the most part, the Congress allows the President broad discretion in selecting the officials who will run the departments. No qualifications are necessary. Small wonder, then, that none of them ever turns out to be disqualified.

CATEGORY 2—RESPECT OF THE PUBLIC

A nominee who has lost the respect of the public should rarely be pressed forward, even if that loss is the consequence of events beyond the control of the nominee. The view of the public matters because, in a democracy, it is the public's respect for our institutions that must ultimately give them their authority. (The main alternative, as practiced in much of the world, is authority at the point of a gun.) If a significant segment of the public loses (or never possesses) respect for the nominee, and if that lack of respect is likely to rub off on the relevant institution itself, the nomination should be withdrawn or, if the nominee insists on a vote, defeated.

This is not a comment on the quality of the nominee, because, as we have seen, the public is often wrong in its moral judgments and is even sometimes ashamed of them later. Thus, for example, Zoe Baird may have been right to withdraw as nominee for attorney general because the public response, even if unfair, would have hindered her ability to do her job. And despite the anguish it created in Lani Guinier's supporters (myself included), President Clinton may have been correct when he made the choice to withdraw her nomination if he thought the vicious campaign against her had made it impossible for her to do the job effectively. Similarly, President Carter was right to withdraw Sorensen and President Reagan was right to withdraw Gates. For the same reason, President Reagan would have done better to withdraw Bork's name in 1987, as President Johnson did in 1968 with the doomed nomination of Abe Fortas as Chief Justice. (Fortas, of course, asked the President to withdraw his name. Bork insisted on a vote, but a nominee has no entitlement.)

Sometimes, nominees who seem to have been damaged by the campaigns against them are nevertheless confirmed, but the controversy that caused the difficulties does not always end with a Senate vote. Edwin Meese, for example, was at last confirmed as attorney general, almost a year after being nominated, but the same questions about his financial affairs that held up the Senate vote plagued him throughout his tenure as attorney general. Joycelyn Elders, who was confirmed in 1993 as President Clinton's surgeon general, has been unable to escape lingering suspicions from many Christian Evangelicals and Roman Catholics based on some troubling comments that she made about both religious groups. And there is every reason to think that skepticism over Clarence Thomas's denial of Anita Hill's charges will follow him for years to come.

Nominees who have faced the often vicious attacks that characterize our confirmation processes understandably desire to fight it out in order to gain personal vindication. But facing down one's enemies or even preserving one's reputation does not always mean achieving the office one seeks; in many cases, honor requires that the desires for vindication and perhaps for personal accomplishment be placed to one side, that the integrity of the institution come first. That is why some Thomas supporters suggested that he should have withdrawn as a nominee for the Supreme Court, even if he was telling the truth, because enough of the public disbelieved him that his effectiveness as a Justice and, perhaps, the legitimacy of the Court itself might be compromised.

However, unlike the fundamental lack of qualifications, a loss of public respect should, in rare cases, be considered curable. The low-risk cure is for the President to spend scarce political capital making a public case for the nominee. This, of course, Presidents have been willing to do only infrequently, because they need their energies for other battles. But if a President is so sure of the nominee's importance and qualities that he wants the person in government despite public skepticism or hostility, he should be willing to put his own reputation on the line. Many conservatives criticized President Reagan for failing to do this with sufficient enthusiasm when Robert Bork's nomination ran into trouble; and many liberals criticized President Clinton for the same failure on behalf of Lani Guinier. Those failures of support may suggest, however, that each President had what he considered more important fish to fry. Establishing priorities is part of the job.

The high-risk cure is for the senators to invest their own political capital by voting to confirm the nominee because of a faith that the nominee's performance will be so spectacular that the public will quickly regain the faith it has lost. Some of Clarence Thomas's supporters, in explaining their affirmative votes in the face of strong public opposition, made precisely this argument. Supporters of Edwin Meese also insisted that once he had the chance to serve, the public criticism—seen as whipped up by a biased media—would fall away. And many fans of Lani Guinier argued that if she simply had the chance to do the job, the public reaction would turn around.

The confirmation of an unpopular nominee is a high-risk cure because it requires a difficult prediction regarding future events. A public servant mired in public "scandal" cannot easily, in our mass media culture, trumpet the outstanding job that he or she may be doing. Too often, senators who explain their votes on the ground that scandal will be forgotten are probably more wishful than certain. But our government institutions are at risk when the public has grave doubts about the nominee, and wishfulness is no substitute for the cold calculation that sometimes requires politicians to realize that getting their way will cause more harm than good.

CATEGORY 3—IMMORAL CONDUCT

Despite what I have said above about disqualifying factors, I should remind the reader that I think personal morality *does* matter, and matter greatly, when one is deciding how to staff the government (see chapter 5). Even though I question whether we have always in the past correctly identified what should count as immoral, I do not dispute the proposition that consideration of the candidate's moral uprightness is a part of the task of both President and Senate.

The way one might put the question is this: Has the candidate acted, outside of his or her official capacity, in a way that does not violate any laws and does not violate any professional norms but that nevertheless displays moral obtuseness? The charges that Clarence Thomas sexually harassed Anita Hill would fit into this category. So might the matter of the offensive jokes told by Earl Butz, who was shortly forced to resign as President Ford's secretary of agriculture, and James Watt, also forced to step down as President Reagan's secretary of the interior. To be sure, the jokes in question were told while Butz and Watt were serving in office, but had similar material come to light during confirmation hearings, the Senate would have acted properly in taking it into account. Consider once more Joycelyn Elders, President Clinton's nominee for surgeon general, the nation's leading public health authority. Prior to her nomination, she had suggested that religious opponents of abortion should "end their love affair with the fetus"[14]—which was, even in its context, a horribly offensive use of her wit. Had she been white and made a comment of similar magnitude about, say, African Americans, she would doubtless have been criticized as racist. Evidence of religious bias should be taken as seriously as evidence of racial bias. However, although a pattern of bias should be disqualifying on its face, a single comment should not; it should be balanced against the qualities that the nominee might bring to the office. As Elders was confirmed, one assumes—hopes?—that the Senate weighed matters out that way.

Personal immorality can also take other forms. As I mentioned in chapter 1, Roberta Achtenberg, President Clinton's nominee for a position in the Department of Housing and Urban Development, was essentially charged with immoral conduct when opponents pointed to her sexual orientation as the ground for their negative votes.[15] That the charge was made says something unhappy about our society: we still cher-

ish our discriminatory impulses against people who are different, and we often do it by calling difference a moral issue.*
Fortunately, the majority of the Senate saw matters otherwise,
and Achtenberg was confirmed. Had she been rejected, the
trend might have had no logical stopping point: one can imagine an argument by some at the extreme end of the pro-life
movement that a nominee who has had an abortion should
not be confirmed. But that argument would probably fail, as
did the argument against Achtenberg, which illustrates the
point I made in the previous chapter about the moral consensus: it is not possible to create one. We must deal with the
consensus that already exists. Thus, the rejection because of
gross immorality in conduct should be limited to what I proposed in the previous chapter—conduct outside the existing
societal consensus.

Immoral conduct should be curable in some cases; that is,
it should not be as difficult to cure as lack of qualification
(which should not be curable) and loss of public respect
(which should rarely be curable). An exceptionally able public
servant might be more readily forgiven than an undistinguished
one, simply because of the cost to the nation when the outstanding nominee must go away. We must be cautious, however, about what we label a cure. For example, when nominees
are members of all-white clubs—that is, when they have made
a lifelong habit of relaxing in the company of people who, by
choice, avoid people of color—we allow them to cure this act
of immorality by the expedient of resignation. Canon 2(c) of

* I do not deny that people of good will may sincerely and reasonably hold
a variety of positions on the morality of homosexual conduct. But it is not
clear that even the view that the conduct is immoral means that potential
public servants should be subjected to discrimination on this basis. For example, it is my personal view that the use of tobacco products is immoral, as are
other acts of self-destruction, but I would not support a ban on smokers from
positions requiring Senate confirmation.

the Code of Conduct for United States Judges states flatly that a judge may not be a member of such a club, and a resolution of the Judiciary Committee requires nominees holding such memberships to relinquish them. But it is the habit of mind that makes membership possible and comfortable, not the fact that the membership exists, that is the problem.[16]

True, membership in an all-white club is not like membership in the Nazi party. But our willingness as a society to tolerate it, in the name of personal privacy, in those who aspire to public service—while we will not tolerate, to take the most obvious case, the employment of illegal aliens—shows a bizarre moral calculus. Trying to make the best child-care arrangements one can is disqualifying; enjoying the fruits of the nation's odious history of discrimination deserves no more than a nod and a wink. Indeed, if there is reason to doubt the capacity of the Senate to make serious judgments about moral worthiness, the tolerance for nominees who have spent much of their leisure time in affectionate company with those who discriminate by choice provides the best evidence.

CATEGORY 4—ILLEGAL CONDUCT

It might seem surprising that I have placed this category next to last, but, as will become clear, there are reasons for it. Obviously, we should be wary about staffing the government with people who have broken the law. It is possible to say what Oliver Wendell Holmes did about the law and see it as putting the citizen to a choice—obey the law or pay the penalty— which leads to an image of societal indifference as to whether the law is broken or not as long as the criminal is punished. But criminal laws are not tort laws; their purpose is to deter crime, not to force the criminal to reimburse the victim, thereby internalizing the costs of the illicit activity. Put otherwise, a criminal law states a moral sentiment and its violation is often an immoral act.

Nevertheless, it would be an error to ban from government service anyone who had ever broken any law, and violations of law should often be curable. Not every violation of the law is a crime and not every crime is of equal severity. A conviction for driving sixty-five miles per hour in a fifty-five-mile-per-hour zone simply is not in the same category as a conviction for beating one's spouse. One must see violations as existing along two axes—the importance of the law in question and the severity of the violation. In fact, we might need to plot the problem in three dimensions, because illegalities near the core of the duties we expect the nominee to perform might be more serious than illegalities in areas wholly divorced from those duties. President Clinton's letter accepting Zoe Baird's withdrawal as his potential attorney general implied that the brouhaha surrounding her household help might have been less serious had she been nominated for a different post. There is obviously something to this: other nominees with nanny problems have been confirmed.

Thus, in addition to asking whether the nominee has violated any laws, we must determine whether the law involved is related to the task for which the individual has been nominated, whether those violations are consequential or inconsequential, how those who violate the laws in question are generally treated (which tells us something about the depth and profundity of moral judgment the laws involve), and whether the nominee has made appropriate amends for the illegality. I am not proposing, strictly speaking, a balancing test; I do not argue that each of these questions must receive a particular answer for a "No" vote to be justified. But inquiries of this kind must be undertaken before we can decide how much weight to give to the underlying violation of law.

On this test, some violations would never be curable. Murder, rape, armed robbery, and other harms that are recognized by all as evil would obviously fall into this category. Adultery (illegal in many states), although a dreadfully serious breach of trust, probably would not. Illegal drug use might be somewhere in the middle. True, Douglas Ginsburg, when nominated for the Supreme Court, was pilloried for marijuana use many years before, and zero tolerance might after all be the most sensible policy—not only are drugs dangerous, but those who use them, even, as it is said, "recreationally," support a vicious, murderous subculture that leaves our young people dead in the streets. But it blinks at reality to deny, given the self-indulgence of the baby-boom generation, that our government is likely chock-full of people who tried drugs as teens or even as adults. In all likelihood, many of our public servants use drugs now—a scary thought, but one that seems statistically correct. What we should do about it I am not quite sure.

Although legal violations surrounding her employment of a nanny shot down Zoe Baird, it does not appear after all that this will be taken to disqualify future candidates. I have already mentioned that other appointees have had similar legal difficulties (one of them is now—I am not joking—the head of the Social Security Administration) and the Senate has taken the view that as long as they pay the taxes and penalties due, they will be eligible for confirmation. Perhaps the laws that Baird violated, which are not criminal statutes, should not fall into the category of automatic disqualifications; on the contrary, for reasons to which I shortly turn, perhaps they should be easily curable. In which case, our national silence on the "nannygate" violations of other government officials might be our way of admitting that we are ashamed of the way we acted the first time around.

CATEGORY 5—UNPROFESSIONAL CONDUCT

Finally, we come to a category that will sometimes—not always—be easiest to cure: Has the candidate violated any norms of the profession, or violated any ethical standard to which we generally hold public officials? I here have in mind the existence of actual standards, with precedents that enable them to be applied in difficult cases. The easiest case to determine is one in which the nominee has actually been adjudged by a competent authority to have violated an ethical norm. This will be true only if the nominee is a member of a self-regulating profession, such as law or medicine, or if, in government service or private life, the nominee has been employed by an institution that promulgates and enforces a code of conduct.

Although some breaches of professional standards are so severe that they should plainly be disqualifying, ethical norms do not represent societal judgments, which is why I suggest that violating them will generally be more easily curable than the immoral conduct constituting Category 3 or the illegal conduct constituting Category 4. (To be sure, many serious ethical breaches may fall into one of those categories.) In particular, we might want to distinguish between a pattern of ethical violations and a single professional breach, already the subject of discipline and never repeated.

Still, ethical violations are serious matters, and to say that they are often more easily cured than immoral or illegal acts is not to say that the cure should be easy. A professional enters law or medicine or whatever the field might be with eyes wide open. Rare is the professional who, when caught, can honestly say, "But I didn't know it was wrong!"—and, were we to honor that excuse, we would provide an incentive not to find out the rules. Moreover, public service has ethical codes of its own, both written and unwritten. Past ethical violations may be the best predictor of the likelihood of further ethical violations while in government service, a factor that goes to the heart of the ability to do the job well.

Many nominees have been accused of ethical violations. Abe Fortas was said to have violated professional norms by accepting a substantial fee for conducting a university seminar while serving as a Justice of the Supreme Court; as a result, his nomination as Chief Justice stalled. Subsequently, *Life* magazine reported that he had a hefty consulting agreement with a private foundation—a clearly serious ethical breach, probably not curable, which finally forced him to resign. Theodore Sorensen was accused of converting secret government documents to his own use; his nomination as director of Central Intelligence was withdrawn. Edwin Meese was accused of arranging government jobs for individuals to whom he owed money, but his nomination as attorney general succeeded.

As one might imagine, history is replete with instances of ethical improprieties by presidential appointees. For example, Samuel Swartout, chief customs inspector for the Port of New York (a federal appointment) stole $1.2 million from 1829 to 1838, before fleeing to England.[17] (We are talking here about early–nineteenth-century dollars.) In 1850, the administration of Zachary Taylor ordered the payment of $235,000 to settle a claim against the United States government—without revealing that Taylor's own secretary of war, in private practice, had received a fee of $95,000 to represent the very claimant on the identical claim.[18] Just before the Gold Panic of 1869, which was caused by the federal government's decision to put up for sale millions of dollars worth of gold, the assistant treasurer of the United States borrowed $1.5 million to speculate in the gold market, and the President of the United States, Ulysses S. Grant, wrote to his own sister, urging that her husband, an associate of financier Jay Gould, get out of the market.[19]

I mention these instances (which of course include nominees already confirmed) because many of them illustrate the concept of "honest graft" that dominated the second half of the nineteenth century and is even raised today, albeit not under that name, by almost any President whose associates are accused of unethical activity. "Honest graft" was the name given to the use of one's government service to benefit one's friends and clients. It was graft because it was unseemly, but it was honest because it was not against the law. ("Dishonest graft" encompassed bribery, theft, and the like.) Nowadays, what used to be called honest graft frequently *is* against the law, as it should be, which leads to one of our principal confusions about the role of ethics in government: when investigation (for example, by a court-appointed independent counsel) determines that an office-holder has violated no *law*, we treat that result as a vindication, and the accused public servant hangs onto the job. We forget in our investigations of the already confirmed what we try hard to remember in our investigations of the nominated: a wrong that is not illegal may yet be unethical, and a wrong that is unethical, unless balanced by some positive good, should serve as a bar to public service.

SUMMARY

Lest we forget, categorizing the wrong the candidate has done is not the end of the story. For my basic proposal is that we should balance what good the candidate might do when serving in the position against the evil that the putatively "disqualifying" factor represents. To summarize, there are five categories of potentially disqualifying facts, which I have listed in order of the relative ease of cure:

1) —Lack of qualifications	Never curable
2) —Loss of public respect	Very rarely curable
3) —Immoral conduct	Rarely curable
4) —Illegal conduct	Occasionally curable
5) —Unprofessional conduct	Somewhat more frequently curable

Looking at recent nomination battles, then, one would say, for example, that Zoe Baird fell into Category 4, which might have been curable, but also into Category 2, which was not curable without a presidential effort that was not forthcoming. Clarence Thomas, for those who believed Anita Hill, fell into Category 3 and perhaps Category 5. Whatever one's views on the charges, the controversy certainly placed him in Category 2, but significant presidential support was forthcoming and he was confirmed. Edwin Meese was either in Category 5 or in none of the categories, so his confirmation is not surprising. Lani Guinier fell into Category 2, so without the President's fervent support, she had no hope of confirmation. Robert Bork also fell into Category 2 and had relatively little presidential support, although studies of past confirmation fights suggest it is unlikely that a President in the next-to-last year of his term could stem the tide of opposition. As for Thurgood Marshall, opponents tried to place him in Category 1, which is not curable, and Category 5, which few people care about, and, in the end, did not even succeed in placing him in Category 2, which is why he was confirmed.

A CLOSING WORD ON NANNYGATE

In light of this analysis, it is useful to return for a moment to the matter of the many potential public servants felled by the nanny problem. Although I have placed these individuals in Category 4—illegal conduct—there is an argument to be made that such illegalities as existed were at the very fringe of appropriate public scrutiny. To see why this is so, suppose a nominee who had broken a very different law, as proposed in my discussion of Category 3. Imagine a nominee who had obtained an abortion at a time and place where the practice was illegal or who had engaged in consensual sexual activity with an adult of the same sex at a time and place where such activity was illegal. It is difficult to believe that we would have had a remotely comparable brouhaha about the *illegality* of the conduct. On the contrary, we would presumably have been told that for the Senate even to inquire into such matters would violate a fundamental norm of privacy—and I think that argument would be correct. Therefore, it is not the case that every violation of law should lead to a moral judgment of unfitness for office. In the examples mentioned, the privacy right of the nominee would intervene.

Very well, what about what has come to be called the nanny problem? The answer resides in separating the three most common nanny problem offenses, for they are not the same. One is the failure to pay Social Security on the sitter's wages. Another is the failure to report to the Internal Revenue Service the sitter's wages. A third is the knowing decision to hire an alien who lacks proper documentation (or, what is also a legal violation, the failure to determine prior to employment whether the nanny is legally in the country).

Are any of these also covered by privacy rights? The answer depends critically on one's view of the home and the life of the family. In our traditional legal iconography, home and family life have been deemed central to civil society. In his separate opinion in *Poe v. Ullman*,[20] the second Justice John Marshall Harlan, certainly no liberal activist, argued that the Court should apply the strictest scrutiny when the state seeks to regulate what goes on in the privacy of the home. He added that the Third and Fourth Amendments protect "the physical curtilage of the home . . . as a result of solicitude to protect the privacies of life within." Harlan was writing about contraception, and he specified that the "privacies" in question involved only the sexual relationship of husband and wife. But it is difficult to see why our constitutional solicitude for choices about childbearing should be greater than our constitutional solicitude for questions about child rearing. After all, the Supreme Court said in *Meyer v. Nebraska*[21] that among the most fundamental of constitutional rights are the rights "to marry, establish a home, and bring up children."

Bring up children. Once one accepts that the home is the rock on which the society is built, the nanny problem begins to lose the elegant simplicity that helps sustain the outrage. Matters are much more complex. We are, fortunately, well past the days when it was said that the king's writ did not run into the home—which meant that husbands could beat wives and children without official restraint—but the home, quite sensibly, is still surrounded by a political and philosophical mystique. Just as fortunately, we are past the days when only one form of human arrangement was described as the "family" on which the idea of home critically rests. These positive changes make no essential difference in the importance of home as a place free of all but the most vital state intrusions. Thus, even today, the state should intervene rarely and, when it does, it should do so only for the protection of someone else; never, in Kantian terms, to make people into means rather than ends.

Some courts, recognizing the specialness of the home,

have ruled that the state lacks power to regulate the posses-sion or use of otherwise illegal drugs within those four walls. One need not share that overly zealous view to understand that the home, in our jurisprudence, remains clothed in a spe-cialness that other venues lack. Indeed, when the Supreme Court in *Griswold v. Connecticut*[22] sustained the right of mar-ried couples to use contraceptives, Justice Douglas's majority opinion concluded with a rhetorical question—and a firm answer: "Would we allow the police to search the sacred precincts of marital bedrooms for telltale signs of the use of contraceptives? The very idea is repulsive to the notions of pri-vacy surrounding the marriage relationship." A few years later, when the Court upheld in *Stanley v. Georgia*[23] the right of individuals to possess obscene materials in their homes, Justice Thurgood Marshall wrote for the unanimous Court: "[I]f the First Amendment means anything, it means that the State has no business telling a man, sitting alone in his own house, what books he may read or what films he may watch."

None of this is to say that a state decision to regulate parts of a family's child-rearing choices is unconstitutional. But when set against the moral traditions of the nation, the state interests in enforcing the various laws at issue must at least be considered somewhat weaker. Thus, even if the laws do not offend the Constitution, moral and political questions remain to be resolved.

Given this analysis, the safest answer is that only the first of the three offenses—failure to pay the nanny's Social Secu-rity taxes—is obviously the government's business. The reason is that the requirement that the employer pay Social Security taxes is intended to protect the employee; the fact that the employment takes place within the four walls of the house and in the context of child rearing, over which the parents enjoy plenary authority, does not give the parent-employer any right to take advantage of the employee. The same would be true for minimum-wage or maximum-hour laws. In other words, to protect employees from abuse, the sovereign's writ runs into the home.*

But the other two requirements—that families report to the IRS what their nannies earn and that they ascertain their nannies' immigration status—would, in a sensible society, be beyond the government's power, except perhaps for the most extreme cases. In demanding that parent-employers check the nanny's work eligibility or report the nanny's earnings, the government is not seeking to protect against abuse *of* the employee; rather, the government is seeking to protect against abuse *by* the employee. In other words, the government is forcing the family to help it to ensure that the nanny does not escape the tax or immigration laws. Enforcing those laws is of course the government's business; but conscripting families, in the privacy of their homes and the sanctity of their child rearing, into assisting in that enforcement is not.[24]

To paraphrase Douglas, would we allow the police to search the sacred precincts of children's bedrooms for telltale signs of illegal employment? One would hope not; one would like to keep the home, and the choices a family makes about child rearing, sacrosanct. It is no answer to say that there is no physical search but only a reporting or payment requirement, for even in Justice Douglas's lyrical opinion in *Griswold,* the image of the search was only a metaphor for the intrusion itself. Consequently, if we now share a sense of national embarrassment rather than national outrage about the nanny problem, we have taken a very long step toward respecting a lost sense of privacy.

---

* Although the state may have a valid interest in enforcing its Social Security laws for individuals who provide child care in the home, it is not clear that the state always *should* do so. As the law now stands, the requirement is triggered whenever the worker—say, the baby-sitter—earns $50 in any quarter.

CODA: REPENTANCE AND SIN

I have argued that the search for disqualifying factors takes us down a dangerous road. I have further suggested that if we are to play that game, we should do it right, which means struggling for consistency and striving for a sense of balance. People, after all, are complicated, and the wrongs that we do in our lives are only part of our characters.

The American mind, someone has written, is literal: Americans are less ideological than pragmatic and, therefore, value the concrete over the abstract, the plain meaning over the metaphor. That, perhaps, is why we often show so little patience with wrongdoing by those who are in public life: we are unable to get our minds around such abstractions as the concept of sin.

Christian theology teaches that human sin is a consequence of our freedom—and that the burden of sin is too great for us to lift alone. In the Christian vision, redemption is possible only through God. The reason Christian theologians write of guilt as "threatening" is that the believer always feels the need to justify himself or herself before God, which is, for the sinful, impossible to do.[25] But sin is ever-present in human existence, which means that the fear of God is also ever-present, which is why human beings are in constant need of God's forgiveness.

One need not be a Christian—or even believe in God—to see the radical possibilities of this model. If the capacity to do wrong is ever-present, then we must accept that any one of us

---

The Social Security payroll tax is a regressive transfer of income in the best of cases (lower-wage workers pay a higher percentage of their income than higher-wage workers), but to require part-time baby-sitters who earn $50 in a single quarter to help support older individuals who have already recovered all of their Social Security contributions, plus interest, is not simply regressive. It is a cruel disincentive to work, so cruel that it is hard to see why disobedience *at the employee's behest* should be considered immoral.

(not merely those nominated for judicial or executive posts) may, at any moment, fall into sin. If that is so, we surely have a larger obligation toward the wrongdoer—the sinner—than a simple condemnation and, in the case of a confirmation fight, a negative vote. In particular, recognizing our shared sinfulness, we might instead have the moral obligation to listen for the possibility of genuine contrition, which might in turn demand of us a degree of forgiveness. This, surely, is the point of Lincoln's epigram that I quoted in chapter 2: "On principle, I dislike an oath which requires a man to swear he *has* not done wrong. It rejects the Christian principle of forgiveness on terms of repentance. I think it enough if a man does no wrong here*after*." Forgiveness in this sense might not necessarily mean confirmation, but it might mean that even upon detecting sin, we could be more loving, and less vicious, in our decision against a nominee. We could reject potential Justices or cabinet officers as sinners without rejecting them as monsters.

Unfortunately, we seem to prefer to think of sin as wrongdoing—the violation of some duty, whether written down somewhere or not—which means that we reject the concept of sin as something ever-present in all of us. Because we reject that concept in our national dialogues over morality, we are unable to encompass in those dialogues the more complex metaphorical possibilities of contrition, redemption, and forgiveness. Although, as I have made clear, I thought Anita Hill told the unvarnished truth and Clarence Thomas lied when he denied her charges, I would genuinely rather live in a world in which a Thomas who found himself able to say "Yes, it happened, and I am terribly sorry, but it was a long time ago in a difficult time and I am a different man" might have found an audience willing to listen. Listening, even forgiving, does not entail reward. A world in which people might have listened would not necessarily be one in which his contrition would have led to his confirmation. (Indeed, waiting for confirmation time to make acts of contrition is always a reason for suspicion.) But vindication should not be the highest value, and nobody holds an entitlement to confirmation. On the other hand, vindication is not trivial either. But it is sometimes found in what one does later rather than in one's confirmation vote. For example, Hugo Black apologized for his membership in the Ku Klux Klan and was easily confirmed; but had his subsequent career as ardent civil libertarian not made plain the sincerity of his apology, he might today be remembered not as the great liberal but as the Court's only avowed Klansman. So in the case of Clarence Thomas, had he apologized as I suggest he should have, he might or might not have been confirmed, but at least the question before the Senate could then have been, empirically, a prediction of future behavior (metaphorically, a judgment on the sincerity of his contrition) rather than a need to impose punishment for his past.

But we do not reward contrition. Zoe Baird, who was the one who brought up her nanny problem in the first place, apologized for it and was thrown overboard. Given that the Senate had treated with less hostility individuals who have denied wrongdoing that many people believed they had committed, the message of the way we now conduct our affairs is surely that one should deny and deny and accuse and accuse. Better to blame your problems on the world than to take a hard look into your own soul—because if you admit what you have done wrong, even if you apologize for it, the word passes swiftly along the televised backyard fence, and you might lose the resume race.

We do have an alternative to the way we have lately been doing business. We could try, possibly for the first time in our history, to treat public service as a calling rather than a reward. Rather than thinking of service on the Supreme Court or at the Justice Department as a device to add points to the resume, we can treat it as an opportunity to labor on behalf of the country, to offer a fair return for what the nation has given. The question, then, should not be whether the nominee "deserves" the position, as though the job is a quid pro quo for years of moral rectitude. The question should be whether this person is capable of honorable service of which, in the future, we will be glad.

Or we can go on as we have been. We can refuse to develop a sense of balance and continue to provide incentives to dissemble and conceal. We can say to those who are nominated to serve us that the best strategy, if accused of any wrongdoing, is to stonewall if possible, to lie if necessary—for we will reward you if you allow us to continue deluding ourselves, but we will never forgive you if you force us to face our own very human capacity for sin.

7

Some Modest Proposals, Reviewed

REFORMING our understanding of what disqualifies a nominee from public service will not eliminate the bloodbaths that are all too frequent when the contest involves a seat on the Supreme Court. Given the vast power that the Justices will continue to exercise in American society, one can hardly avoid the bitter battles that have characterized some 40 percent of the nominations since *Brown v. Board of Education*[1] was decided in 1954. After all, when a seat falls vacant, there is much at stake—especially as one's most hated or loved decisions slip from a majority of 7 to 2 to one of 6 to 3 to the tantalizing 5 to 4.

The most obvious way to avoid leaving blood on the floor is to name individuals of the highest caliber and experience, with much less attention paid to their likely votes. The proper model might be the one followed by Gerald Ford, in uncovering the gem of John Paul Stevens. Ford, insisting that "ideological grounds" are not proper in judicial selection, was evidently quite serious when he instructed his attorney general—the formidable, non-political Edward Levi—to make recommendations without regard to the political views of the nominee, for the list of finalists was remarkably diverse. The

Stevens nomination had opponents at the ideological extremes—Bella Abzug and Pat Buchanan were both sharply critical—but the great middle, which includes the moderate right and the moderate left, found little problem with Stevens, who was confirmed by a vote of 98–0.[2]

President Clinton plainly had something similar in mind when he selected Ruth Bader Ginsburg in 1993, choosing, so news reports had it, between her and one other finalist, Judge Stephen Breyer. Both are judges of considerable ability who, like Stevens, are respected across the political spectrum. By limiting his choice to such individuals, he successfully resisted the pressure to select someone who could be counted on more reliably to vote into constitutional law his party's platform—which is approximately what Democrats accused Republicans of doing in the decade betweeen 1981 and 1991. And although there was some conservative carping, Ginsburg was confirmed by a vote of 96–3.

Perhaps unsurprisingly, critics of recent confirmation fights seem unwilling to contemplate the possibility that the selection of nominees was an important part of the problem. They have focused instead on what has happened after the announcement of a nomination and have set forth a number of proposals that would, they believe, reduce the amount of blood on the floor. However, as will be seen, only one of them—the least likely to be adopted—would make a genuine difference in the likelihood of a vicious struggle. The trouble with the proposals for reform is that none goes to the heart of the trouble: our attitudes toward the Court as an institution and the work it does for the society. Although we try mightily to resist the temptation, we continue to view the Court as a servant, charged with handing down decisions that most people want; when it fails to do so, we grow furious, and promise to remake it, which is, we insist, our prerogative. We demand a degree of judicial accountability, which is another way of saying that we are unhappy with genuine judicial independence. If we are unable or unwilling to alter those attitudes, then we ought to consider a quite different and more radical shift in how we think about choosing our Justices. I say this without any enthusiasm for tampering with the Constitution, least of all with the delicate balance involved in the appointment process; yet in the way we think, talk, and act on the selection of Supreme Court Justices, we the people have, in effect, already altered the original constitutional arrangements. All we have failed to do is codify our new understanding.

PROPOSALS THAT REQUIRE NO CONSTITUTIONAL AMENDMENTS

Many recently proposed changes would require no tampering and a few of them might even help make matters a bit more congenial. For example, the Senate, in an effort to give teeth to the constitutional notion of "advice," could assert its institutional prerogatives by sending the White House a list of possible nominees from which the President would be urged to make his choice.[3] A Senate willing to behave as an institution—a branch of the national government rather than a branch of the White House[4]—could even insist on its list, by informing the President that nobody not on the list would be confirmed. But the realities of public perception being what they are, it is possible that a Senate willing to make such a move would emerge smelling like a sewer, for voters might believe (wrongly) that the Senate was involved in a power grab. Besides, the nature of modern partisan politics makes this unlikely: members of the President's party will not want to oppose him without very strong reasons. The nature of the modern sound bite makes it less likely still: through the alchemy of television, a candidate who looked very strong when the senators compiled their list might wind up looking like a monster by the time the hearings were through. Something much like this happened in 1987, for Judiciary Committee Chairman Joseph Biden had been quoted the previous year as rebutting charges of partisanship with the suggestion that if President Reagan nominated a "principled conservative," the nominee would be confirmed with no difficulty. His example of such a principled conservative was Robert Bork.

Similarly, some critics have proposed that the Senate adopt a "merit selection" process like the one used in many of the states. In a process of this kind, a commission, comprising both lawyers and lay people, presents the appointing authority with a list of candidates, selected, it is said, solely on the basis of their individual merit. The appointing authority (usually the governor) then nominates one of them, who ordinarily must then face hearings in the legislature prior to confirmation.

The Carter Administration experimented with merit-selection panels to choose nominees for the federal courts of appeals, and the Senate by law has established such a plan for selecting the local judges for the District of Columbia. However, the experience of the states has been uneven, and critics have charged that the merit-selection panels are masks for secret rather than public ideological battles. Only the identity of the players, it is said, has changed. The Carter Administration panels, although they produced some of the finest federal judges in the country, also faced criticism on the ground that politics rather than merit was too often decisive.[5] Besides, it is famously difficult to define the term *merit* (although the relevant statutes usually make a game try), and, in any event, even a nominee from such a list could wind up, as they say, being borked.

Other proposals to "reform" the confirmation process without amending the Constitution would do no good, because they attack the wrong enemies. Our battles over Supreme Court nominees leave so much blood on the floor because so much is seen to be at stake. This perception is independent of the selection process. When a seat falls open, what hangs in the balance is nothing so arcane as the correct approach to interpretation. What hangs in the balance, rather, is the list of rights to be protected or unprotected, depending on one's preference. As I have explained in the previous chapters, the public—and, for the most part, the activists who struggle titanically over what they insist are questions of judicial philosophy—do not particularly care *how* the nominee will reach her results. The public cares only about what results the nominee will reach. And as long as our national attitude about the Supreme Court holds that only the bottom line matters, the battles over every vacancy are going to stay bloody. Which is, in a nutshell, why the confirmation process can't be fixed.

Let me try to demonstrate the point by running through a series of proposals for reforming the process that have popped up since the Bork and Thomas hearings. Each would inevitably fail, and the reasons for the predicted failure coincide with my principal thesis.

Proposal 1—The nominee testifies immediately upon nomination, and others testify months later.

This proposal, which arose in 1991, would accomplish nothing, except to force a poorly prepared nominee to go before the television cameras and face close Senate scrutiny, and then to give opponents several months to pick apart the transcript before trotting out their own testimony.[6] The proposal assumes, wrongly, that the White House "handlers" are somehow to blame for what has gone wrong. But there is nothing wrong with giving the nominee a chance to practice before appearing on national television—conceivably for the first time—and facing a committee that may include members who are skeptical or even hostile, and who are fed a constant stream of questions by their eager staffers. As long as our vision of the Court requires senators to ask about judicial philosophy, we would do well to give the nominee a chance to prepare.

Proposal 2—Only those with personal knowledge of the nominee are allowed to testify, that is, no "groups."

This proposal would also accomplish nothing. The interest groups that supply both senators and commentators with forgotten articles and long-lost after-dinner speeches by the nominee have a legitimate role to play in the process. The intensity of their efforts helps to signal members of the Senate on the likelihood of public opposition, for when the groups lobby hard, they are likely to take their cases to the voters.[7] Even when the rhetoric of the groups gets out of hand (as it frequently does), even when the press conferences and press releases and commercials go overboard, as they did in the campaign against the Bork nomination, the activity of the interest groups is only a symptom; it is not the problem. The reason the groups that make everyone so angry take so ardent a part is the perfectly sensible perception that much is at stake. The problem is what is thought to be at stake, not who gets involved in the fighting. When one's favorite decision seems to be hanging by a single vote, it is hard to sit passively and watch.

Besides, even if it were true that the activity of the groups was itself a problem, banning their testimony would make no difference. The testimony is not the problem either, and, indeed, with some notable exceptions, the hearings themselves are conducted with considerable decorum. True, many of the most vicious racist innuendos about Thurgood Marshall came in the hearing or even on the Senate floor, but the senators, not the many groups battling against the nomination, were the culprits. The cruelest comments about Robert Bork came outside the hearing rooms, where a ban on testimony by the groups would do nothing to affect the carnival atmosphere: the silly press conferences, the ridiculously overblown claims by supporters and opponents, and the media's absurd and dangerous penchant for reducing complex issues to sound bites and applause lines.

Proposal 3—The nominee does not testify.

As noted in chapter 3, no Supreme Court nominee had ever appeared at his own confirmation hearing until 1925, when Harlan Fiske Stone's nomination ran into trouble on the Senate floor because of the opposition of an angry senator whose conduct Stone, as attorney general, had investigated. When President Coolidge refused to withdraw the nomination, the Judiciary Committee reconvened to hear what he had to say. He was confirmed by a vote of 71 to 6.[8]

After that, nominees appeared intermittently. Felix Frankfurter tried to refuse the committee's invitation to attend, citing a sensible concern for judicial independence, but he caved in when friends warned him that he might not be confirmed if he stuck to his principles. And since 1955, when John Marshall Harlan, the first post-*Brown* nominee, was required to face a skeptical Judiciary Committee that wanted to see whether he would continue the civil rights revolution that Senate conservatives abhorred, every nominee has testified. I am no great fan of requiring nominees to testify, but at this point in our history, this change would cause more problems than it would solve. The Court is a powerful entity in our politics and recognized by the public as such; the people of the United States understandably want what passes for exposure (bits and pieces on the television news) to the individuals who might be wielding that power. The nation might be better off with a Court less central to the making of public policy, but that is not the Court we have, and we should make no pretense to the contrary.

Proposal 4—No television cameras at the hearings.

The presence of television cameras probably makes everyone behave worse, but the main damage is done not through televising the hearings but televising the charges and countercharges.[9] No rule about coverage of the hearings would alter that. Besides, as long as the Court exercises as much power as it does, the public understandably would not (if the reader will pardon the expression) sit still while the plug is pulled.

Proposal 5—No public hearings.

See Proposal 4.[10] And also consider the conspiracy theories. Opponents would be certain that a deal was being struck behind closed doors; supporters would insist that their candidate was being trashed in secret.

This was a particular problem during the Thomas hearings in the fall of 1991, when friends of both Clarence Thomas and Anita Hill complained that the hearings should have been closed. Why, both sets of partisans asked, should our friend be smeared (as each side separately saw it) on national television? The answer, of course, was that once the allegations became public knowledge, the accuser and the accused both, in a sense, became public property—and the public would not have stood for closed hearings. But in another sense, this was to the good: no matter what the outcome, had the hearings been held behind closed doors, supporters of the losing side would have been certain that the fix was in.

Proposal 6—No hearings.

Yeah, right.[11]

In sum, none of these proposals would make any difference because none of them reduces the stakes that all sides have in each nomination. In consequence, they aim at the wrong villains. As long as the stakes remain as high as they are, the nomination and confirmation of Supreme Court Justices will remain a mess.

PROPOSALS THAT WOULD REQUIRE CONSTITUTIONAL AMENDMENTS

Anyone who takes our constitutional republic seriously will have difficulty accepting the possibility of tampering with the Supreme Court. It is easy enough to see why the independence of the Court as an institution matters. For reasons that are obscure, however, our political iconography holds that the Court's very structure is somehow beyond question. Nine Justices, for example, has become a kind of magic number, as Franklin Roosevelt learned to his chagrin when he attempted the ill-fated court-packing plan.

Of course, in an important sense, Roosevelt was right. There is no reason that the Court must comprise nine Justices, and for most of our history, it did not. The Constitution specifies no number. The Judiciary Act of 1789 allocated six. Subsequent legislation decreased the number to five, increased it to eight, increased it to ten, reduced it to seven, and, in 1869, increased it to nine, where it has remained for well over a century. But that magic number, nine, is only tradition; it has been altered before, often in the service of politics, and can be altered again. Yet we are sensibly reluctant to consider change.

Our fixation on the number of Justices is a mask for something deeper: an understanding of the Court's terrible fragility. And because we are unwilling to do anything serious to preserve the image of judicial independence—for example, restraining our natural impulse to treat the Justices as servants—we cling to a cluster of formalisms instead. The number is sacred, and so is the jurisdiction: the last thing most of us seem to want is to read the Constitution as it is plainly written, to allow the Congress to strip the Supreme Court of the ability to hear whole categories of cases. But tampering with the Constitution, no matter how little we might like to do it, could point us toward at least a partial resolution of the Supreme Court confirmation mess.

Proposal 7—Supermajority requirement.

One obvious solution would be to raise the threshold vote necessary for confirmation from a simple majority of the Senate to two-thirds. This change, it is said, would force the President to find a potential Justice not strongly identified with an ideological movement, because the nominee would be unable to squeak by. By this standard, note its supporters, Robert Bork (defeated by 42 to 58) and Clarence Thomas (confirmed by 52 to 48) would never have been nominated, because each of them certainly began with one-third of the Senate in opposition, and although William Rehnquist might still have been nominated for Chief Justice in 1986, he would have been rejected, because the vote in favor was 65 to 33—1 vote short of two-thirds. Bork, Rehnquist, and Thomas are generally described as conservatives (although Bork prefers to call himself a "classical liberal"), and critics of this proposal have suggested that it is simply designed to screen conservatives out. Besides, they argue, a two-thirds requirement might make scare tactics more appealing, because the number of senators who would have to be persuaded to vote no is so much smaller.

Still, the bottom line is this: had the required vote for Supreme Court confirmations been two-thirds of the Senate, Ronald Reagan would never have dared nominate Robert Bork. This would have denied the nation his services, but those services were denied in any case, and even if the Reagan Administration was unable to predict that Bork's hearings would be quite so testy, it might have been somewhat easier to predict that he would not gain a two-thirds majority. Faced with a supermajority requirement, and already having obtained easy confirmations for Sandra Day O'Connor and Antonin Scalia, Reagan might have done initially what he did in the end: nominated a thoughtful, conservative-leaning centrist like Anthony Kennedy. When you add in other admired Justices—John Paul Stevens, for example, was confirmed by 98–0—it is plain that although the supermajority requirement would screen out nominees who were perceived, rightly or wrongly, as narrow-minded, it would not screen out quality. On the contrary: it might well screen out mediocrity. Surely if Richard Nixon in 1971 had been faced with the two-thirds hurdle, he would not have nominated Carswell, who generated Senator Roman Hruska's famous epigram: "Even if he is mediocre there are a lot of mediocre judges and people and lawyers. They are entitled to a little representation, aren't they . . . ?"[12] Were the nominee required to gain the affirmative votes of two-thirds of the senators (the same plurality required for treaties), the answer to Hruska's question would be an easy no.

So the two-thirds standard *could* work, as long as it encouraged the President to seek a nominee respected on all sides, able to garner votes even from those who disagree sharply on philosophy—a nominee, for example, like Ruth Bader Ginsburg (confirmed 96 to 3) or Antonin Scalia (confirmed 98 to 0). Requiring a supermajority for confirmation, in other words, would encourage consensus candidates rather than predictable ideologues. Certainly we *could* nevertheless have a bitter battle over confirmation, but a confrontation would not be likely unless the President tried to pack the Court as part of an ideological crusade.

Those most likely to oppose the two-thirds requirement (other than such curmudgeons as I, who worry about whether we should *ever* amend the Constitution) are those who think it useful that we have the occasional Justice who only squeaks by. However, the only utility in having Justices confirmed by very close votes is that very slightly qualified or very controversial figures can make it to the Court. It is not clear why this is an advantage. Besides, one can be a bit controversial and still win confirmation by a comfortable margin—the final vote on Thurgood Marshall's nomination, for example, was 69 to 11—but in the era of the sound bite, a supermajority requirement would coax Presidents away from figures whose public lives had made enemies. Right now, with the confirmation process so riven with strife, this might not be a bad thing.

WHY NOT ELECTION?
MORE MODEST PROPOSALS

Committed activists are unlikely to support a two-thirds rule, at least when their parties are in the White House, because the proposal would make it harder to pack the Court. But if we are to go on as we have been, voting for Presidents because of their promises to staff the Supreme Court with people who have already made up their minds, then we should give serious thought to taking the game outside the Beltway. After all, even though opinion surveys influence Senate confirmation votes, the arguments and the decisions are made by Washington activists and Washington staff members. The surveys are no substitute for direct citizen participation. Usually, one is warned at this point in the argument that allowing some kind of direct popular vote on the Justices would represent too much public influence. With that sentiment I heartily agree. I simply fail to understand why simple candor—doing honestly what we now pretend not to do—would not be an improvement.

I also wonder why so many of today's supporters of democratic checks seem to have such short historical memories. I confess to a bias in the matter: I served as law clerk to Thurgood Marshall, one of the great figures of American legal history, and any system that would have denied the nation his services strikes me as crazy. But under the contemporary theory that insists on discarding any nominee whose views are out of step with the public's, a Marshall could never have been confirmed.

Still, if a democratic check is truly needed, consideration of a handful of modest proposals that *would* require constitutional amendments might be in order.

Proposal 8—Term limits.

Back in chapter 3, I suggested it would be easier to support the view that each political generation should have the chance to enshrine its programs as fundamental constitutional law if the Justices served limited terms—say, eight or twelve years.

When I speak of limited terms, I do not mean that the Justices should be eligible to succeed themselves, to sit for what we might call reconfirmation. That possibility, it should be unnecessary to note, would pose a terrible threat to judicial independence. (We have some recent experience with reeligibility at the state level, and although some of it is encouraging, much of it is horrendous.)[13] No, when I refer to term limits, I mean the real thing—you put in your twelve years and you're gone, to private law practice or to academia or politics or a speaking tour—even to a lower federal court. (Indeed, one possibility would be to rotate the Justices from lower federal court posts, with the understanding at the time of each elevation that the judge selected for the Supreme Court would ultimately return.) The point would be that no jurist could twice serve on the Supreme Court.

Life tenure for our judges has obvious virtues. It allows the accumulation of wisdom and experience. It promotes independence. And a less remarked advantage of life tenure is that its existence encourages life service, thereby avoiding a variety of potential improprieties. For example, the *New York Times* accused federal district judge Royce Savage of "poor judgment" that tended "to lessen public confidence in the independence and integrity of the Federal Judiciary" when he left the bench in 1961 to become general counsel of Gulf Oil Corporation, which, two years earlier, he had acquitted of charges of violating the antitrust laws. President John Kennedy remarked at the time: "I don't think that anyone should accept a Federal judgeship unless prepared to fill it for life because I think the maintenance of the integrity of the Judiciary is so important."[14]

Still, it is curious that with so many people shouting about term limits for the Congress, where (barring overdrafts) incumbents seem to endure forever, nobody has the courage to point to the strangest incumbency that we have. Absent voluntary retirements, we return upward of 90 percent of the Congress year after year—but we return 100 percent of the Justices. Once a Justice, always a Justice. One can at least hypothesize the defeat of an incumbent member of the Congress. Supreme Court Justices, wielding far greater power per member, are simply there, year after year after year. Perhaps term limits would do the Court some good. Certainly term limits are sensible if we are to go on picking the Justices the way that we do.

After all, if the Justices served for limited terms, it would be far easier for passing political majorities to enshrine their views as fundamental law. One would not need to engage in the extended and unseemly deathwatch to which various interest groups now subject the Court—*which one will die next? will we be in power? whom can we appoint?* If passing political majorities really have the right to pack the Court, it hardly seems fair that the only ones to get Justices of their own are those who happen to be in power when a vacancy happens to occur. Much fairer, surely, to give everybody a chance. That is, much fairer if we truly intend to go on picking Justices the way we do, through trying to craft a Court full of people whose minds are already made up.

But must we go on picking Justices the way that we do? Maybe not. If we really want a democratic check—if we really think the Court should reflect the fundamental values of the American people—why not let the people choose? Again, I remind the reader that I think popular choice of Justices a terrible idea—but I think it just as bad to encourage the President and the senators to talk, nominate, and vote as though public opinion should rule constitutional law. Most voters—and certainly most politicians—seem to accept the contrary view, that their opinions on constitutional interpretation should carry some weight. It is that reality that the notion of popular choice would reflect. Let us now travel down that road briefly and see how the scenery looks.

Proposal 9—Judicial elections.

In an electoral democracy, when one speaks of letting the people choose, one is speaking of election. The matter of what elections might look like—while still preserving the bedrock principle of judicial independence—is what leads to my next set of modest proposals. I will mention here two general models, one of them drawn from the experiences of the states, one of them rather uniquely federal.

PROPOSAL 9-A—CONTESTED ELECTIONS.   First, drawing on the tradition in many states, we could fill vacancies on the Supreme Court through *contested elections*.   When a vacancy occurs, each party could nominate a candidate, who would, after a suitable interval, stand for election before the national voting public. Perhaps there would be third-party candidates as well. Press conferences would be held; television commercials would run. I imagine that quotes from old opinions (if the candidate is a judge) or from old articles (if the candidate is a scholar) would be splashed misleadingly across the front pages of the nation's newspapers, or edited down to tightly deceptive sound bites. ("High Court candidate once questioned right to private property. At 11.") There would be attack ads, and bumper stickers, perhaps even a debate or two. In short, up until the time of the vote itself, things would be pretty much as they are now.

But the vote is where things would be different: sooner or later, we the people would have to make a choice. We might try the simple popular vote, but that would run contrary to deep-seated American traditions. No national question is decided by a national majority vote. So, very likely, we would have to trot out the strange but magnificently agonizing state-by-state calculus we use when selections are made by what we are pleased to call the electoral college. There are quadrennial demands for reform or abolition of the college, but they never come to much. The mechanism is cumbersome, but we get by with it for mere Presidents; very likely, we would get by with it for Justices of the Supreme Court as well.[15]

PROPOSAL 9-B—REFERENDA. Does it sound awful? There's worse. If you dislike the idea of contested elections, there is a *second* possibility as well: referenda.

This is the way it would work. When a vacancy occurred,

the President would nominate a candidate who, instead of facing a candidate from the other party, would face only the voters, who would be entitled to cast a *yes* or a *no*. The election
would not be contested. Either the voters would endorse—that
is, confirm—the nominee, or the President would be forced to
go back and start anew with another candidate. We would still
have the press conferences and the attack ads and all the rest,
so democracy would continue to receive its due. But there
would be only a single candidate.

This system would, in effect, be the same as what we do
now, except that the confirmation battle would take place in
the court of public opinion rather than in the Senate. We
would simply be doing directly what we now do indirectly:
using all means, fair or foul, to influence public opinion. The
difference would be that we would suddenly be honest about
what we are doing—and that the public opinion itself would
be decisive rather than merely influential.

BUT WHAT ABOUT INDEPENDENCE?

One might object that all this talk of election constitutes a threat
to judicial independence. In principle, I certainly agree; and yet
the election systems that I have described are less different
from what we do now than they may seem. Right now, when
controversy erupts over a Supreme Court nomination, we ask
the voters what they think. We fight for their opinions with television commentaries, newspaper columns, planted stories of
scandal or defense, even paid advertisements. Of course, under
the current system, much of the work, and all of the voting, is
concentrated inside the Beltway. Were we to elect the Justices
directly, rather than by proxy, the principal change would be
that this game of democratic checkery, of having the chance to

enshrine the values of a passing political majority as fundamental constitutional law, would be opened up to the entire voting
public, to all of us—all of "we, the people"—rather than limited
to the liberal and conservative Beltway activists who speak with
perfect sincerity in the people's name.

One who rejects these modest proposals, then, either (1)
believes that potential Justices should be screened for their
fidelity to "our" values, but that the people in whose name it is
done are not competent to take part in it, or (2) rejects the
conventional wisdom holding that the screening is appropriate
to begin with. The first option reduces the screening to an elite
phenomenon—in effect, an "undemocratic" check, in which
small interest groups work to gain seats on the Court in order
to work their will on the nation. The second option is more
sensible. Indeed, the true solution to the Supreme Court confirmation mess lies in our ability to develop a public rhetoric
about the Constitution that does not treat the Court as though
the results it reaches are all that matters. And that change
would require that we rethink our attitude about the Court and
its place in our society.

What is wrong with our attitude about the Court? Three
things, all of them staples of polemics from the left or the right.
First, as many commentators have argued, we rely too heavily
on the Justices to correct what we often view as the errors of the
other branches of government, including the state and local
entities where most lawmaking takes place. Second, and perhaps as a consequence of the first, we have become so bound
up in the rhetorical habit of referring to constitutional rights that
we have virtually lost the ability to engage in public dialogue
about tough moral questions. Third, we have developed so
much political machinery designed to control or influence the
Justices that we have lost sight of the principal means through
which change must come in a democracy, if the change is to
have lasting effect: the persuasion of our fellow citizens.

Yielding these myths will not be easy; in fact, it may not be possible. Which is why, here, as so often, one finally longs for the good old days, not because the country was better then—it was, in nearly every respect, far worse—but because they have a mythos of their own, and one from which we can learn much. I have in mind the era when President James Madison, for political reasons, desperately sought a New Englander to replace Justice Cushing. As Prof. Charles Warren narrates the tale, the following events then transpired: first, Madison found Levi Lincoln and nominated him, without first advising him that he was the candidate. The Senate swiftly confirmed. And when Lincoln at last discovered what was happening up on Capitol Hill, he . . . *declined to serve.*

So Madison, working hard, sent up the name of John Quincy Adams, and Adams was swiftly confirmed, and when he learned of all this, Adams said . . . *no thanks.*

A third nominee was rejected by the Senate, on the ground that he had, as a government lawyer, enforced a law that the Senate majority didn't like.[16]

Which left for the Court the happy circumstance of Madison's fourth nominee, Joseph Story, who was confirmed—and who, as Prof. Paul Freund reminds us, then proceeded, during his three decades on the Court, to vote against everything that Madison, who nominated him, and Madison's Senate, which confirmed him, held dear and true.[17] All that hard work, Madison must have groaned, just to produce a traitor. But that, it seems to me, is the Supreme Court confirmation process at its best, a process that will work only when we learn once more to treat the role of Justice as simply a job. Not a prize, but a job—a job not everybody wants—and a job that, if done well, will mean working without a scintilla of loyalty to movement or cause.

And it can work that way again if we surrender the bold and exciting image of the Supreme Court as national policymaker and recapture in its stead the more mundane and lawyerly image of the Supreme Court as—dare I say it?—a court.

If it ain't broke, runs the old saw, *don't fix it*—and despite all the worry about blood on the floor and smears and sound bites, our processes for nominating and confirming Supreme Court Justices and other public officials are not really broken, which is why so few of the proposed repairs would make much difference. The trouble, rather, is in our attitudes—the way we think about public service in general, and the Supreme Court in particular.

If we stop thinking of public service as a reward for good behavior and begin again to think of it as a calling; if we stop asking whether our nominees have ever sinned and begin again to ask whether they will be good at the job; if we stop envisioning the Supreme Court as a democratically selected body and begin again to envision it as a check on what the democratically elected branches do; if we can make all these changes in our attitudes, then, and only then, can the confirmation process be fixed. Otherwise, we will certainly muddle through—but we will leave lots of blood along the way.

NOTES

CHAPTER 1: THE TELEVISED BACKYARD FENCE

1.   Clinton and Rehnquist quoted in Joan Biskupic, "Thurgood Marshall, Retired Justice, Dies," *Washington Post,* January 25, 1993, p. A1.

2.   Ethan Bronner, *Battle for Justice: How the Bork Nomination Shook America* (New York: Norton, 1989), pp. 334–35.

3.   The American people evidently understood the distinction, which some commentators insisted they would not, between hiring an illegal alien illegally and hiring an illegal alien legally. In a *USA Today*/CNN/Gallup poll, 65 percent of respondents said Wood (never formally nominated) should not have pulled out. Richard Benedetto, "Fallout Continues In and Out of White House: Wood, Baird Cases Different, Most Say," *USA Today,* February 9, 1993, p. 4A.

4.   Meg Greenfield, "Only Kidding," *Newsweek,* July 5, 1993, p. 66.

5.   For example, a writer in *The Nation,* after attending a service at Thomas's church in which "the faithful sang, 'We've got our marching orders. Now is the time to carry them for-

ward,'" sounded a slightly hysterical call to arms: "Shouldn't Thomas be asked if he accepts any marching orders other than to preserve and protect the Constitution of the United States?" David Corn, "Believing Thomas," *The Nation,* August 12, 1991, p. 180. The columnist Judy Mann also argued that the nation had a right to know how Thomas's religious views would influence his judging, at least on the abortion issue. Judy Mann, "Thomas's Abortion Views," *Washington Post,* July 5, 1991, p. D3. For further samples of this debate, see David S. Broder, "Wilder Urges Scrutiny of Thomas on Abortion," *Washington Post,* July 3, 1991, p. A14; A. L. May, "Thomas's religion looms as an issue," *Atlanta Journal-Constitution,* July 21, 1991, p. A1; and Walter V. Robinson, "Thomas's church has antiabortion ties," *Boston Globe,* July 17, 1991, p. 8.

For general discussion of the interplay between a judge's religious belief and judicial craft, see Stephen L. Carter, "The Religiously Devout Judge," *Notre Dame Law Review* 64 (1989): 932; and Scott C. Idleman, "The Role of Religious Values in Judicial Decision Making," *Indiana Law Journal* 68 (1993): 433.

6. Robert Bork, *The Tempting of America: The Political Seduction of the Law* (New York: Free Press, 1990), p. 337.

7. For discussions of this history, see, for example, Joseph P. Harris, *The Advice and Consent of the Senate* (Berkeley: University of California Press, 1953); Neil D. McFeeley, *Appointment of Judges: The Johnson Presidency* (Austin: University of Texas Press, 1987); Laurence H. Tribe, *God Save This Honorable Court: How the Choice of Supreme Court Justices Shapes Our History* (New York: Random House, 1985).

8. Of course, such difficulties as may exist in the backgrounds of most nominees will never be discovered. Limited time and resources mean that relatively few presidential nominees receive serious Senate scrutiny and the overwhelming majority are confirmed without trouble. Over 80 percent of nominees surveyed say that they were treated well by the Senate. For discussions of these and other data, see Christo-

pher J. Deering, "Damned If You Do and Damned If You Don't: The Senate's Role in the Appointments Process," in G. Calvin MacKenzie, ed., *The In-and-Outers: Presidential Appointees and Transient Government in Washington* (Baltimore: Johns Hopkins University Press, 1987), p. 100.

9. See Jeffrey Segal, "Senate Confirmation of Supreme Court Justices: Partisan and Institutional Politics," *Journal of Politics* 49 (1987): 998.

10. See, for example, Martin Shapiro, "Interest Groups and Supreme Court Appointments," *Northwestern University Law Review* 84 (1990): 935.

11. Ted Harbert, president of the entertainment division of ABC, quoted in Ken Auletta, "What Won't They Do?" *The New Yorker,* May 17, 1993, pp. 45, 53.

CHAPTER 2: OF NANNIES, SOUND BITES, AND CONFIRMATION NONSENSE

1. Ruckelshaus is discussed in Anthony Lewis, "It's Gender, Stupid," *New York Times,* February 8, 1993, p. 17. To be fair, one must add that the Ruckelshaus "nanny problem" was discovered after his confirmation, not before. However, given the atmosphere that prevailed early in 1993, he would have been asked and, had he answered truthfully, he would not have been nominated.

2. For a sample of the debate, compare "Questions for Ms. Baird," *New York Times,* January 19, 1993, p. 20, with Murray Kempton, "A Woman in Distress," *Newsday,* January 22, 1993, p. 102.

3. See Stuart Taylor, "Inside the Whirlwind," *American Lawyer,* March 1993, and Sidney Blumenthal, "Adventures in Babysitting," *The New Yorker,* February 15, 1993, p.53.

4. Lest the reader protest that homosexuals have done nothing wrong whereas such cabinet nominees as Zoe Baird have broken the law, I would remind that there are many places where sexual relations between adults of the same sex are

illegal. These laws are cruel, and the Supreme Court, in my judgment, erred in failing to rule them unconstitutional in *Bowers v. Hardwick*, 478 U.S. 186 (1986), but that does not change the fact that they are the laws. Most of the offenses charged against Zoe Baird (as will be seen in chapter 6) also fall into the category of violation of cruel laws.

5. Quoted in Harold H. Hyman, *To Try Men's Souls* (Berkeley: University of California Press, 1959), p. 188 (emphasis in original).

6. See James D. King and James W. Riddlesperger, Jr., "Senate Confirmation of Appointments to the Cabinet and Executive Office of the President," *Social Science Journal* 28 (1991): 189.

7. See Harris, *The Advice and Consent of the Senate*, pp. 79–98.

8. See Robert N. Roberts, *White House Ethics: The History of the Politics of Conflict of Interest Regulation* (Westport, Conn.: Greenwood Press, 1988), p. 26.

9. Clint Bolick, "Clinton's Quota Queens," *Wall Street Journal,* April 30, 1993, p. A12.

10. See, for example, remarks of Robert Novak, CNN, *The Capital Gang* (transcript no. 75), broadcast June 5, 1993: "He [Clinton] should never have nominated a radical like that." Compare Joe Klein, "Principle or Politics?" *Newsweek,* June 14, 1993, p. 29: "The dirty little secret of the Lani Guinier debacle is that she is, as she insists, firmly in the mainstream of the civil rights movement—but the movement has gone off the deep end."

11. See editorial, "Withdraw Guinier," *The New Republic,* June 14, 1993, p. 7; Stuart Taylor, "Who's Fooling Whom About Justice Nominee's Views?" *Legal Times,* May 31, 1993, p. 27.

12. See, for example, Stuart Taylor, "DOJ Nominee's 'Authentic' Black Views," *Legal Times,* May 17, 1993, p. 23.

13. See, for example, Abigail Thernstrom, "Guinier Miss," *The New Republic,* June 14, 1993, p. 16; George Will, "Sympathy for Guinier," *Newsweek,* June 14, 1993, p. 78.

14. For a depressing analysis of how so many misstatements about Guinier's record were reported uncritically by journal-

ists, see Laurel Leff, "From Legal Scholar to Quota Queen: What Happens When Politics Pulls the Press Into the Groves of Academe," *Columbia Journalism Review,* October 1993.

15. Some media observers got this point right. See, for example, editorial, "The Destruction of Lani Guinier," *Chicago Tribune,* June 6, 1993, p. 2: "Right or wrong, scholars ought not be punished for the sin of unconventional thinking—or else good scholars will never be allowed into public office."

16. Lani Guinier, "The Triumph of Tokenism: The Voting Rights Act and the Theory of Black Electoral Success," *Michigan Law Review* 89 (March 1991): 1077. See also Lani Guinier, "No Two Seats: The Elusive Quest for Political Equality," *Virginia Law Review* 77 (1991): 1413. These two articles, both long, both complex, and neither one much amenable to being chopped into sound bites, were the principal focus of the critics. Guinier has a much larger opus, but these articles were, at the time of her nomination, the most important.

17. Some of Guinier's more thoughtful critics conceded this point. See, for example, Thernstrom, "Guinier Miss." The usually perspicacious Thernstrom, however, does make an analytical error in her discussion of cumulative voting. The problem, she writes, is that Guinier would not leave the choice of whether to implement cumulative voting "to the voters themselves"; rather, Guinier "would have courts and Justice Department attorneys make such decisions for them." But why in the world would voters in any majority—whether white Republicans or black Democrats or whomever—voluntarily accept a scheme that would reduce their own clout? Guinier raises the notion of cumulative voting as a *remedy* for ineffective voting by minorities. One may of course argue over whether it matters that votes be "effective"—but if they should be, then here, as on so many other matters, the remedy will come about by the usual tools, legislation or litigation.

18. See Stephen L. Carter. *Reflections of an Affirmative Action Baby* (New York: Basic Books, 1991), chap. 2.

19.   See Taylor, "DOJ Nominee's 'Authentic' Black Views," and "Who's Fooling Whom About Justice Nominee's Views?"

20.   Guinier, "Triumph of Tokenism," p. 1108.

21.   Unfortunately, consistent polling data certainly bear out the notion that a majority of white Americans harbor racist attitudes. See, for example, "Poll Finds Whites Use Stereotypes," *New York Times,* January 10, 1991, p. B10, which discusses the depressing results of the 1990 General Social Survey of the University of Chicago's National Opinion Research Center.

22.   For a list of some Reagan sub-cabinet rejections, see Herman Schwartz, *Packing the Courts: The Conservative Campaign to Rewrite the Constitution* (New York: Scribner's, 1988), p.52. Reagan's nominees, interestingly, were not attacked only for conservatism and they were not attacked only by the left. Some were actually defeated or forced to withdraw because of suspicion that they were too liberal, and even some of those who made it through faced the skepticism of right-wing activists: Justice Sandra Day O'Connor was thought to be "soft on abortion," Secretary of State Alexander Haig to be "soft on Moscow," Attorney General William French Smith to be "soft on affirmative action." See Laurence I. Barrett, *Gambling With History* (Garden City, N.Y.: Doubleday, 1983), p.60. As none of the three is exactly a hero to the American left, it is plain that confirmation politics depend a good deal on where one stands.

23.   Michael Pertschuk and Wendy Schaetzel, *The People Rising: The Campaign Against the Bork Nomination* (New York: Thunder's Mouth Press, 1989).

24.   741 F.2d 444 (D.C. Cir. 1984).

25.   Quoted in Bronner, *Battle for Justice,* p. 179.

26.   See Pertschuk and Schaetzel, *The People Rising,* p. 138, and Bronner, *Battle for Justice,* pp. 178–79.

27.   Bork did not help matters with his offhand suggestion during his confirmation hearings that the women were evidently "glad to have the choice," which led to swift, sensible action by the Coalition: a telegram from one of the women

explaining the horror of the choice. See Bronner, *Battle for Justice*, pp. 236–37; Pertschuk and Schaetzel, *The People Rising*, pp. 224–25. In his own book on the hearings, Bork says what I suspect he meant with the unfortunate and perhaps insensitive choice of the word "glad": "[S]ome of the women apparently wanted to keep these jobs, and the company informed them that sterilization was an option. Five of them chose that option." Bork, *Tempting of America*, p. 327. The distortion of his use of the word "glad" was not, perhaps, as severe as the distortion of Lani Guinier's use of the word "authentic," but in the context, it is plain that he did not mean what his detractors said.

28.   *American Cyanamid*, 741 F.2d at 445.

29.   Quoted in Bronner, *Battle for Justice*, p. 39.

30.   Quoted in Pertschuk and Schaetzel, *The People Rising*, p. 250.

31.   Quoted in ibid., p. 224.

32.   Robert Bork, "Civil Rights: A Challenge," *The New Republic*, August 31, 1963, p. 22. The first year of the Clinton Administration brought another interesting twist on the Bork battle. In 1987, many Bork supporters found the use of the 1963 *New Republic* article particularly irksome. They described the piece, published almost a quarter century earlier, as the work of a different Bork in a different era. This raises the question of whether there should be a statute of limitations on the paper record, a time period beyond which past opinions no longer matter. In 1993, when President Clinton nominated Morton Halperin to a high position in the Department of Defense, conservatives attacked him in terms suggesting that he was, in effect, soft on the Cold War, because of what they saw as his activism against the terms and instruments of American foreign policy (especially the use of force) from the seventies to the early nineties. In the end, Halperin was forced to withdraw.

In Halperin's case, as in Bork's, questions were raised about using older views as the basis for current criticism. True, the passage of time was much less, and Halperin did not suggest that his views had changed. On the other hand, the Cold War was over. Halperin would never have been nominated had the nation still worried about the Soviet Union; Bork would not have been nominated were the country still deeply divided over basic civil rights. This judgment has nothing to do with the personal decency of either man, a characteristic to which legions of friends attest; it is related instead to a simple measurement of the paper record.

33. Bronner, *Battle for Justice,* p. 231.
34. Quoted in Garry Wills, *Under God: Religion and American Politics* (New York: Simon & Schuster, 1990), p. 262.
35. Speech of Senator Kennedy, Cong. Rec. 113 (1987): 18519, quoted in Bronner, *Battle for Justice,* p. 98.
36. Henry J. Abraham, *Justices and Presidents: A Political History of Appointments to the Supreme Court,* 3d ed. (New York: Oxford University Press, 1992), p. 357.
37. "Inside Politics" (CNN), transcript of June 2, 1993 (No. 345–2).
38. Pertschuk and Schaetzel, *The People Rising,* p. 102.
39. A powerful account of the nation's love-hate affair with the Constitution is Michael Kammen, *A Machine That Would Go of Itself: The Constitution in American Culture* (New York: Knopf, 1986).

CHAPTER 3: OF LITMUS TESTERS AND STEALTH CANDIDATES

1. Quoted in Penny Bender, "Judiciary Panel Unanimously Endorses Ginsburg for High Court," *Houston Post,* July 30, 1993, p. A8. For a similar expression of frustration, with reference to earlier confirmation hearings, see David A. Strauss and Cass R. Sunstein, "The Senate, the Constitution, and the Confirmation Process," *Yale Law Journal* 101 (1992): 1491, 1492.
2. Federal News Service, *Hearings of the Senate Judiciary Com-*

mittee on the Nomination of Judge Ruth Bader Ginsburg to the United States Supreme Court (July 1993), p. 194. (Available on Nexis).

3. See Alexander Bickel, *The Least Dangerous Branch: The Supreme Court at the Bar of Politics* (New Haven: Yale University Press, 1962), p. 1: "The least dangerous branch of the American government is the most extraordinarily powerful court of law the world has ever known."

4. 112 S. Ct. 2791 (1992).

5. Christopher Cox, "The Sad Career of the Reagan Justices," *Wall Street Journal,* July 1, 1992, p. A14.

6. 410 U.S. 113 (1973).

7. See, for example, Eleanor Clift, "Interview: 'Change Is Very Painful,'" *Newsweek,* July 20, 1992, pp. 28, 29. See also "Bush v. Clinton: The Candidates on Legal Issues," *American Bar Association Journal,* October 1992, p. 37.

8. Abortion rights supporters are not alone in these explicit campaign promises. For example, Jack Kemp told the annual meeting of Iowans for Life in 1987 that he would if elected appoint "pro-life, pro-family conservative judges to all the courts in America." Quoted in Patrick B. McGuigan and Dawn M. Weyrich, *Ninth Justice: The Fight for Bork* (Washington, D.C.: Free Congress Research and Education Foundation, 1990), p. 95.

9. Paul Gewirtz, "A Litmus Test for Judges? Legal Views Do Matter," *New York Times,* April 28, 1993.

10. I do not mean to suggest that *all* Americans or even *most* Americans believe in asking these seemingly inevitable questions. One 1990 survey indicated that 43 percent of respondents thought nominee David Souter should disclose his position on abortion rights and 49 percent thought he should not; another found that 65 percent thought he should disclose and 31 percent thought he should not. (Both are cited in Dennis Steven Rutkus, *Questioning Supreme Court Nominees: A Recurring Issue* [Washington, D.C.: Congressional Research Service, Sept. 9, 1990], p. 36*n*147.)

Whatever the true figures, the Senate understandably listens to those who are politically active, and who are thus the most likely to want the question answered.

11. Harlan transcript, p. 174.

12. 410 U.S. 113 (1973). For another example of conservative support for asking questions that will help predict future votes, see Grover Rees III, "Questions for Supreme Court Nominees at Confirmation Hearings: Excluding the Constitution," *Georgia Law Review* 17 (1983).

13. See Ruth Marcus, "Thomas Affirms Right to Privacy: Nominee Deflects Abortion Question," *Washington Post,* September 11, 1991, p. A1.

14. See Al Kamen, "No 'Fixed View' on Abortion: Confirmation Hearings Open as Court Splits 4–4 in Illinois Case," *Washington Post,* December 15, 1987, p. A1.

15. Roger J. Miner, "Advice and Consent in Theory and Practice," *American University Law Review* 41 (1992): 1075, 1083–84. The article is sharply critical of the process for selecting judicial nominees, especially in the Bush Administration. Because Judge Miner was appointed by President Reagan and was mentioned as a finalist for Supreme Court vacancies during the Reagan and Bush presidencies, the mainstream media took notice of his article. See, for example, David Margolick, "Biting the hand that fed him, a federal judge criticizes the judicial selection process," *New York Times,* August 21, 1992, p. A21.

16. Laurence H. Tribe, *God Save This Honorable Court: How the Choice of Supreme Court Justices Shapes Our History* (New York: Random House, 1985), p. 137.

17. 384 U.S. 436 (1966).

18. *Nomination of Thurgood Marshall to Be Associate Justice of the Supreme Court of the United States: Hearings Before the Senate Committee on the Judiciary,* 90th Congress, 1st Sess. (1967), pp. 12–13.

19. 113 *Congressional Record* 24, 639–40 (1967).

20. Remarks of Senator Tower, 113 *Congressional Record* 24,646 (1987).

21. See Rutkus, *Questioning Supreme Court Nominees.*

22. Remarks of Senator Kennedy, 113 *Congressional Record* 24,647 (1967).

23. Remarks of Senator Thurmond, 113 *Congressional Record* 24,648 (1967).

24. 347 U.S. 483 (1954).

25. *Nomination of William Joseph Brennan To Be Associate Justice of the Supreme Court of the United States: Hearings Before the Senate Committee on the Judiciary,* 85th Congress, 1st Sess. (1957), pp. 18, 38.

26. *Nomination of Potter Stewart To Be Associate Justice of the Supreme Court of the United States: Hearings Before the Senate Committee on the Judiciary,* 86th Congress, 1st Sess. (1959), p. 62. In the transcript, this exchange follows 26 pages of wrangling over McClellan's inability to get an answer to his question. Stewart, to his credit, although sticking to his refusal to answer, insisted on a very firm last word: "I would not like you to vote for me . . . because I am for overturning that decision, because I am not" (p. 63).

27. Tribe, *God Save This Honorable Court,* p. 89.

28. 60 U.S. 393 (1856).

29. See Peter G. Fish, "Spite Nominations to the United States Supreme Court: Herbert C. Hoover, Owen J. Roberts, and the Politics of Presidential Vengeance in Retrospect," *Kentucky Law Journal* 77 (1989): 545.

30. Quoted in Paul Simon, *Advice & Consent: Clarence Thomas, Robert Bork and the Intriguing History of the Supreme Court's Nomination Battles* (Washington, D.C.: National Press Books, 1992), p. 33.

31. For a provocative suggestion that selecting judges according to political party is sometimes unconstitutional, see Michael E. Solimine, "Constitutional Restrictions on the Partisan Appointment of Federal and State Judges," *University of Cincinnati Law Review* 61 (1993): 955.

32. See Henry J. Abraham, *Justices and Presidents: A Political History of Appointments to the Supreme Court,* 3d ed. (New York: Oxford University Press, 1992), p. 68.

33. Party compatibility is also important in other presidential appointments, although some studies have found that Democrats are more likely to appoint strong Republicans to their administrations than Republicans are likely to appoint strong Democrats. See data discussed in Christopher J. Deering, "Damned If You Do and Damned If You Don't: The Senate's Role in the Apointments Process," in G. Calvin Mackenzie, ed., *The In-and-Outers: Presidential Appointees and Transient Government in Washington* (Baltimore: Johns Hopkins University Press, 1987), p. 100.

34. Larry C. Berkson and Susan B. Carbon, *The United States Circuit Judge Nominating Commission: Its Members, Procedures, and Candidates* (Chicago: American Judicature Society, 1980).

35. For a detailed, but highly partisan, review of the Reagan judicial appointments, see Herman Schwartz, *Packing the Courts: The Conservative Campaign to Rewrite the Constitution* (New York: Scribner's, 1988). The political scientist Sheldon Goldman said of the Reagan judicial appointments: "Not since the Roosevelt Administration have we seen such a systematic attempt to place on the bench people whose judicial and political views are compatible with those of the Administration." Quoted in Robert E. Norton, "Reagan's Imprint on the Courts," *Fortune,* November 24, 1986, p. 121.

36. Roger J. Miner, "Advice and Consent in Theory and Practice," pp. 1080–81.

37. See Bronner, *Battle for Justice,* p. 40.

38. William H. Rehnquist, *The Supreme Court* (New York: William Morrow, 1987), pp. 235–36.

39. See, for example, Tribe, *God Save This Honorable Court.*

40. Quoted in Richard Kluger, *Simple Justice* (New York: Knopf, 1975), p. 142.

41. Quoted in Abraham, *Justices and Presidents,* p. 202.

42. Kluger, *Simple Justice,* p. 144.

43. See Jeffrey A. Segal and Harold J. Spaeth, *The Supreme Court and the Attitudinal Model* (Cambridge, England: Cambridge University Press, 1993), pp. 134–35.

44. For general discussions of the Fortas confirmation battle, see Abraham, *Justices and Presidents,* pp. 285–92; John Massaro, *Supremely Political: The Role of Ideology and Presidential Management in Unsuccessful Supreme Court Nominations* (Albany: State University of New York Press, 1990), pp. 12–77; and Robert Shogan, *A Question of Judgment: The Fortas Case and the Struggle for the Supreme Court* (Indianapolis: Bobbs-Merrill, 1972).

45. *Marshall Hearings,* p. 176.

46. Remarks of Senator Eastland. *Congressional Record* 13 (1967): 24, 642–43.

47. *Marshall Hearings,* pp. 163, 164.

48. See Abraham, *Justices and Presidents,* p. 112.

49. 347 U.S. 483 (1954).

50. For a thoughtful survey of the history, much of which relies on original documents, see William G. Ross, "Participation by the Public in the Federal Judicial Selection Process," *Vanderbilt Law Review* 43 (1990): 1. For a contemporaneous observer's view of the changes during the 1970s, see L. A. Powe, Jr., "The Senate and the Court: Questioning a Nominee," *Texas Law Review* 54 (1976).

51. The shift was so distinct that with Fortas, Haynsworth, and Carswell, the Senate, for the first and only time in history, rejected three high court nominees in three years. See Donald G. Tannenbaum, "Explaining Controversial Nominations: The Fortas Case Revisited," *Presidential Studies Quarterly,* p. 573.

52. See Charles Cameron, Albert D. Cover, and Jeffrey A. Segal, "Senate Voting on Supreme Court Nominees: A Neoinstitutional Model," *American Political Science Review* 84 (1990): 525.

53. 347 U.S. 483 (1954).

54. Senator Kennedy stated that Rehnquist was "too extreme to be Chief Justice." Quoted in Stuart Taylor, "Senate Opens Rehnquist Hearings, and the Lines of Battle Are Drawn," *New York Times,* July 29, 1986, p. 1.

55. Rutkus, *Questioning Supreme Court Nominees,* pp. 11–19.

56. Albert P. Melone, "The Senate's Confirmation Role in Supreme Court Nominations and the Politics of Ideology

Versus Impartiality," *Judicature* 75 (August–September 1991): 68, 79.

57. Jeffrey A. Segal and Albert D. Cover, "Ideological Values and the Votes of Supreme Court Justices," *American Political Science Review* 83 (1989): 557. See also Cameron et al., "Senate Voting on Supreme Court Nominees," p. 525.

58. Rehnquist, *The Supreme Court,* p. 235.

59. Melone, "Senate's Confirmation Role," p. 79 and nn. 96, 97.

60. During the Court's 1992–93 term, Justice Thomas voted with Justice Scalia 86 percent of the time—more frequently than any other two members of the Court. "The Supreme Court, 1992 Term—Leading Cases—The Statistics," *Harvard Law Review* 107 (1993): 372, 373.

61. For example, the constitutional scholar Bruce Ackerman, certainly no fan of the Bork nomination, readily concedes that Bork came to the Supreme Court with one of the strongest resumes of any nominee in this century. Bruce Ackerman, "Transformative Appointments," *Harvard Law Review* 101 (1988): 1164. The intriguing if ultimately unpersuasive thesis of Ackerman's rewarding essay is that nominations with the potential for markedly changing the Court's direction—he saw Bork in these terms—raise special problems of review that ordinary nominations do not.

62. Miner, "Advice and Consent in Theory and Practice," p. 1084.

63. See, for example, "Remarks by Senator Orrin G. Hatch (R–Utah) During Floor Debate Regarding Confirmation of Nomination of Clarence Thomas to the Supreme Court," *Federal News Service,* October 3, 1991.

64. Not all movement conservatives were happy with Thomas's performance. One remarked after the *Roe* discussion, "By the second day, Clarence Thomas had begun to sound too much like David Souter to be Clarence Thomas." Quoted in Timothy M. Phelps and Helen Winternitz, *Capitol Games: Clarence Thomas, Anita Hill, and the Story of a Supreme Court Nomination* (New York: Hyperion, 1992), p. 194.

CHAPTER 4: OF JUDICIAL PHILOSOPHY AND
DEMOCRATIC CHECKERY

1. Harry H. Wellington, *Interpreting the Constitution: The Supreme Court and the Process of Adjudication* (New Haven: Yale University Press, 1990), p. 153.

2. Laurence Tribe, *God Save This Honorable Court* (New York: Random House, 1985) (emphasis in original).

3. William H. Rehnquist, *The Supreme Court* (New York: William Morrow, 1987), p. 235.

4. Ibid.

5. Mark Tushnet, *Red, White, and Blue: A Critical Analysis of Constitutional Law* (Cambridge, Mass.: Harvard University Press, 1988), p. 201.

6. Rehnquist, *The Supreme Court,* p. 236.

7. For commentary on this phenomenon, see, for example, John Massaro, *Supremely Political: The Role of Ideology and Presidential Management in Unsuccessful Supreme Court Nominations* (Albany: State University of New York Press, 1990), pp. 8–24.

8. See the data discussed in Roger Rosenblatt, *Life Itself* (New York: Random House, 1992), and Ronald Dworkin, *Life's Dominion: An Argument About Abortion, Euthanasia, and Individual Freedom* (New York: Knopf, 1993). Although I do not agree with all of Dworkin's interpretation of the data, I am quite sure that he is correct to insist that majority opinion must not guide constitutional analysis. For a discussion of more recent (1992) data, see E. J. Dionne, Jr., "Abortion Rights Supporters Claim Election Gains: Exit Polls Indicate That a Majority of Voters Favor Access, but with Some Restrictions," *Washington Post,* November 9, 1992, p. A9.

9. I have in mind particularly *Miranda v. Arizona,* 384 U.S. 436 (1966), which requires that criminal suspects be informed of their constitutional rights prior to interrogation, and *Mapp v. Ohio,* 367 U.S. 643 (1961), which enunciated the general use of the "exclusionary rule." Although there is little evidence that either decision has interfered significantly with law

enforcement, politicians run against them routinely.

10. The unpopular flag-burning decision is *Texas v. Johnson,* 491 U.S. 397 (1989).

11. The Supreme Court decisions known collectively as the "school prayer cases" include: *Engel v. Vitale,* 370 U.S. 421 (1962) (no state-drafted prayer in public schools); *Abington School District v. Schempp,* 374 U.S. 203 (1963) (no devotional Bible readings in public schools); *Stone v. Graham,* 449 U.S. 39 (1980) (may not post Ten Commandments in classroom without clear secular purpose); *Wallace v. Jaffree,* 472 U.S. 38 (1985) (no moment of silence in public schools if used as subterfuge for prayer); and *Lee v. Weisman,* 112 S. Ct. 2649 (1992) (no nondenominational prayer at graduation).

12. See Stephen L. Carter, *The Culture of Disbelief: How American Law and Politics Trivialize Religious Devotion* (New York: Basic Books, 1993), chaps. 6 and 10.

13. The 1983 survey is a Gallup poll, reported in *The Gallup Report,* no. 217 (October 1983), pp. 17–19. The 1992 survey is a *USA Today*/CNN/Gallup survey, reported in Richard Benedetto, "Economy Shakes American Dream," *USA Today,* January 16, 1992, p. 5A.

14. The proposition that constitutional interpretation should in some sense reflect the moral sense of the community (sometimes called "conventionalism," although the term is put to other uses as well) has its many forms and its many defenders. See, for example, Ronald Dworkin, *Law's Empire* (Cambridge, Mass.: Harvard/Belknap, 1986); Laurence H. Tribe, *Constitutional Choices* (1985); Owen Fiss, "The Supreme Court, 1978 Term—Foreword: The Forms of Justice," *Harvard Law Review* 93 (1979): 1; Thomas Grey, "Do We Have an Unwritten Constitution?" *Stanford Law Review* 27 (703): 70. Indeed, liberal scholars have flocked to it since the Supreme Court in *Roe v. Wade,* 410 U.S. 113 (1973), created the constitutional right to abortion but made no serious effort to ground its opinion in the text or history of the Constitution. For a devastating critique of the basic proposition

that the community's moral sense should be a guide—a cri-
tique that has, to my mind, never been refuted—see Paul
Brest, "The Fundamental Rights Controversy: The Essential
Contradictions of Normative Constitutional Scholarship,"
Yale Law Journal 90 (1981): 1063. For a more measured, but
equally effective, assault, see John Hart Ely, *Democracy and
Distrust* (Cambridge, Mass.: Harvard University Press, 1908).

15. For my efforts to preserve the distinction between political
powers simpliciter and constitutional law, see, for example,
Stephen L. Carter, "Constitutional Improprieties: Reflections
on *Mistretta, Morrison,* and Administrative Government,"
University of Chicago Law Review 57 (1990): 357; and
Stephen L. Carter, "Constitutional Adjudication and the Indeterminate Text: A Preliminary Defence of an Imperfect Muddle," *Yale Law Journal* 94 (1985): 821.

16. Ginsburg's criticism of the Court's decision in *Roe v. Wade*
stretches back to the mid-eighties. See Ruth Bader Ginsburg,
"Some Thoughts on Autonomy and Equality in Relation to
Roe v. Wade," *North Carolina Law Review* 63 (1985): 375;
Ruth Bader Ginsburg, "A Moderate View on *Roe*," *Constitu-
tion*, Spring–Summer 1992, p. 17; and Ruth Bader Ginsburg,
"Madison Lecture: Speaking in a Judicial Voice," *New York
University Law Review* 67 (1992): 1185.

President Clinton, obviously aware of the possibility that
some would find Ginsburg's views on *Roe v. Wade* troubling, insisted when he announced her nomination that she
was "clearly pro-choice." He added, "She disagrees with the
rationale of the decision. I'm not sure I agree with her, as a
matter of fact, on that issue, but I thought it was a very
provocative and impressive argument." Quoted in "Excerpts
from Clinton's News Conference at the White House," *New
York Times,* June 16, 1993, p. 20.

17. The broader language of the old canon was deleted because
the drafting committee concluded that it constituted "an
overly broad restriction on speech." *Model Code of Judicial
Conduct as Submitted for Consideration,* Appendix C, p. 72.

18. 347 U.S. 483 (1954).

19. Quoted in Taylor Branch, *Parting the Waters: America in the King Years 1954–63* (New York: Simon and Schuster, 1988), p. 380.

20. See, for example, *Orleans Parish v. Bush,* 188 F. Supp. 916 (E.D. La. 1960), affirmed, 364 U.S. 500 (1960).

21. Quoted in J. W. Peltason, *Fifty-Eight Lonely Men: Southern Federal Judges and School Desegregation* (New York: Harcourt, Brace & World, 1961), p. 236. The Peltason book, with its catalog of official efforts to sway the courts, is a powerful reminder of why liberals traditionally resisted the idea of a democratic check on the judiciary.

22. Quoted in ibid., p. 238.

23. For a particularly sparkling discussion, see Gordon S. Wood, *The Radicalism of the American Revolution* (New York: Knopf, 1992), pp. 322–25.

24. The historical accounts in this section are drawn primarily from the following sources: Simeon Baldwin, *The American Judiciary* (New York: Century, 1905); Susan B. Carbon and Larry C. Berkson, *Judicial Retention Elections in the United States* (Chicago: American Judicature Society, 1980); and Evan Haynes, *The Selection and Tenure of Judges* (National Conference of Judicial Councils, 1944). The sources are not separately noted.

25. See, for example, *Martin v. Hunter's Lessee,* 14 U.S. (1 Wheat.) 304 (1816) (affirming national Supreme Court's sovereignty over state courts); *McCulloch v. Maryland,* 17 U.S. (4 Wheat.) 316 (1819) (restricting state power to tax federal entities); *Green v. Biddle,* 21 U.S. (8 Wheat.) 1 (1823) (striking down a state land initiative as violating the rights of property owners).

26. Haynes, *Selection and Tenure of Judges,* p. 90. Many of the examples in this section are taken from Haynes's remarkable book.

27. 21 U.S. (8 Wheat.) 1 (1821).

28. The accounts in text of the Kentucky case are drawn from Baldwin, *The American Judiciary,* pp. 113–16; Haynes, *Selection and Tenure of Judges,* pp. 92–93; and Bethurum,

"The Old and New Court Controversy," *Kentucky Law Journal* 6 (1918): 173.

29. Baldwin, *The American Judiciary*, p. 115.

30. The decisions known together as the *Cherokee Cases* are *Cherokee Nation v. Georgia*, 30 U.S. (5 Pet.) 1 (1831) and *Worcester v. State of Georgia*, 31 U.S. (6 Pet.) 515 (1832).

31. The story is nicely told in Charles Warren, *The Supreme Court in United States History*, rev. ed., 2 vols., vol. 1 (Boston: Little, Brown, 1926), pp. 729–79.

32. *National Intelligencer*, March 5, 1802, quoted in Warren, *The Supreme Court in United States History*, vol. 1, p. 209 (emphasis added).

33. 2 U.S. (2 Dall.) 419 (1793).

34. Haynes, *Selection and Tenure of Judges*, p. 91.

35. 60 U.S. (19 How) 393 (1856).

36. 74 U.S. (7 Wall.) 506 (1868).

37. See, for example, Akhil Amar, "A Neo-Federalist View of Article III: Separating the Two Tiers of Federal Jurisdiction," *Boston University Law Review* 65 (1985): 205; Lawrence Sager, "The Supreme Court, 1980 Term—Foreword: Constitutional Limitations on Congress' Authority to Regulate the Jurisdiction of the Federal Courts," *Harvard Law Review* 95 (1981): 17.

38. 71 U.S. (4 Wall.) 475 (1867).

39. Id., pp. 500–501.

40. 5 U.S. (1 Cranch) 137 (1803).

41. See the discussion in Warren, *The Supreme Court in United States History*, vol. 1, pp. 222–30.

42. In different ways, many theorists reach this point. They tend to disagree on the mechanics of the exercise. To take three examples, Ronald Dworkin would argue for enforcement of the Founders' broad concept rather than their narrow conception. See Dworkin, *Law's Empire*. Robert Bork would prefer that the courts not make value choices beyond those fairly implied in those concrete expectations (which is not the same as enforcing only the expectations themselves). See Bork, *The Tempting of America: The Political Seduction*

of the Law (New York: Free Press, 1990). Bruce Ackerman would insist that the judges search for the relevant principles in a richer understanding of the contemporaneous political battles in which every movement for constitutional change is embedded. See Ackerman, *We, the People: Foundations* (Cambridge, Mass.: Harvard University Press, 1991). But despite these different interpretive visions, all three theorists would agree with the Supreme Court's decision to outlaw racial segregation in public schools as a violation of the Fourteenth Amendment's equal protection clause, even though most of those who wrote and ratified it expected school segregation to continue. Dworkin would say that the Court properly enforced the Founders' broad principle of equality rather than their concrete expectation that one could achieve equality in a nation with segregated schools. Bork would argue that in order to resolve an internal tension in the Founders' views, the Justices could reasonably choose to enforce one aspect of their understanding, even at the expense of another. And Ackerman would insist that only an end to segregation could harmonize the constitutional vision of the Founders with the rather different constitutional vision of the New Deal generation.

43. U.S. (4 Wall.) 2 (1866).

44. 410 U.S. 113 (1973).

45. What I am describing is entirely independent of which version of constitutional interpretation one finds attractive. It is also independent of whether one believes in the possibility of a form of interpretation that one might call relatively objective. Rather, the effort to recognize and overcome one's own biases is itself an important disciplining tool. For discussions of this point, in the particular context of constitutional theory, see Ronald Dworkin, *Law's Empire*; Owen Fiss, "Objectivity and Interpretation," *Stanford Law Review* 34 (1982): 739; Robert Bennett, "Objectivity in Constitutional Law," *University of Pennsylvania Law Review* 132 (1984): 445.

46. See the discussion in Evan Haynes, *The Selection and*

Tenure of Judges (National Conference of Judicial Councils, 1944), pp. 55–61.

47.   347 U.S. 483 (1954).

48.   410 U.S. 113 (1973).

49.   See *Engel v. Vitale,* 370 U.S. 421 (1962); *Abington School District v. Schempp,* 374 U.S. 203 (1963); *Stone v. Graham,* 449 U.S. 39 (1980); *Wallace v. Jaffree,* 472 U.S. 38 (1985); and *Lee v. Weisman,* 112 S. Ct. 2649 (1992).

CHAPTER 5: OF *BROWN* . . . AND BEING
MORALLY OFF LIMITS

1.   347 U.S. 483 (1954).

2.   Compare Randall Kennedy, "The Political Court," *The American Prospect* , Summer, 1993, p. 96.

3.   William H. Riker, *The Theory of Political Coalitions* (New Haven: Yale University Press, 1962), pp. 174–87.

4.   For a thoughtful discussion of the strategy of the portrayal, and of these words, see Ethan Bronner, *Battle for Justice: How the Bork Nomination Shook America* (New York: Norton, 1989).

5.   Edwin Meese, while serving as attorney general, argued that the Supreme Court that decided *Brown* rediscovered the ideal of color blindness that the authors of the Fourteenth Amendment meant to lay down. See Edwin Meese, "The Battle for the Constitution," *Policy Review* (Winter 1986): 32. Bork, in his book, notes the difficulty with this position: "The inescapable fact is that those who ratified the amendment did not think it outlawed segregated education or segregation in any aspect of life." Bork, *The Tempting of America: The Political Seduction of the Law* (New York: Free Press, 1990), pp. 75–76. This is common ground. See, for example, William Nelson, *The Fourteenth Amendment: From Political Principle to Judicial Doctrine* (1988), pp. 96–100, and the sources there cited. See also Alexander Bickel's seminal article, "The Original Understanding and the Segre-

gation Decision," *Harvard Law Review* 69 (1955). But when the school cases arose, says Bork, the Court was not required to follow that plain original view: "The court's realistic choice . . . was either to abandon the quest for equality by allowing segregation or to forbid segregation in order to achieve equality. Either choice would violate one aspect of the original understanding." Bork, *The Tempting of America*, p. 82.

The trouble with Meese's solution is that it is ahistorical. The trouble with Bork's is that it violates a rule he lays down elsewhere in the book: "The role of a judge committed to the philosophy of original understanding is not to '*choose* a level of abstraction.'" Ibid., p. 149. For an originalist who accepts Bork's constraints, the meaning of the equal protection clause as applied to segregated schools is not in the least unclear. An originalist who, as Bork does, denies the freedom of the interpreter to choose among competing levels of abstraction should find the *Brown* result legally indefensible. (See, for example, Robert Nagel, *Constitutional Cultures* [1989], pp. 4–5.) The expectation among those who drafted and ratified the equal protection clause that its guarantees did not apply to schools could hardly be clearer, and the changing role of education, and of race, does nothing to change that original expectation.

Yet a more sensitive originalism than Meese's or Bork's would easily find *Brown* to be rightly decided. The proper focus of the originalist judge should be on the broad but often clear values that the Framers sought to enact, rather than on their concrete expectations. The question then is not *What did the drafters expect to happen?* but *What were the drafters trying to accomplish?* (This is analogous to the method proposed by the legal scholar Ronald Dworkin in his *Taking Rights Seriously* [Cambridge, Mass.: Harvard University Press, 1977] and *Law's Empire* [Cambridge, Mass.: Harvard/Belknap, 1986] and elsewhere.) This approach readily accommodates *Brown* because, although the value choice of the Framers—the elimination of racial oppression—is still the same, the society in which it is applied is a different one from the society that the Framers of the Fourteenth Amendment understood. This approach is consistent with the rules for reading statutes, for it is a commonplace of statutory interpretation that every part of a statute shall be read in a way that gives effect to the legislature's purpose. Bork's approach, I fear, would lead to a Constitution that would slowly lose its significance, because the concrete expectations of the authors would so far diverge from the world in which their document must be applied. As a sometime originalist, I do not believe that this was the original plan. See my discussion in Stephen L. Carter, "Bork Redux, or, How the Tempting of America Led the People to Rise and Battle for Justice," *Texas Law Review* 69 (1991): 759.

6. Riker, *Theory of Political Coalitions,* pp. 178–80.

7. See Henry J. Abraham, *Justices and Presidents: A Political History of Appointments to the Supreme Court,* 3d ed. (New York: Oxford University Press, 1992), pp. 178–80. When Felix Frankfurter was appointed to succeed Brandeis, McReynolds refused to attend the official robing ceremony, reportedly exclaiming, "My God, another Jew on the Court!" Ibid., p. 179.

8. Riker, *Theory of Political Coalitions,* p. 181.

9. Bork, *The Tempting of America,* p. 337.

10. Ibid., p. 343.

11. Michael Pertschuk and Wendy Schaetzel, *The People Rising: The Campaign Against the Bork Nomination* (New York: Thunder's Mouth Press, 1989), p. 254.

12. Ibid., p. 15.

13. Of course, as anti-Bork activists have generally conceded, the votes of Justice Kennedy have been about as "bad" as the votes of Robert Bork were expected to be. See, for example, Pertschuk and Schaetzel, *The People Rising,* p. 327. (Kennedy, along with Justices Souter and O'Connor, has held the middle ground on abortion, but to pro-choice activists, as well as pro-life activists, the middle is the wrong place to be.)

14. Pertschuk and Schaetzel, *The People Rising,* pp. 102, 124–25.

15. The best book of the many books on the hearings is Bronner, *Battle for Justice,* which struggles mightily to be fair to both sides. For more partisan, but still compelling, assessments of the many misstatements in the campaign against Bork, see Bork, *The Tempting of America,* pp. 323–36; and Patrick B. McGuigan and Dawn M. Weyrich, *Ninth Justice: The Fight for Bork* (Washington, D.C.: Free Congress Research and Education Foundation, 1990), pp. 73–103.

16. Editorial, "The Bork Nomination," *Washington Post,* October 5, 1987, p. A14.

17. Pertschuk and Schaetzel, *The People Rising.*

18. Quoted in Bronner, *Battle for Justice,* p. 178.

19. Although the tide of public opposition finally washed over the Bork nomination, the early forecasts were for fairly placid weather. According to an ABC News–*Washington Post* poll in August of 1987, well after the nomination was announced, most of the public had never heard or read of Robert Bork. See "Voters View Bork Nomination as Political Battle, Pollster Says," *Washington Post,* August 26, 1987, p. A4. On the eve of the hearings, most of the public still had little interest: at that time, 11 percent of the public favored confirmation, 12 percent opposed it, and an astonishing (in retrospect) 77 percent had no view. "Bork Sinks in Poll," *Detroit Free Press,* September 24, 1987. On the eve of the vote, however, all of that had changed, as 57 percent opposed confirmation, 29 percent favored it, and only 14 percent were undecided. "Poll Finds 57 Percent Want Senate To Reject Bork," *Newsday,* September 28, 1987.

20. Said Marshall of Bork: "I thought he got a bum deal." Quoted in Stuart Taylor, Jr., "Glimpses of Thurgood Marshall," *The American Lawyer,* March 1993, p. 36. (Lest one worry about journalistic bias, Taylor was an opponent of the Bork nomination.)

21. See, for example, "Mr. Marshall's Nomination," *Washington Evening Star,* June 15, 1987 (editorial), reprinted in *Congressional Record* 113 (1967): 16,138; James J. Kil-

patrick, "Marshall's Appointment Upsets Court Balance," *Washington Evening Star,* June 18, 1967, reprinted in *Nomination of Thurgood Marshall to be Associate Justice of the Supreme Court of the United States: Hearings Before the Senate Committee on the Judiciary,* 90th Congress, 1st. Sess. (1967), p. 45 [hereafter cited as *Marshall Hearings*]; and White, "Marshall to the Court—Can Moderation Survive?" *Washington Post,* June 19, 1967, reprinted in *Marshall Hearings,* p. 48.

22. 410 U.S. 113 (1973).

23. 388 U.S. 307 (1967).

24. See, for example, "Dr. King's Conviction," *Washington Evening Star,* June 15, 1987 (editorial), reprinted in *Congressional Record* 113 (1967): 16,138. See also *Congressional Record* 113 (1967): 24,643 (remarks of Senator Eastland).

25. Senate Committee on the Judiciary, *Report on the Nomination of Robert Bork To Be an Associate Justice of the United States Supreme Court,* 100th Congress, 1st Sess. (1987), pp. 11–13, 33.

26. Remarks of Senator Ervin, *Congressional Record* 113 (1967): 24,590.

27. Quoted in Pertschuk and Schaetzel, *The People Rising,* p. 22.

28. Remarks of Senator Ervin, *Congressional Record* 113 (1967): 24,589. See also remarks of Senator Holland, *Congressional Record* 113 (1967): 24,635. Marshall's lifelong civil rights activism moved one senator to ask him during the hearings whether he was "prejudiced against white people in the South" and whether, if confirmed, he would give white Southerners "fair and square treatment," *Marshall Hearings,* p. 161 (Senator Eastland). For similar remarks, see *Congressional Record* 113 (1967): 15,968 (remarks of Senator Rarick) (accusing Marshall of "contempt, open ridicule, and hatred of white southerners").

29. Philip Kurland, quoted in Pertschuk and Schaetzel, *The People Rising,* p. 24.

30. For further discussion, see Stephen L. Carter, "The Confirmation Mess, Revisited," *Northwestern University Law Review* 84

(1990): 962.

31. Judith N. Shklar, *Ordinary Vices* (Cambridge, Mass.: Harvard/Belknap, 1984), pp. 65–66.

32. 410 U.S. 113 (1973).

33. Some black supporters of Thomas have since stated that they were wrong, because his votes on the Court, they say, have been much worse than they expected. See Trevor W. Coleman, "House Negro: Clarence Thomas's ex-supporters repent," *Emerge* (November 1993): 38. (I should add that although the Coleman article is nicely researched, fairly presented, and quite powerfully written, its title and the accompanying cover art—a drawing of Thomas with a handkerchief wrapped around his head—are indescribably offensive.) For example, Thomas was one of two members of the Court to argue that the Eighth Amendment's prohibition on cruel and unusual punishment is not violated when a prisoner is severely beaten by his guards, an opinion that the Founders would have found incredible. He joined a majority in *Presley v. Etowah County Commission,* 112 S. Ct. 820 (1992), in holding that a county does not violate the Voting Rights Act when it strips from the only black member of its governing commission virtually all his independent authority, a reading of the statute that might charitably be described as implausible. (The plaintiff, Presley, had supported Thomas during his confirmation struggle.)

Some observers have speculated that Thomas's bitterness over the confirmation battle is one reason that he has voted as he had. See, for example, Jeffrey Toobin, "The Burden of Clarence Thomas," *The New Yorker,* September 27, 1993, pp.38, 42. That analysis, if accurate, implies that he was too severely wounded to be confirmed—a judgment that in no way turns on one's view of the relative veracity of Thomas and Hill. On the other hand, even if worried about Thomas's possible bitterness, one should not make the mistake of supposing that the votes he has cast are themselves evidence of his unfitness for office; in the particular example of the *Presley* case, although the outcome seems plainly wrong,

Thomas was part of the majority—and one suspects that anyone appointed to that seat by President Bush would have voted the same way. Although it is possible to describe a majority of the Supreme Court as a group of dangerous radicals, outside the mainstream—the way many conservatives routinely did during the era of the Warren Court—rhetorical flourishes of that kind are principally political tools and raise no intellectually interesting questions.

34. I discuss some of these criticisms in my review essay, "The Candidate," *The New Republic* (February 22, 1993), p. 29. Because of his conservative views on racial issues, Thomas was subjected to very harsh criticism by black activists long before his Supreme Court nomination. See the discussion in my *Reflections of an Affirmative Action Baby* (New York: Basic Books, 1991), pp. 136–38, and elsewhere. Because I defended Thomas from these criticisms in my book, which was published shortly after his nomination was announced, I was widely described as a supporter of his. But the distinction between *supporter* and *defender*—between saying, "I think he should be confirmed" and "I think he is being badly treated"—is one that the present book is trying to recover.

35. The argument that Thomas was dangerous because of his embrace of natural law (an embrace that had troubled *conservatives* at the time of his nomination for a seat on the Court of Appeals for the District of Columbia Circuit) was bizarre. Natural law reasoning is often associated with Thomas Aquinas, and the process of natural law reasoning is one means by which the Roman Catholic Church concludes that abortion is wrong. Some Thomas opponents therefore suggested that if the nominee seriously meant to be guided by natural law, he would, in effect, be using a religious form of reasoning. But although natural law reasoning is certainly part of the Roman Catholic tradition, it is not religious doctrine. It is, rather, a way of arguing to moral truths by observing what seems self-evident in the world. It is the stuff of very serious secular scholarship, one well-known example being John Finnis's book *Natural Law and*

Natural Rights (1980). Certainly one need not be a Catholic—or even a Christian—or believe in God at all—to accept the idea that there is a natural moral order that can be discerned through study of what is. See Rogers Smith, *Liberalism and American Constitutional Law* (Cambridge, Mass.: Harvard University Press, 1985), chap. 7. On the other hand, one might perfectly well reject the view that natural law exists or that it can form a stable basis for judicial decision making; but the fact that some will accept it and some will reject it has nothing to do with whether using it as a tool is the same thing as using religious doctrine.

Indeed, natural law, although not always under that name, is a staple of contemporary constitutional argument. See, for example, the thoughtful discussion in Frederick Schauer, "Constitutional Positivism," *Connecticut Law Review* 25 (1993): 797. Indeed, as Michael McConnell has pointed out, Robert Bork was criticized precisely for denying what Thomas was said to have affirmed. Michael McConnell, "Trashing Natural Law," *New York Times,* August 16, 1991, p. A23.

36. Quoted in Timothy M. Phelps and Helen Winternitz, *Capitol Games: Clarence Thomas, Anita Hill, and the Story of a Supreme Court Nomination* (New York: Hyperion, 1992), p. 104.

37. On this point, compare E. J. Dionne, *Why Americans Hate Politics* (New York: Simon and Schuster, 1991).

38. See Orlando Patterson, "Race, Gender, and Liberal Fallacies," *New York Times,* October 20, 1991, p. E15.

39. Perhaps members of the Judiciary Committee understood this, which would explain why, as one commentator noted, although the senators called her many things, "[t]hey did this behind her back, after she had left the witness stand"—perhaps because "none of them could look her in the eye and say she was lying." Jim Dwyer, "Lies Litter Path To Confirmation," *Newsday,* October 16, 1991, p. 4. Indeed, one wonders why, if Thomas's official supporters were so certain that Thomas was telling the truth, Hill was never indicted (or,

evidently, investigated) for perjury. After all, in 1991, when
the hearings occurred, the Democrats were not yet in the
Justice Department.

40. See the discussions in Anthony Gale, ed., *The Polygraph Test*
     (London: Sage Publications, 1988), and James Allen Matte,
     "Defence Access to Police Polygraph Tests," *New York State
     Bar Journal* 65 (August 1993): 36.

41. Some of those who voted against Thomas cited this as cru-
     cial evidence. Wrote Sen. Paul Simon later, "My experience
     is that people who are lying do not volunteer to take poly-
     graph tests." Paul Simon, *Advice & Consent: Clarence
     Thomas, Robert Bork and the Intriguing History of the
     Supreme Court's Nomination Battles* (Washington, D.C.:
     National Press Books, 1992), p. 140.

42. As a number of reviewers have pointed out, this is not the
     only point on which Brock is mistaken. See, for example,
     Jane Mayer and Jill Abramson, "The Surreal Anita Hill," *The
     New Yorker*, May 24, 1993, p. 90. Indeed, as one who has
     personal knowledge of some of the events and many of the
     people Brock discusses, I am quite certain that he is wrong
     on a central claim of his book—that there was any signifi-
     cant relationship between Anita Hill and Jim Brudney, a
     Capitol Hill staffer whom Brock sees as a key to the pur-
     ported conspiracy, other than the simple fact that they over-
     lapped as students at the Yale Law School. (I was, during
     the period that Brock describes, a close friend of both.)

     Moreover, although Brock insists that he was unable to
     find anybody who knows both Hill and Thomas who
     believed Hill and not Thomas, I am not an investigative
     journalist and have not even been searching, but I have had
     no trouble finding several such people, including some who
     have known Thomas for many years, personally as well as
     professionally. In fact, I have come across a number of peo-
     ple who know Thomas and do not know Hill or know her
     only slightly who believed Hill and not Thomas. The fact
     that I have found such people does not mean that they are

right; our courts sensibly do not admit evidence on whether a defendant's friends believe that he is guilty. My point is that the fact that Brock, who says he looked hard, was unable to find them raises serious questions about the accuracy of other parts of his account.

43. See George Lardner, Jr., "Weinberger Passes Lie Detector Test; Senators Also Back Former Defence Chief's Veracity on Iran Arms Deal," *Washington Post,* May 21, 1992, p. A4.

44. For example, although an ABC News–*Washington Post* poll at the time of the hearings found that 46 percent believed Thomas and only 24 percent believed Hill, an NBC News–*Wall Street Journal* poll one year later found that 44 percent believed Hill and 34 percent believed Thomas. A December 1992 Gallup poll found that 51 percent believed Hill and 34 percent believed Thomas. Despite these numbers, a *U.S. News and World Report* poll in late 1992 found that 51 percent of respondents agreed that the Senate "did the right thing" in confirming Thomas. (All surveys are available through Westlaw in the Polls database.)

The apparent discrepancy between the percentage stating that Thomas lied and the percentage stating he should have been confirmed is easily accounted for: many people believe that the charges were not disqualifying or that Hill should not have come forward after so much time had passed. See Alex Kozinski, "Thomas Affair: A Valuable Civics Lesson," *Wall Street Journal,* October 24, 1991, p. A16.

45. Simon, *Advice & Consent,* p. 145. See also David A. Strauss and Cass R. Sunstein, "The Senate, the Constitution, and the Confirmation Process," *Yale Law Journal* 101 (1992): 1491.

46. Laurence Tribe, in defending the Senate's independent role in the confirmation process, has written to similar effect. See Tribe, *God Save This Honorable Court.* He and I part company, as I have already noted, on the matter of what this independent role entails.

47. For a critique of the "resume-review" model of the Senate's role, see Stephen L. Carter, "The Confirmation Mess," *Har-*

vard Law Review 100 (1988): 1185. For a response to my argument, see Bruce Fein, "A Circumscribed Senate Confirmation Role," *Harvard Law Review* 102 (1989).

48. Alexander Bickel, *The Morality of Consent* (New Haven: Yale University Press, 1975), p. 111.

49. 111 S. Ct. 1759 (1991).

50. For recent theoretical treatments of the dialogic metaphor, see, for example, Barry Friedman, "Dialogue and Judicial Review," *Michigan Law Review* 91 (1993): 578; Christopher L. Eisgruber, "Is the Supreme Court an Educative Institution?" *New York University Law Review* 67 (1992): 961; and Stephen L. Carter, "The Morgan 'Power' and the Forced Reconsideration of Constitutional Decisions," *University of Chicago Law Review* 53 (1986): 819.

51. John Rawls, *Political Liberalism* (New York: Columbia University Press, 1993), pp. 213, 235. As Rawls himself notes, his ideas are anticipated in Ronald Dworkin, *Law's Empire,* and Bruce Ackerman, "Constitutional Politics/Constitutional Law," *Yale Law Journal* 99 (1989): 453. See also Bruce Ackerman, *We the People: Foundations* (Cambridge, Mass.: Harvard University Press, 1991). Of course, the distinction Rawls (and Ackerman) draw between the sorts of reasons that should count for ordinary political discourse and the sorts of reasons that should count for higher (constitutional) discourse is (as Rawls notes) at least as old as Locke, and even has an early-twentieth-century anticipator in Simeon Baldwin, *The American Judiciary* (New York: Century, 1905).

52. The legal scholar Bruce Ackerman has recently adopted a quite similar metaphor. Bruce Ackerman, "Constitutional Politics/Constitutional Law," pp. 546–47.

53. See Mark Tushnet, "Following the Rules Laid Down: A Critique of Interpretivism and Neutral Principles," *Harvard Law Review* 96 (1983): 781, 823–24.

54. The problem of indeterminate meaning is particularly acute with respect to interpretation of the relatively open-textured clauses of the Constitution that deal with individual rights.

On this point, the much-maligned scholars of the Critical Legal Studies movement seem to me to have a very good argument. For particularly lucid and forceful presentations of the indeterminacy thesis, see Mark Tushnet, "Following the Rules Laid Down: A Critique of Interpretivism and Neutral Principles," *Harvard Law Review* 96 (1983): 1781; and Paul Brest, "The Fundamental Rights Controversy: The Essential Contracictions of Normative Constitutional Scholarship," *Yale Law Journal* 90 (1981): 1063. For more detailed explications of my own view, see Stephen L. Carter, "Constitutional Improprieties: Reflections on *Mistretta, Morrison,* and Administrative Government," *University of Chicago Law Review* 57 (1990): 357; and Stephen L. Carter, "Constitutional Adjudication and the Indeterminate Text: A Preliminary Defense of an Imperfect Muddle," *Yale Law Journal* 94 (1985): 821.

55. See *Texas v. Johnson,* 491 U.S. 397 (1989).

56. See *Brown v. Board of Education,* 347 U.S. 483 (1954).

57. See *Ange v. Bush,* 752 F. Supp. 509 (D.D.C. 1990).

58. See *Nixon v. Sirica,* 487 F.2d (D.C. Cir. 1973).

59. Sen. Paul Simon has made a similar argument. See Simon, *Advice & Consent.*

60. The political scientist Gregory A. Caldeira has been a particular proponent of the thesis that American public respect for the Court is based principally on the results that the Justices reach. See, for example, Gregory A. Caldeira, "Public Opinion and the U.S. Supreme Court: FDR's Court Packing Plan," *American Political Science Review* 81 (1987): 1139; and Gregory A. Caldeira, "Neither the Purse Nor the Sword: Dynamics of Public Confidence in the Supreme Court," *American Political Science Review* 80 (1986): 1209. Notes the legal scholar Mary Ann Glendon, "Supreme Court decisions these days . . . have surprisingly wide readership among nonlawyers" and "an even wider public follows them through secondary sources." Mary Ann Glendon, *Rights Talk: The Impoverishment of Political Discourse* (New York: Free Press, 1991), pp. 94–95.

CHAPTER 6: THE DISQUALIFICATION PROBLEM, REVISITED

1. I have argued elsewhere that the Constitution grants to the Congress considerable authority to balance the executive, if the Congress will but use it. See, for example, Stephen L. Carter, "Constitutional Improprieties: Reflections on *Mistretta, Morrison,* and Administrative Government," *University of Chicago Law Review* 57 (1990): 357; Stephen L. Carter, "The Independent Counsel Mess," *Harvard Law Review* 102 (1988): 105; and Stephen L. Carter, "From Sick Chicken to Synar: The Evolution and Subsequent De-Evolution of the Separation of Powers," *Brigham Young Law Review* (1987): 719. In this, I am much affected by the work of Professor Charles Black. See Charles L. Black, Jr., "The Working Balance of the American Political Departments," *Hastings Constitutional Law Quarterly* 1 (1974): 13. See also Peter M. Shane, "The Separation of Powers and the Rule of Law: The Virtues of 'Seeing the Trees,'" *William and Mary Law Review* 30 (1989): 375.

2. For a perhaps overheated discussion of the reasons for my concern, see Stephen L. Carter, *Reflections of an Affirmative Action Baby* (New York: Basic Books, 1991), chap. 2.

3. 347 U.S. 483 (1954).

4. Felix Frankfurter, "The Supreme Court in the Mirror of Justice," *University of Pennsylvania Law Review* 105 (1957): 781. Frankfurter, of course, had a certain bias in the matter, having had no judicial experience before taking the bench.

5. I remind the reader that I fear that left and right alike use the term "closed-minded" as a synonym for "doesn't agree with me."

6. Quoted in *Nomination of Clarence Thomas To Be an Associate Justice of the United States Supreme Court, Hearings Before the Committee on the Judiciary,* S. Hrg. 102–1084, part 2 (1991), p. 244.

7. Bruce Fein, "A Court of Mediocrities," *American Bar Association Journal,* October 1991, p. 75.

8. See, for example, Bruce Fein, "The ABA: Just Another Interest Group," *The Texas Lawyer,* October 21, 1992, p. 14.

9. *Public Citizen v. Department of Justice,* 491 U.S. 440 (1989).

10. Quoted in Timothy Phelps and Helen Winternitz, *Capitol Games: Clarence Thomas, Anita Hill, and the Story of a Supreme Court Nomination* (New York: Hyperion, 1992), p. 199.

11. See Larry C. Berkson and Susan B. Carbon, *The United States Circuit Judge Nominating Commission: Its Members, Procedures, and Candidates* (Chicago: American Judicature Society, 1980).

12. See, for example, David Alpern, "The CIA: The First Defeat," *Newsweek,* January 31, 1977, p. 30.

13. See 28 U.S.C. 505.

14. Quoted in Laurie Goodstein, "Nominee Draws Attacks, Support From Religious Groups," *Washington Post,* July 24, 1993, p. A8.

15. See Al Kamen, "Helms on Nominee—'She's a Damn Lesbian,'" *Washington Post,* May 7, 1993, p. A21.

16. In the early seventies, one scholar pointed out (correctly) that banning from the Court those whose background makes them appear to be racist would have denied the nation the services of such great civil libertarians as Hugo Black (formerly a member of the Ku Klux Klan) and Earl Warren (who, as governor of California, presided over the World War II internment of Japanese-Americans). Thomas Halper, "Senate Rejection of Supreme Court Nominees," *Drake Law Review* 22 (1972): 102, 107. But the seventies are not the nineties, and the detrimental effects of racial exclusion are far more widely accepted today than they once were. In other words, there is no longer any excuse.

17. Robert N. Roberts, White House Ethics: *The History of the Politics of Conflict of Interest Regulation* (Westport, Conn.: Greenwood Press, 1988).

18. Roberts, *White House Ethics,* pp. 9–10.

19. Ibid., pp. 14–15.

20. 367 U.S. 497 (1961).

21.   262 U.S. 390 (1923).

22.   381 U.S. 479 (1965).

23.   394 U.S. 557 (1969).

24.   Consequently, Washington now seems to have things precisely upside down. The White House, Senate, and media have chosen to be forgiving for failures to pay Social Security taxes, but seem adamant—as witness Kimba Wood's unfortunate experience—on the issue of the employment of illegal aliens.

25.   See, for example, Karl Rahner, *Foundations of Christian Faith,* tr. William V. Dych (New York: Crossroad, 1986), pp. 91–106.

CHAPTER 7: SOME MODEST PROPOSALS,
REVIEWED

1.   347 U.S. 483 (1954).

2.   See David M. O'Brien, "Filling Justice William O. Douglas's Seat: President Gerald R. Ford's Appointment of Justice John Paul Stevens," Supreme Court Historical Society Yearbook Annual (1989): 20. See also Victor H. Kramer, "The Case of Justice Stevens: How To Select, Nominate, and Confirm a Justice of the United States Supreme Court," *Constitutional Commentary* 7 (1990): 325.

3.   For lively discussions of this and other ways to beef up the "advice" side of "advice and consent," see David A. Strauss and Cass R. Sunstein, "The Senate, the Constitution, and the Confirmation Process," *Yale Law Journal* 101 (1992): 1491; Glenn Harlan Reynolds, "Taking Advice Seriously: An Immodest Proposal for Reforming the Confirmation Process," *Southern California Law Review* 65 (1992): 1577; and Charles McC. Mathias, Jr., "Advice and Consent: The Role of the United States Senate in the Judicial Selection Process," *University of Chicago Law Review* 54 (1987): 200. See also the less optimistic view of independent Senate power in Charles L. Black, Jr., "A Note on Senatorial Consid-

eration of Supreme Court Nominees," *Yale Law Journal* 79 (1970): 657.

4. For a thoughtful appreciation of how our politics might be very different if the Congress were to act as an independent branch of government, see Charles L. Black, Jr., "The Working Balance of the American Political Departments," *Hastings Constitutional Law Quarterly* 1 (1974): 13.

5. See Larry C. Berkson and Susan B. Carbon, *The United States Circuit Judge Nominating Commission: Its Members, Procedures, and Candidates* (Chicago: American Judicature Society, 1980).

6. See, for example, Stuart Taylor, Jr., "Confirmation Process Flawed . . . By Senate Cowardice." *New Jersey Law Journal,* November 21, 1991.

7. See Martin Shapiro, "Interest Groups and Supreme Court Appointments," *Northwestern University Law Review* 84 (1990): 935.

8. On this proposal, see, for example, Donald J. Devine, *Reform the Judicial Process Now: Five Proposals for a Return to Senate Comity,* Heritage Lecture No. 351 (Washington, D.C.: Heritage Foundation, November 12, 1991). For detail on the Stone story, see Henry J. Abraham, *Justices and Presidents: A Political History of Appointments to the Supreme Court,* 3d ed. (New York: Oxford University Press, 1992), pp. 195–97.

9. See, for example, Devine, *Reform the Judicial Process Now.*

10. Sen. Alan Simpson, among others, has suggested this. Jeffrey Stinson, "Is Confirmation Process In Need of Revamping?" *Gannett News Service,* October 16, 1991.

11. See, for example, Devine, *Reform the Judicial Process Now.*

12. Quoted in Abraham, *Justices and Presidents,* p. 17. Hruska added: "We can't have all Brandeises, Cardozos, and Frankfurters, and stuff like that there."

13. The most notable recent example involved a retention election rather than a re-election, but nevertheless serves as a model for what might happen. In 1987, California voters, furious at a series of criminal procedure decisions by the

state Supreme Court, voted not to retain three incumbents. (In retention elections, incumbents are unopposed and voters are offered the choice of keeping them in office or turning them out.) In what must have been a bitter irony, given that the purpose of judicial elections is to control judges, when two justices who were accused of thwarting the imposition of the death penalty voted to sustain a death sentence shortly before the election, they were accused by their opponents of acting on the basis of politics rather than principle. See Grodin, "Developing a Consensus of Constraint: A Judge's Perspective on Judicial Retention Elections," *Southern California Law Review* 61 (1988): 1969.

14. President Kennedy and the *Times* are both quoted in Emily Field Van Tassel, "Why Judges Resign: Influences on Federal Judicial Service, 1789–1992," in *Research Papers of the National Commission on Judicial Discipline and Removal*, vol. II (Washington, D.C., 1993), pp. 1137, 1159.

15. As long as we are engaging in this thought experiment, it is worthwhile to mention a problem that has occurred at the state level that might make national judicial elections well-nigh impossible: election funding. For commentary on the problem of fundraising by state judges who must run for their offices, see Patrick M. McFadden, *Electing Justice: The Law and Ethics of Judicial Election Campaigns* (Chicago: American Judicature Society, 1990), pp. 23–66; and Schotland, "Elective Judges' Campaign Financing: Are State Court Judges' Robes the Emperor's Clothes of American Democracy?" *Journal of Law and Politics* 2 (1985): 57.

16. This story is delightfully told by Professor Charles Warren in his book *The Supreme Court in United States History*, rev. ed., vol. 1 (Boston: Little Brown, 1926), pp. 400–415.

17. See Paul Freund, "Appointment of Justices: Some Historical Perspectives," *Harvard Law Review* 101 (1988): 1146, 1148.

INDEX